CSR, Sustainability, Ethics & Governance

In recent years the discussion concerning the relation between business and society has made immense strides. This has in turn led to a broad academic and practical discussion on innovative management concepts, such as Corporate Social Responsibility, Corporate Governance and Sustainability Management. This series offers a comprehensive overview of the latest theoretical and empirical research and provides sound concepts for sustainable business strategies. In order to do so, it combines the insights of leading researchers and thinkers in the fields of management theory and the social sciences and from all over the world, thus contributing to the interdisciplinary and intercultural discussion on the role of business in society. The underlying intention of this series is to help solve the world's most challenging problems by developing new management concepts that create value for business and society alike. In order to support those managers, researchers and students who are pursuing sustainable business approaches for our common future, the series offers them access to cutting-edge management approaches. CSR, Sustainability, Ethics and Governance is accepted by the Norwegian Register for Scientific Journals, Series and Publishers, maintained and operated by the Norwegian Social Science Data Services (NSD).

Yifei Yang

Corporate Collapse and Corporate Governance

Analysis from Corporate Constitutional Perspective

Springer

Yifei Yang
School of Law
Capital University of Economics
and Business
Beijing, China

ISSN 2196-7075 ISSN 2196-7083 (electronic)
CSR, Sustainability, Ethics & Governance
ISBN 978-981-96-9665-9 ISBN 978-981-96-9666-6 (eBook)
https://doi.org/10.1007/978-981-96-9666-6

This Springer imprint is published by the registered company Springer Nature Singapore Pte Ltd.
The registered company address is: 152 Beach Road, #21-01/04 Gateway East, Singapore 189721, Singapore

Preface

We are living in an era of recurring corporate collapses—some sudden, others slow-burning. Each time a major company goes to bankruptcy, it leaves behind not only financial wreckage but also social and institutional scars. Shareholders lose investments, employees lose livelihoods, pensioners lose security, and public trust is eroded. We always ask the familiar questions: What went wrong? Who is responsible? And how can it be prevented next time? Too often, our answers circle around the same themes such as improved oversight, more regulation, better transparency, while leaving untouched the deeper architecture of corporate governance itself. These responses may provide comfort, but they rarely confront the underlying assumptions that shape our understanding of the modern companies. At the core of these failures lies something more fundamental than poor judgement or weak enforcement. There is a structural problem in how we conceive of companies, their purpose, and the legitimacy of the power they exercise.

This book is an attempt to take a step back and ask whether our prevailing theoretical foundations are adequate for the complex, global, and politically entangled corporate world we now inhabit. The dominant model of corporate governance which is rooted in contractualism, efficiency, and shareholder primacy, has long shaped how we design institutions, interpret responsibility, and measure success. However, this model increasingly reveals its inadequacies, both in its failure to account for and in its inability to resolve the persistent governance breakdowns that continue to emerge across different contexts. Taking the collapse of Carillion Plc as a starting point, this book seeks to challenge the conceptual and normative assumptions underpinning corporate governance in the UK and beyond. The failure of Carillion is illustrative not only because of its scale and the catastrophic consequences it triggered, but because it exposes how deeply the current system struggles to detect, respond to, or restrain harmful corporate practices before it is too late.

To move forward, we need more than reformist tweaks or technical adjustments. What is needed is a fundamental shift in the prevailing conceptual approach. This book explores one such alternative—corporate constitutionalism. Corporate Constitutional framework treats companies not merely as economic actors or contractual networks, but as governance institutions that operate within a broader social and political order. As such, their power must be subjected to the same types of scrutiny, legitimacy, and accountability that we expect from public institutions. By drawing from constitutional thinking, particularly the principles of accountability, deliberation, and contestability, this approach enables us to reimagine corporate governance in political, not just financial, terms. Importantly, this book does not purport to deliver a fixed institutional blueprint or a comprehensive legal solution. Instead, it offers a thought experiment: a conceptual inquiry into what it might mean to take seriously the governance function of the corporation. It invites reflection on the institutional conditions under which corporate power can be justified, limited, and redirected in the service of broader societal interests.

If this book resonates with those who are grappling with the limitations of the current system—academics, regulators, policymakers, legal scholars, and corporate leaders alike—then it will have served its purpose. And if it prompts deeper inquiry into the constitutional dimensions of corporate life, then perhaps it can also be a small contribution toward building a more responsible and resilient framework of corporate governance.

Beijing, China
April 2025

Yifei Yang

Acknowledgements First and foremost, I owe my deepest gratitude to Professor Charlotte Villiers, Professor Paddy Ireland, Professor Tony Prosser, Professor Shijun Zhang and Professor Lerong Lu. Their intellectual generosity, incisive insights, and kind encouragement have profoundly shaped not only this book but also my broader academic outlook. Professor Villiers, in particular, has been a guiding force throughout my scholarly journey—her unwavering belief in my ideas, even at times when I struggled to believe in them myself, has left an enduring mark. I feel deeply privileged to have learned from such brilliant and generous minds.

I also wish to thank the many friends, colleagues, and fellow scholars who have walked alongside me on this path. In particular, Professor Xiang Hu, Dr. Wenna Wang, Dr. Lin Zhang, Dr. Yefan Xu, Dr. Jiabin Lai and Dr. Yihui Wang have offered invaluable support—through thoughtful conversations, feedback on early drafts, or moments of levity when they were most needed. Academic work can often feel solitary, but thanks to their companionship, I have never truly been alone.

My heartfelt thanks go to my parents and my husband, whose unwavering love, quiet patience, and constant support have sustained me through every step of this journey. Their belief in me has never wavered, even in the most challenging moments. They are, and always will be, my greatest source of strength and resilience.

This book is dedicated to the memory of my beloved grandparents—my "Ye Ye" and "Nai Nai". Though they passed away in 2011 and 2017, their presence continues to live on in my heart and in the values they instilled in me. They were my first teachers in the truest sense, nurturing my curiosity, discipline, and sense of justice. Their gentle wisdom and quiet strength remain a constant source of inspiration. It is to them that I owe the earliest seeds of this intellectual journey.

Funding Information This book is funded by the Start-up Research Project for Early-Career Faculty of Capital University of Economics and Business (Project Number: XJ2024000502).

Competing Interests The author has no competing interests to declare that are relevant to the content of this manuscript.

Contents

Chapter 1
Corporate Collapse and Corporate Governance

1.1 Introduction

1.1.1 Research Background

This book is going to tell a story about a giant company's collapse. Carillion Plc, one of the biggest UK suppliers of public sector services, suddenly went into liquidation in early 2018, leaving nearly £7 billion liabilities and only £29 million assets in cash.[1] The compulsory liquidation of Carillion had catastrophic consequences for the tens of thousands of workers and sub-contractors across public services, constructions and transport infrastructures; for countless clients, public bodies and end users that relied on Carillion's services; and for the financial system in the UK as a whole. It was estimated that, after its bankruptcy, there were over 2000 people losing jobs; £2.6 billion pension shortfalls; and nearly £2 billion liability to its suppliers, sub-contractors and other short-term creditors.[2]

Lessons and analyses from different perspectives have sought to shed light on the fundamental issues behind Carillion's winding-up. Particularly, in reaction to the disruption, Business, Energy and Industrial Strategy and Work and Pensions Committees issued a joint report (or the Second Joint Report) highlighting the problems leading to Carillion's downfall.[3] The Second Joint Report effectively "pierced the veil" of Carillion's failure, so that the public could gain access to details about what was going wrong inside the company. The Second Joint Report began by pointing

---

[1] House of Commons Business, Energy and Industrial Strategy and Work and Pensions Committees, *Carillion*, Second Joint Report from the Business, Energy and Industrial Strategy and Work and Pensions Committees of Session 2017–2019, HC 769, 16 May 2018, at 3, https://publications.parliament.uk/pa/cm201719/cmselect/cmworpen/769/769.pdf. Accessed 31 October 2023.

[2] Ibid.

[3] In the following context, Business, Energy and Industrial Strategy (BEIS) and Work and Pensions Committees may refer to the abbreviation of "the Committees"; their report may refer to "the Second Joint Report".

Y. Yang, *Corporate Collapse and Corporate Governance*, CSR, Sustainability, Ethics & Governance, https://doi.org/10.1007/978-981-96-9666-6_1

out that Carillion's rise and fall was a story of "recklessness, hubris and greed".[4] As revealed, Carillion's business approach was "a relentless dash for cash"—rapid expansion and acquisitions which were mainly financed by debt; thin profit margins and inadequate allowances for loss-making projects, coupled with steadily rising dividend payouts that were largely disconnected from the company's unstable financial performance; an irresponsible board of directors who blocked multiple chances to raise new cash into the company; excessive reliance on suppliers; and little concern for pensions.[5]

Whom should we blame for the company's winding-up? And whom should we blame for the consequent huge losses of creditors and workers, and the subsequent social and financial turmoil? The Second Joint Report has placed the blame liberally across Carillion's internal controls, including the boardroom, internal auditors; and the external checks and balances, including the investors, auditors, advisors, pension trustees, pension regulator, FRC, the government, and the corporate law.[6] Indeed, Carillion's corporate governance arrangement was highly dysfunctional and was severely at fault in permitting the company to act wrongfully. Internally, Carillion collapsed as a result of "selfishness", "ignorance", "lies" and "irresponsibility". In the wake of a company's collapse, focus is usually concentrated, with substantive reasons, on the company's internal governance mechanism—especially including the directors and managers who possess great managerial power, and the auditors who are asked to take up a gatekeeping role on accounting issues. Carillion's boardroom (including the Chief Executive, Finance Director and five non-executive directors) was concerned more about increasing the directors' remuneration and bonus payments, without giving enough attention to the company's problematic status. Six months before Carillion's breakdown, the Chairman, Philip Green, made a misleading statement that Carillion was advised to issue an optimistic and confident statement, highlighting the company's strengths and positioning it as a strong and appealing business opportunity;[7] all three finance directors, Richard Adam (former finance director from 2007 to 2016), Zafar Khan (nine-month finance director for nine months until September 2017) and Emma Mercer (the last finance director appointed after Carillion's crisis broke) performed at a level that was inadequate or even worse. Among those finance directors, only Emma Mercer had a real understanding of Carillion's financial dilemma and pointed out Carillion's aggressive accounting problem.[8] The audit committee, the internal auditors (Deloitte), the external auditors (KPMG)

---

[4] House of Commons Business, Energy and Industrial Strategy and Work and Pensions Committees, *Carillion*, Second Joint Report (n 1) 3.

[5] Krish Bhaskar and John Flower, *Financial Failures and Scandals: From Enron to Carillion* (Routledge 2019), 68–72.

[6] Rob Davies, 'Key Findings from the MPs' Report into Carillion's Collapse' *The Guardian* (15 May 2018), https://www.theguardian.com/business/2018/may/16/mps-dole-out-the-blame-over-carillions-collapse, accessed 29 December 2023.

[7] Simon Goodley, 'Carillion Chair Planned "Upbeat" Message before £845 m Writedown' *The Guardian* (1 March 2018), https://www.theguardian.com/business/2018/mar/01/carillion-chair-planned-upbeat-message-before-845m-writedown, accessed 27 December 2023.

[8] Bhaskar and Flower (n 5) 81.

and the financial advisor (EY) significantly misstated Carillion's profits and assets. Even though Carillion's Chairman maintained that the company adhered to corporate governance principles such as accountability, transparency, integrity, and a commitment to the organisation's long-term sustainable success,[9] the board of directors, the subordinate committees, especially the audit committee, and the internal and external auditors seemed all to fail in performing appropriately and responsively.

Externally, there was also a systematic dysfunctionality of the external checks and balances. According to the Second Joint Report, even though the investors had figured out Carillion's accounting issues at an early stage, they failed to exert sufficient influence on the board; the auditors, internally and externally, made inadequate checks of the accounts; and the Financial Reporting Council (FRC), who acted in a passive manner, also failed to identify, intervene and challenge Carillion's financial misdeeds.[10] The Second Joint Report also criticised the government because it "lacked the decisiveness or bravery" to tackle a culture of corporate recklessness and it should have taken ultimate responsibility regarding a series of questions about public interest protection.[11]

The Second Joint Report undoubtedly has offered a comprehensive analysis of Carillion's failure and has provided a series of workable recommendations on the subsequent reforms of UK's corporate governance system. As observed by the Report, Carillion's collapse represented more than the downfall of a single company; it exposed a broader systemic failure in corporate accountability—one that frequently allows top executives and their surrounding advisory firms to emerge unscathed or even rewarded, while the broader group of stakeholders bears the consequences.[12] Indeed, Carillion's scandal is a familiar story along with the history of corporate failures. From the collapse of Enron in the United States to the failures of BHS and Carillion in the United Kingdom, corporate scholars have become all too familiar with the recurring elements of such downfalls: employees and suppliers find their futures uncertain, pension scheme members suffer reduced benefits offset by burdens on other schemes, and misled shareholders face significant losses. Public confidence in business takes yet another blow, much to the frustration of responsible corporate leaders, while the state is left to bear the financial burden of maintaining critical public services.[13]

We seem to be trapped inside a circle in which we have never been tired of learning lessons from corporate collapses, but the collapses appear never to be stopped. Someone may claim it is usual that some obsolete economic patterns are

---

[9] 'Oral Evidence—*Carillion*—6 Feb 2018' Q418, http://data.parliament.uk/writtenevidence/committeeevidence.svc/evidencedocument/work-and-pensions-committee/carillion/oral/78103.html, accessed 27 December 2023.

The corporate governance standards can be seen from Financial Reporting Council, '*UK Corporate Governance Code 2016*' Para. 4.

[10] House of Commons Business, Energy and Industrial Strategy and Work and Pensions Committees, *Carillion*, Second Joint Report (n 1) 61.

[11] Ibid., 85.

[12] Ibid., 68.

[13] Ibid.

being eliminated. But the mystery is that, as the Second Joint Report pointed out at the very beginning, it is unusual that Carillion, with such an unsustainable business model, could keep running for so long.[14] In other words, before Carillion's problem turned out to reveal a systematic turmoil, it seems strange that there was no efficient mechanism to detect, deter and correct its problems until it was too late. There is, ultimately, a question mark over the whole system which tolerated Carillion's dysfunctional behaviours for so long.

Could a Carillion-style collapse have been prevented? Under the UK's existing corporate governance system, this book answers "no". The MPs' report has also warned that without corporate governance reforms, "Carillion could happen again, and soon".[15] The string of spectacular corporate failures, from Enron in the US to Carillion in the UK and beyond, highlights persistent flaws in the current corporate governance system—a system located within a contractual paradigm with efficiency and profit maximisation as priority.[16]

1.1.2 Beyond Carillion's Collapse

As time passes, post-collapse reflections tend to become diluted, yet the underlying systemic issues remain unresolved. This book, completed six years after Carillion's collapse, traces the aftermath over this period. It highlights not only the profound impact of Carillion's failure on society, but also how easily the disaster has been forgotten in the passing of time, and how quickly the same catastrophe strikes again. For instance, in September 2024, the UK construction giant ISG entered administration with nearly £1 billion in debt, affecting numerous public sector projects and leading to widespread redundancies.[17]

To address such systematic problems, this book is therefore not only concerned with the collapse of Carillion itself. Rather, by utilising Carillion Plc as a starting point, it seeks to go further and deeper, and to provide insight into the critiques and challenges currently facing the UK's corporate governance system and corporate governance theories. In particular, it adopts "corporate constitutionalism"—a framework first systematically and paradigmatically introduced by Stephen Bottomley—as a foundation for critiquing the dominant "corporate contractualism".

By re-conceptualising the corporate governance system in political terms, Bottomley's corporate constitutional framework provides a different approach to

---

[14] House of Commons Business, Energy and Industrial Strategy and Work and Pensions Committees, *Carillion*, Second Joint Report (n 1) 3.

[15] Ibid., 86.

[16] The present corporate governance system is mainly within a contractual paradigm. See Stephen Bottomley, 'From Contractualism to Constitutionalism: A Framework for Corporate Governance' (1997) 19 *Sydney L. Rev.* 277, 279.

[17] The Sunday Times Business team, 'ISG Goes Bust: After Carillion, How Has This Happened Again?' (21 September 2024), https://www.thetimes.com/business-money/companies/article/isg-goes-bust-after-carillion-how-has-this-happened-again-35l9tn5c0, accessed 17 March 2025.

thinking about the operation and effect of corporate governance and how companies might be controlled and regulated, although political ideas and values may be presented differently in their "formulations, applications, and consequences" when applied to corporate life.[18]

In the context of the corporate constitutional framework, this book examines the extent to which the dysfunctionality of both Carillion and the UK's corporate governance system could be reformed. It begins with the assertion that further corporate collapses similar to Carillion's cannot be prevented under the UK's current corporate governance system. This is because the practices of public companies are underpinned by a contractarian theory of the corporate form, in which the interests of investors—and, by extension, short-term profits—are prioritised over other concerns, such as labour rights, prudent pension fund governance, and fair treatment of suppliers. The aim of this book, therefore, is to offer a critical analysis of the corporate governance system and explore the potential outcomes of applying the alternative framework of corporate constitutionalism to a publicly held company, using Carillion Plc as a case study.

1.1.3 Book Description and Chapter Overview

This book offers a thorough investigation into the relationship between the UK's dominant corporate governance regime and a notable corporate collapse within the country. It explores whether a corporate constitutional paradigm can provide fresh insights into corporate failures and inspire substantial reforms to the UK's current shareholder-oriented, contractual governance system. The book argues that the dysfunctionality of the UK's corporate governance framework is the primary and direct cause of corporate collapses. It posits that differing paradigms or frameworks of corporate governance lead to distinctly different corporate behaviours and outcomes. To address these systemic issues, the book advocates for a fundamental shift in the paradigm that underpins the UK's corporate system. The structure of the book is as follows.

1.1.3.1 Part I: Theoretical Foundations and Paradigm Comparison

Part I, spanning Chapters 2 through 4, establishes the theoretical foundation. Chapter 2 explores corporate contractualism as the dominant theoretical framework in the UK's corporate governance. It begins with an explanation of corporate contractual theory, a paradigm that underpins many contemporary governance systems by framing the corporation as a private entity driven by economic efficiency and market dynamics, thereby justifying corporate power through contractual principles. The chapter critically examines the core assumptions of corporate contractualism,

---

[18] Ibid., at 278.

positioning it as both a pivotal and flawed foundation of contemporary governance systems. This analysis sets the stage for exploring alternative paradigms, such as corporate constitutionalism, which seeks to address the inherent shortcomings of contractualism by integrating stakeholder accountability and democratic principles into corporate governance frameworks.

Chapter 3 introduces corporate constitutionalism as a transformative framework for corporate governance. Grounded in the principles of accountability, deliberation, and contestability, corporate constitutionalism shifts the focus from shareholder primacy to a more inclusive and participatory model. Drawing on the works of scholars such as Stephen Bottomley, Frederic Maitland and Lawrence E. Mitchell, and tracing the evolution of corporate constitutionalism, the chapter demonstrates how this paradigm can amplify the voices of stakeholders traditionally excluded from decision-making processes. It argues that corporate constitutionalism addresses the failures of shareholder-centric governance by embedding democratic principles within corporate structures, offering a pathway toward sustainable and equitable corporate practices.

Chapter 4 compares and contrasts corporate contractualism and corporate constitutionalism to understand more fully the differences and similarities of these two frameworks. It can be seen that both theories are significantly different in their ideal origins, methodology, and ideas towards the arrangements and relations of the internal corporation, their ideas towards the relationships between corporations and the state, and the resulting outcomes likely under the guidance of these two theories. The compare and contrast approach could therefore highlight the unique character of corporate constitutionalism which may then provide a new direction for examining and solving Carillion's and the overall systematic problems of corporate governance.

1.1.3.2 Part II: The Carillion Case: History, Governance, and Collapse

Part II, consisting of Chapters 5 and 6, presents a case study on Carillion. Chapter 5 narrates the story of Carillion's downfall, providing a detailed description of the company, including the services it offered, its operational history, and the consequences of its bankruptcy. Chapter 6 offers a comprehensive analysis of Carillion's collapse, examining how both internal corporate controls and external governance arrangements contributed to the company's failure. Internally, this chapter provides an in-depth exploration of Carillion's governance structure, focusing on key decision-making processes. It also examines the external regulatory mechanisms that applied to Carillion, with a particular emphasis on corporate governance systems. While acknowledging the significant role of government in the external regulatory framework, the chapter predominantly focuses on the corporate governance system.

1.1.3.3 Part III: Applying Corporate Constitutionalism: Hypothetical Evaluation and Critical Reflection

Part III, consisting of Chapter 7 and Chapter 8, rethinks corporate governance and analyses corporate collapse through the lens of corporate constitutionalism. Chapter 7 revisits Carillion's collapse, examining its governance failures and extracting broader lessons. It reflects on how a lack of accountability, transparency, and effective stakeholder engagement contributed to the company's downfall. The chapter demonstrates how corporate constitutionalism, with its emphasis on stakeholder involvement, could have prevented such a collapse by fostering a more balanced and accountable governance framework. The chapter also challenges the traditional notion of corporate membership, which typically limits participation to shareholders. It advocates for a more inclusive approach, recognising stakeholders such as employees, suppliers, and communities as integral members with a voice in corporate decision-making. The concept of "procedural justice" is explored, emphasising the importance of fairness in decision-making processes, rather than focusing solely on "substantive justice," which centres on decision outcomes.

Chapter 8 delves into the application of corporate constitutionalism to corporate governance, using Carillion Plc as a case study to highlight the failures of both internal controls (shareholders, directors, auditors) and external regulations. This analysis builds on the findings from Chapter 7, where Carillion's collapse was attributed to a lack of accountability, transparency, and effective stakeholder engagement. Corporate constitutionalism offers a shift from the traditional contractual model to one based on power dynamics, emphasising the need for accountability, deliberation, and contestability within corporate structures. Chapter 8 argues that shareholders must evolve from passive entities to active participants in corporate governance, a principle that aligns with the inclusive approach advocated in Chapter 7. In this new framework, shareholders are not absolved of responsibility but are legally and morally compelled to engage in decision-making processes. Moreover, by integrating Environmental, Social, and Governance (ESG) factors into decision-making, corporate constitutionalism can address broader societal concerns, fostering sustainability and long-term value. This integrated approach, combining shareholder engagement with wider stakeholder involvement, serves as a preventive measure against corporate failures like Carillion's, reinforcing the need for systemic reform to ensure accountability, fairness, and sustainable governance practices.

1.1.3.4 Part IV: Conclusion

Chapter 9, the conclusion, expands the discussion to include other corporate failures, drawing key conclusions about the need for governance reforms to prevent future crises. The book concludes by advocating for a paradigm shift from contractarian to constitutional models to prevent similar corporate failures in the future. The concluding chapter offers broad reflections, highlights limitations and gaps within

Bottomley's theory, and considers the future of both the theory itself and corporate governance more generally, proposing directions for future research.

1.2 Research Objective, Originality and Methodology

1.2.1 Research Objective

This book aims to present a critical analysis of the existing UK's corporate governance system by examining, analysing and re-thinking Carillion's failure. It seeks to offer a thought experiment on ***whether corporate constitutionalism presents a viable framework for addressing governance failures***.

1.2.2 Originality

This book acknowledges that Bottomley's corporate constitutionalism, which inserts political values into the corporate sector, is not a novel observation. By tracing the formation processes of corporate constitutionalism, this book identifies that there is a rich literature viewing corporations as political entities or utilising public thought to analyse corporate conducts. For example, in 1960, Elles recognised an inadequate level of study on the political dimension of corporations. As he noted, while extensive research has explored the economic role of corporations, much less attention has been given to understanding the corporation as a largely self-regulating entity characterised by distinct internal power dynamics and authority structures.[19] Stevenson expressed a similar perspective, asserting that corporations are as much political entities as they are economic ones.[20] However, what is novel in Bottomley's idea is that, drawing from those predecessors' thoughts on corporate polity, he develops "corporate constitutionalism" that stands out as an independent and comprehensive framework in evaluating corporate governance issues from a political way of thinking.

Although Bottomley's corporate constitutionalism was raised as early as 1997, his framework has remained relatively under-researched in the years since. Even if not being given enough attention, Bottomley's idea can still open up a new direction for this book to access issues within a corporation that the contract-based models cannot. As Bottomley clearly noted, relying solely on contract-based frameworks is insufficient to manage the complexity, diversity, and dynamic nature of relationships between individuals and corporate organisations, or to address the wide range of

---

[19] Richard Sedric Fox Eells, *The Meaning of Modern Business: An Introduction to the Philosophy of Large Corporate Enterprise* (Columbia University Press 1960) 12.

[20] Russell B Stevenson Jr, 'The Corporation as a Political Institution' (1979) 8 *Hofstra L. Rev.* 39, 40.

organisational structures that emerge as a result.[21] By understanding corporations as political entities, Bottomley's framework turns from the orthodox corporate contractualism to a corporate constitutional way of analysis in which corporate scholars could view a different dimension of corporations and corporate relations.

The originality of this book lies in its novel application of a corporate constitutional framework to analyse and evaluate Carillion's collapse and to consider potential reforms to the UK's corporate governance system. Although there has been a growing body of research and media coverage on Carillion's failure from various perspectives, much of the literature remains entrenched within the traditional contract-based model of corporate governance. Relatively few studies explore alternative frameworks such as corporate constitutionalism in the context of Carillion's downfall.

Furthermore, applying corporate constitutionalism to the Carillion case serves two purposes. First, it employs Bottomley's framework to evaluate whether this alternative approach could have prevented the company's collapse by offering a more sustainable and inclusive model of governance. Second, the Carillion case acts as a lens through which to critique the practical consequences of corporate constitutionalism, exploring how this framework can be further developed and implemented to enhance corporate governance going forward.

While the literature on corporate contractualism, particularly in the US and the UK, is extensive, there is relatively little research that critiques its limitations through concrete empirical examples like Carillion. By addressing this gap, this book makes a substantial contribution to the academic discourse. Furthermore, given the underdeveloped literature on corporate constitutionalism, this work offers valuable insights by illustrating how this alternative approach could have mitigated or prevented the failures that led to Carillion's collapse, paving the way for further exploration of constitutional models in corporate governance.

1.3 Context of the UK's Corporate Governance Framework

Originating from the 1970s, the term "corporate governance" started to rise to prominence in the US amidst increasing attention to managerial accountability of public companies.[22] With the establishment of the Cadbury Committee, the term was first imported to the UK corporate area in the early 1990s. The Cadbury Committee defined "corporate governance" in the Cadbury Report as "the system by which

[21] Stephen Bottomley, The Constitutional Corporation: Rethinking Corporate Governance (Routledge 2016) 31.

[22] Brian R Cheffins, 'The Rise of Corporate Governance in the UK: When and Why' (2015) 68 *Current Legal Problems* 387, 389.

companies are directed and controlled".[23] It was implicitly assumed that only public-traded corporations are the subject to be considered, though since that time the principles have been extended to cover large private limited companies, as we saw, for example, with the introduction of the Wates Corporate Governance Principles for Large Private Companies in 2018.[24]

Dual tracks influence the UK's corporate governance practices—the first refers to the mandatory statutory and judicial laws on responsibilities and accountabilities of directors,[25] and the various financial reporting and disclosure obligations;[26] the second refers to the non-binding UK Corporate Governance Codes. Modern UK corporate governance is guided by the adoption of governance of best practices and the comply-or-explain principle. Codes of good practice in corporate governance have been substantially influenced by agency theory and its emphasis on the superiority of shareholder value tenets.[27] In the first Cadbury Report, the Cadbury Committee put high hopes on the flexibility and shareholder primacy provided by the non-mandatory adoption of the corporate governance and the comply-or-explain principle. Other corporate governance reviews of the 1990s all recommended that shareholders' engagement be placed at the heart of corporate monitoring, alongside increased disclosure requirements.[28] But the most recent Corporate Governance Code (2018) stressed the importance of stakeholders in promoting a sustainable increase of the UK's economy which signals a change in the recent development direction of the corporate governance.

It could be said the development of UK's corporate governance occurred alongside the waves of corporate crises and scandals.[29] One year before the setup of Cadbury Committee, the so-called biggest fraud case in English commercial history—the 1990 bankruptcy of the Polly Peck International Plc food and consumer electronics group occurred, leading to £2 billion shares made worthless.[30] After Polly Peck's collapse, unceasing mega scandals let the commercial world be confronted with a

---

[23] *Report of the Committee on the Financial Aspects of Corporate Governance—Cadbury Report* (Gee and Co. Ltd., London, 1992) Para.2.5.

[24] Financial Reporting Council, *The Wates Corporate Governance Principles for Large Private Companies*, December 2018, https://www.frc.org.uk/getattachment/31dfb844-6d4b-4093-9bfe-19cee2c29cda/Wates-Corporate-Governance-Principles-for-LPC-Dec-2018.pdf, accessed 28 May 2023.

[25] For example, Companies Act 2006 Sections 171–177.

[26] For example, Companies Act 2006 Section 417, Section 463 and Sections 854–859.

[27] Luh Luh Lan and Loizos Heracleous, 'Rethinking Agency Theory: The View from Law' (2010) 35 *Academy of Management Review* 294, 294.

[28] Janet Williamson, "Beyond Shareholder Primacy—The Case for Workers' Voice in Corporate Governance" (2017) in *Shaping the Corporate Landscape Towards Corporate Reform and Enterprise Diversity*, Eds. Boeger and Villiers, (Hart Publishing, 2018) 173.

[29] Klaus J Hopt, 'Comparative Corporate Governance: The State of the Art and International Regulation' (2011) 59 *The American Journal of Comparative Law* 1, 5.

[30] Gareth David, 'Polly Peck: From £2 Billion to Zero' *Sunday Times* (London, 28 October 1990) II 8; see also Andrew Davidson, 'Scandal' *Sunday Times* (London, 29 October 1991) 3, citing from Cheffins (n 22) 410.

severe credit crisis. Especially in 1991, the year of the Cadbury Committee's formation was called an "unprecedented year for scandal".[31] In this year, due to improper arrangement of pension funds and an illegal share price support scheme, two public companies under Robert Maxwell's control—Maxwell Communications Corporation and Mirror Group Newspapers Plc collapsed which had a great impact on the whole society.[32] These economic crises that engulfed the UK's financial markets to a large extent catapulted corporate governance to a focal point.

Since the publication of the Cadbury Report which was the UK's first attempt to formalise the best practice and the system of corporate governance in a written document,[33] the corporate governance codes have been regularly reviewed, refined and developed in response to various corporate governance issues.[34] For example, the 1995 Greenbury Report focused on directors' excessive remuneration packages.[35] The Higgs Report (2003) made recommendations on the roles and effectiveness of non-executive directors, the Tyson Report (2003) focused on the non-executives' recruitment and development, and the Smith Report (2003) was concerned with auditors' independence. All these reports were stimulated by the notorious 2001 American giants Enron's and WorldCom's scandals. With a specific concern around the banking sector, the issue background of the Walker Review (2009) was the manipulation of the London Inter-Bank Offered Rate (LIBOR) by several UK and international banks. The Walker Review triggered the development of the Stewardship Code (2010) which aimed to enhance institutional shareholders' participation, dialogue and responsibilities within the company.[36]

After Carillion's downfall, the FRC published the Corporate Governance Code (2018) which indicated certain changes in direction. The new Code turned its sights to the role of stakeholders in the company and called for a corporate culture that fed into corporate integrity, value diversity, and long-term sustainability. It was designed to set higher standards of corporate governance to improve transparency and sustainability in business, and to encourage long-term investments benefiting the economy and wider society.[37] These conducts appeared to be a positive and forward-looking approach for the UK corporate governance practices being revamped to fit corporate needs in the twenty-first century.[38]

---

[31] Davidson (n 30).

[32] Brian R Cheffins, *Company Law: Theory, Structure, and Operation*, vol 361 (Clarendon Press Oxford 1997) 612–613.

[33] Jill Solomon, *Corporate Governance and Accountability* (John Wiley & Sons 2020) 41.

[34] The next report following Cadbury Report is the Greenbury Report issued by the Greenbury Committee with its recommendations on the level of salaries and bonuses being paid to senior executives.

[35] James J Hughes, 'The Greenbury Report on Directors' Remuneration' (1996) *International Journal of Manpower* 4–9.

[36] Solomon (n 33) 52.

[37] Peter Yeoh, 'Corporate Governance Codes in the UK: The Risk of Over-Reliance?' (2019) 40 *Business Law Review* 19, 21.

[38] Ibid., 26.

The Kingman Review, published in 2018, gave a harsh review of the function of the FRC. Given the serious flaws of the audit function in Carillion, and FRC's consistently passive, hesitant, ineffective, and powerless performance in addressing Carillion's issues,[39] the FRC was beyond rescue according to the Kingman Review. A new independent regulator –the Audit, Reporting and Governance Authority (ARGA) therefore was to be established to replace the FRC, being accountable to Parliament and to the Department for BEIS.[40] The Kingman Review also criticised the Stewardship Code (2010) as "not effective in practice" which led to the rectification of the code.[41] In contrast to the Stewardship Code (2010), the 2020 version of the code expands the concept of stewardship and the methods used to advance it beyond the scope of the original version.[42] The Stewardship Code (2020) emphasises five changes in corporate governance which represent the focal points of the further development of the UK's corporate governance, including encouraging investors to integrate environmental, social and governance factors (ESG) into the consideration of investment; giving more focus on investors' purpose, values and culture; for the first time involving the roles of asset owners[43] and service providers[44] in corporate governance; enhancing greater transparency; concerning how investors exercise stewardship across asset classes beyond listed equity.[45] In 2024, the FRC made interim changes to streamline the reporting process for signatories, aiming to reduce the reporting burden while maintaining transparency and accountability.

In a nutshell, the above discussion shows the narrow regulatory spectrum of the UK's corporate governance. The Companies Act 2006 and the body of common law principles, as the hard laws, lay the foundation of the corporate governance arrangement. The soft and flexible corporate governance codes, stewardship codes and takeover code together establish an evolving framework that caters to the development of the corporate world. While both hard and soft laws play crucial roles in shaping corporate governance frameworks, it is the hard laws that provide the foundation for the effectiveness of the latter, establishing the fundamental formal distribution of governance rights between shareholders and the board of directors.[46] The UK's regulatory rules on the whole have created a flexible and free-market-based corporate governance framework which puts high emphasis on efficiency, profit maximisation

[39] House of Commons Business, Energy and Industrial Strategy and Work and Pensions Committees, *Carillion*, Second Joint Report (n1) and John Kingman, *Independent Review of the Financial Reporting Council (Kingman Review)*, December 2018.

[40] Solomon (n 33) 54.

[41] Kingman (n 39) 8.

[42] Paul Davies, 'The UK Stewardship Code 2010–2020 From Saving the Company to Saving the Planet?' (2020) *European Corporate Governance Institute-Law Working Paper* 5.

[43] For example, the pension funds and insurance companies.

[44] For example, the proxy advisers and investment consultants.

[45] 'The Five Most Important Changes to the UK's New Stewardship Code | ACCA Global', https://www.accaglobal.com/ca/en/member/discover/cpd-articles/governance-risk-control/stewardship-codecpd.html, accessed 22 February 2023.

[46] Marc Moore, 'Private Ordering and Public Policy: The Paradoxical Foundations of Corporate Contractarianism' (2014) 34 *Oxford Journal of Legal Studies* 693, 697.

and other economic values. Shareholders' interests (financial interests mainly) are always the prominent interest to be considered in corporate decision making, even without full consideration of other stakeholders' rights.

1.4 Literature Review

A literature study is a necessary step within the doctrinal method which helps trace the key theories of the UK corporate governance and figure out the research gaps of current research.[47] There are a variety of theoretical frameworks that reveal different aspects of corporate governance, through various terminologies and disciplines. The literature review attempts to give an overview of the main scholarship of corporate governance, recognise the rationale behind the existing system, and understand the legal standings towards relevant cases and the theoretical debates in this field. It is suggested that, conducting a literature review does not mean purely tracking down and describing all relevant information, rather it requires a critical analysis of the ideas included therein.[48]

The following literature study provides an initial understanding of the mainstream contractarian theory of the company (or "corporate contractualism") which forms the theoretical underpinnings of UK's corporate governance framework, and other different theoretical approaches which to some extent affect recent years' reform orientation of corporate governance. In essence, these different theories all refer to the fundamental questions of the "ontology of corporations", or the "existence" of companies if drawing on Dine's words.[49] Their different answers and attitudes towards these basic but debatable questions actually impact the extent of the state's interference that is deemed appropriate in the corporate sector, as well as the scope of interests that could be regarded as the corporate interests.[50]

1.4.1 Corporate Contractual Understandings on the Company

Dine divided the "contractual theory" into two strands—"legal contractualism"[51] and "economic contractualism".[52] Therefore, the literature study of corporate contractualism should be tracked from two different perspectives—the traditional legal model, and the law and economics model.

---

[47] Terry Hutchinson and Nigel Duncan, 'Defining and Describing What We Do: Doctrinal Legal Research' (2012) 17 *Deakin L. Rev.* 83, 112.

[48] Nicholas Walliman, *Social Research Methods* (SAGE Publications Ltd 2006).

[49] Janet Dine, *The Governance of Corporate Groups*, vol 1 (Cambridge University Press 2000) 3.

[50] Ibid.

[51] Ibid., 3–8.

[52] Ibid., 8–12.

The concept of the company as a "private association" could be referred to as the formal legal model.[53] It uses the idea of contract to define the nature of the relationship inside the corporation. Given the "traditional logic of ownership",[54] the company law respects that shareholders are entitled to determine the objective of their association through contracts and accepts that by reason of their investments to the company they should be viewed as the owners.[55]

From the legal contractualism model perspective, corporations are regarded as legal entities distinct from their directors and shareholders.[56] It uses the device of contract to define the nature of relations among three sets of legal actors: the corporation, the directors and the shareholders. By using the idea of contract, corporations are simplified as rigorously defined relationships. That is, contractually defined relationships exclude the interests of those who are deemed to be non-contractual parties, and they also exclude what are regarded as the non-corporate-interest parties.[57] According to Bottomley, the legal model concerns the way power is exercised by, and the respective rights and responsibilities of, directors/officers and shareholders.[58]

In the UK, the contractual doctrine now is reflected in Section 33 (1) of the Companies Act 2006 which provides that:

> The provisions of a company's constitution bind the company and its members to the same extent as if there were covenants on the part of the company and of each member to observe those provisions.

The statute uses a contractual term—"covenants"—to describe the effect of a company's constitutional documents on the members (namely shareholders) and the company. A reflection of the contractual expression can also be found in some cases, such as *Foss v Harbottle*, which identifies that the majority decision, taken to the constitutional (contractual) rights of the shareholders, represents the will of the corporation.[59] *Eley v Positive Government Security Life Assurance Co Ltd* is another case that confirmed a company's articles of association as a contract between shareholders and the company.[60]

However, the law and economics model presents a different picture in analysing corporations. The rise and development of corporate contractual theory in the law and economics model is the result of a certain historical stage where the general ideology transited from the "mid- and post-war consensus of state-centric corporatism" to the market-centered "neo-liberalism" since the 1970s onwards.[61] The

[53] JE Parkinson, *Corporate Power and Responsibility: Issues in the Theory of Company Law* (Oxford: Clarendon, 2002) 76.

[54] Adolf Berle and Gardiner Means, *The Modern Corporation and Private Property* (London: Macmillan 1932).

[55] Parkinson (n 53) 75.

[56] *Salomon v Salomon & Co Ltd* [1897] AC 22.

[57] Bottomley (n 21) 25.

[58] Ibid., 20.

[59] *Foss v Harbottle* [1843] 67 ER 189. Citing from Dine (n 49) 7.

[60] *Eley v Positive Government Security Life Assurance Co Ltd* [1875]1 Ex D 88.

[61] Moore (n 46) 699.

American economist Friedman's classic paper "*Corporate Social Responsibility is To Increase Profits*" published in the New York Times, is representative of economic neo-liberalism.[62] In his view, There is only one social responsibility of business: to utilize its resources and participate in activities aimed at increasing its profits, as long as it operates within the rules of the game, meaning it engages in open and fair competition without deceit or fraud.[63] In other words, in a freely operating company, the corporate executives are employees of the owners of the company who should take direct responsibility to their employers. Being subject to the basic rules of society (laws and moral customs), they should conduct business by the will of corporate owners and take all efforts to make profit. Neoclassical economics incorporated the neoliberal philosophy into the discussion of the nature of corporations and corporate governance which laid the foundation of the development of corporate contractualism.

The agency theory and transaction cost economics were prominent in the theoretical analysis of the law and economics contractualism. Although both are different in the views of the firm and managerial behaviours, it is difficult to disentangle these two theories,[64] and they really concern the same question—How can we convince company management to focus on maximizing shareholder value and profits for the company and its shareholders, rather than prioritizing their own self-interest.[65] This question is originated from the separation of ownership and control of modern corporations.

In 1932, two American precursors of modern company law Berle and Means in their classic work—*The Modern Corporation and Private Property*,[66] asserted that the dispersion of shareholdings of modern companies may lead to a separation between ownership and control. Additionally, the introduction of public limited liability could contribute to a congregation of corporate power which may result in oligopolistic corporations. In this sense, they predicted that there could not be effective shareholder control on these modern corporations which possess great powers. As a result, it was the managers, rather than the owners, taking ultimate control of corporations. For providing sufficient protections to shareholders, they argued for a shareholder-centred model of the company which had since then become the "dominant belief system" in Anglo-American company law and economic ideology.[67] The

---

[62] Milton Friedman, 'A Friedman Doctrine—The Social Responsibility of Business Is to Increase Its Profits' *The New York Times* (13 September 1970), https://www.nytimes.com/1970/09/13/archives/a-friedman-doctrine-the-social-responsibility-of-business-is-to.html, accessed 24 February 2023.

[63] Ibid.

[64] Ronald J Gilson and Robert H Mnookin, 'Sharing among the Human Capitalists: An Economic Inquiry into the Corporate Law Firm and How Partners Split Profits Symposium on the Corporate Law Firm' (1984) 37 *Stanford Law Review* 313, 333.

[65] Solomon (n 33) 12.

[66] Berle and Means (n 54).

[67] Gordon Pearson, 'Destruction by Ideological Pretence: The Case of Shareholder Primacy' (2018), in *Shaping the Corporate Landscape Towards Corporate Reform and Enterprise Diversity*, Eds. Boeger and Villiers, (Hart Publishing 2018) 54.

term—"shareholder primacy" elaborated in Johnson's and Millon's 1989 paper has also become a basic element in academic discussions.[68]

The separation of ownership and control gave rise to the conflicts between shareholders and managers, namely the principal-agent conflicts in Jensen and Meckling's analysis. In the work of Jensen and Meckling, corporations are "legal fictions" and "nexus of contracts"—that contractual relations are the essence of the firm among different groups of individuals, including employees, suppliers, customers, creditors, and other parties.[69] They argued that agency costs are an unavoidable result of the relationship between shareholders and managers because managers who possess discretions always expropriate value to themselves at the expense of corporate interests.[70] But agency costs could be minimised if managers' behaviour could be properly monitored.[71] And the solution to shareholder-manager conflicts is to establish a "nexus" of optimal contracts between them to encourage managers to demonstrate to the shareholders that they are responsible and align with shareholder's interests.[72]

The other strand of the theoretical analysis of the law and economics model could be transaction cost theory. Coase, a representative scholar of new institutional economics, was the first to focus on the difference between the market and the firm who asserted that the firm is essentially "a realm beyond contract and the market" in certain respects.[73] In his article *The Nature of the Firm*, Coase proposes that within the firm, market transactions are substituted by the management co-ordinating and controlling production. It is the way in which the firm organised that would decide the boundaries beyond which the firm can control the price and production. Unlike agency theory that regards companies as "nexus of contracts", companies in the eyes of transaction cost theorist are in fact in hierarchical governance structures.[74]

Although agency theory and transaction-cost theory are different in some aspects, they actually share the same contractual ideology—"efficient-contracting orientation"[75]—and are complementary in nature.[76] In the paradigm of transaction cost

[68] Lyman Johnson and David Millon, 'Misreading the Williams Act' (1989) 87 *Michigan Law Review* 1862.

[69] Alchian and Demsetz made a similar statement in an earlier time, that company is a "centralised contractual agent in a team productive process". See Armen A Alchian and Harold Demsetz, 'Production, Information Costs, and Economic Organization' (1972) 62 *The American economic review* 777, 778. However, the contractual approach does not apply to involuntary creditors such as tort victims. See Richard A Posner, *Economic Analysis of Law 7th Ed* (New York: Aspen, 2007) 426.

[70] Shann Turnbull, 'Corporate Governance: Its Scope, Concerns and Theories' (1997) 5 *Corporate Governance: An International Review* 180, 189.

[71] Catherine M Daily, Dan R Dalton and Albert A Cannella, 'Corporate Governance: Decades of Dialogue and Data' (2003) 28 *The Academy of Management Review* 371.

[72] Solomon (n 33) 9.

[73] Paddy Ireland, 'Property and Contract in Contemporary Corporate Theory' (2003) 23 *Legal Studies* 453, 476.

[74] Oliver E Williamson, *The Mechanisms of Governance* (Oxford University Press 1996) 173.

[75] Ibid.

[76] Ibid., 171.

theory, given managers' problems in "bounded rationality" and "opportunism", managers may organise transactions to further their own benefits and discourage potential investment.[77] Thus, like the agency theory, to reduce agency costs or to eliminate management opportunism if in transaction-cost language, such defective behaviours give a reason for managers to be controlled by owners.[78]

In conclusion, the above literature study provides a basic acknowledgement of the traditional legal model and the law and economics model of corporate contractualism. These two models of corporate contractualism are rooted in the same ideology of freedom of contract and they justify the legitimacy of shareholder primacy, but they are also distinct in the aspects of understanding the existence of corporations—whether corporations are legal entities or the aggregation of contracts; the choices of value—the fairness and orders of the legal model or the efficiency and profit maximisation of the law and economics model; the attitudes towards state interference on corporate affairs—taking regulations as a key part of corporate governance or seeking a free market approach;[79] and free from a state's intervention and regulation.[80] According to Bottomley, economic analysis is essentially anti-regulatory with a weak external control approach.[81] Although economic contractualism accepts the role of law, advocates of this approach were calling for the freedom for corporate actors to secede from statutorily or judicially created regulations and to settle their own contractual relations.[82] In this regard, the role of the state was significantly underplayed.[83] And the main mission of the law, company law especially, was to minimise the transaction costs, to substantiate and facilitate corporate contracts, and to correct potential issues that may arise from the agency relationship.[84] These different orientations between the legal model and the law and economics model in fact result in a paradoxical situation of corporate study, court decisions and practical running of companies. The discussion on corporate contractualism will be deepened and furthered in Chapter 3.

---

[77] "Bounded rationality" means that they are intentionally rational but limited doing so. Opportunism means managers are opportunistic in essence. Citing from Solomon (n 33) 12.

[78] Solomon (n 33) 12.

[79] Cheffins (n 32) 119. See also Frank H Easterbrook and Daniel R Fischel, *The Economic Structure of Corporate Law* (Harvard University Press 1996).

[80] Oliver E Williamson, 'Transaction Cost Economics' (1989) 1 *Handbook of Industrial Organization* 135.

[81] Stephen Bottomley, 'Taking Corporations Seriously: Some Considerations for Corporate Regulation' (1990) 19 *Federal Law Review* 203, 205–206.

[82] Bottomley (n 21) 29.

[83] Lan and Heracleous (n 27) 297.

[84] For example, Christopher A Riley, 'Contracting out of Company Law: Section 459 of the Companies Act 1985 and the Role of the Courts' (1992) 55 *The Modern Law Review* 782. And also see Lan and Heracleous (n 27) 297.

1.4.2 Alternative Theoretical Underpinnings of UK's Corporate Governance System

The above literature analysis reveals the contractual model of understanding the existence of companies which consequently affects the extent of the state's intervention and the scope of corporate purpose. However, in recent years, an increasing number of scholars have started to question the theoretical validity of the contractualism theory. They critically evaluate the ambiguity and defects of contractual ideology—such as excessive risk-taking of managerial executives and limited caring for employees and oligopolistic economic organisations.

The concession theory could be regarded as one of the antitheses of the contractual theory.[85] According to Dine, in its most basic form, concession theory regards the creation and operation of a company as a privilege granted by the state.[86] The company thus could grant the ability to trade in the use of the corporate tool, especially operating with limited liability. Bottomley classifies the concession theory of corporations as being situated within the political theory of corporate area,[87] which mainly entails two claims. The first claim regards the corporations as owing their existence to an exercise of state power; while another claim describes the state grant of corporate status as a privilege.[88] The concession theory therefore plays an important role in establishing a theoretical framework sympathetic to state intervention.[89]

However, in the modern era, the concession theory appears to be inappropriate. Many scholars, such as Bratton, Donaldson, and Hartman present critiques suggesting that "privilege" is no longer involved in justifying corporate status and the source of corporates' "economic energy" undoubtedly lies in individual initiative and not in the state.[90]

Some theorists, such as Bainbridge, Blair and Stout recognise the key role of directors who actually embrace the ultimate power in the corporation and those theorists look beyond the classic model of shareholder primacy. They thus propose a new model of corporate governance—the director primacy model in which the board of directors is seen as a key decision-making body.[91]

---

[85] Parkinson (n 53) 14.

[86] Dine (n 49) 21.

[87] Bottomley (n 21) 40.

[88] Ibid.

[89] Parkinson (n 53) 14.

[90] Ibid. See also from William W Bratton Jr, 'The New Economic Theory of the Firm: Critical Perspectives from History' (1989) *Stanford Law Review* 1471, 1475.

See also from Thomas Donaldson, *Corporations and Morality* (Englewood Cliffs, NJ: Prentice-Hall 1982) 3. See also from Edwin M Hartman, 'Donaldson on Rights and Corporate Obligations' (1991) *The Ruffin Series in Business Ethics* 163, 170–172.

[91] Stephen M Bainbridge, 'Why a Board-Group Decisionmaking in Corporate Governance' (2002) 55 *Vand. L. Rev.* 1. See also from Stephen M Bainbridge, *Corporation Law and Economics* (Foundation Press 2002).

For Blair and Stout, the public corporation could be viewed as a team production. This theory does not outright dismiss the contractual perspective; rather, it builds upon it by recognising the limitations of what can be accomplished through explicit contracting.[92] Their analysis rests on the observation that the corporation is a complex productive activity involving several parties.[93] Alongside shareholders, other parties—executives, employees, creditors or the local community—could also make essential contributions to corporate productions and therefore could claim for the residual interests of the corporation.[94] Blair and Stout seek a mediating hierarchy that assigns control rights to a third party, the board of directors, who are largely free to mediate among competing interests and pursue the directions they choose.[95] The board of directors' and managers' discretion to make business judgement should be for the long run health of the entire organisation.

Freeman's stakeholder theory also helps to counter the dominant contractual mindset. Since 1984, his work has developed to re-conceptualise the nature of the firm to encourage consideration of new external stakeholders, beyond the traditional pool—shareholders, customers, employees, and suppliers.[96] Freeman's broader classic definition of stakeholder could be—A stakeholder in an organisation refers to any group or individual who has the ability to influence, or is influenced by, the accomplishment of the organisation's goals.[97] His definition assumes that the consideration of a wider range of stakeholders, enables the maximization of firm value and thus the long-term survival of a firm.[98] For many advocates,[99] the two concepts of corporate social responsibility (CSR) and stakeholder theory are closely

---

[92] Margaret M Blair and Lynn A Stout, 'Team Production Theory of Corporate Law' (1999) 85 *Va. L. Rev.* 247, 320.

[93] Parkinson (n 53) 14.

[94] Margaret M Blair and Lynn A Stout, 'Director Accountability and the Mediating Role of the Corporate Board' (2001) 79 *Wash. ULQ* 403.

[95] Blair and Stout (n 92) 320.

[96] Dima Jamali, 'A Stakeholder Approach to Corporate Social Responsibility: A Fresh Perspective into Theory and Practice' (2008) 82 *Journal of Business Ethics* 213, 217.

[97] R Edward Freeman, *Strategic Management: A Stakeholder Approach* (Cambridge University Press, 2010) 46.

[98] Andreas Georg Scherer, Dorothée Baumann-Pauly and Anselm Schneider, 'Democratizing Corporate Governance: Compensating for the Democratic Deficit of Corporate Political Activity and Corporate Citizenship' (2013) 52 *Business & Society* 473, 491.

[99] Such as Kakabadse pointed that, "CSR aims to define what responsibilities business ought to fulfil, while the stakeholder concept addresses the issue of whom business is or should be accountable to." Cited from Jamali (n 99) 228. See also from Nada K Kakabadse, Cécile Rozuel and Linda Lee-Davies, 'Corporate Social Responsibility and Stakeholder Approach: A Conceptual Review' (2005) 1 *International Journal of Business Governance and Ethics* 277. Brenner and Cochran also stated that "stakeholder theory holds the promise of becoming the theoretical centrepiece in a field that is searching for workable paradigms". Citing from Jamali (n 99) 229. See also from Steven N Brenner and Philip Cochran, 'The Stakeholder Theory of the Firm: Implications for Business and Society Theory and Research', *Proceedings of the International Association for Business and Society* (1991).

related. The adoption of stakeholder theory gives a proper insight for CSR academics and practitioners.[100]

Some scholars acknowledge corporations as powerful actors in public life. They view corporations as political entities because current corporate governance structures and patterns can be assessed using political criteria as much as economic ones.[101] As Blumberg reminded us, a significant degree of politicization of the corporation has already taken place.[102] Similarly, Stevenson also states that all corporations are as much political entities as they are economic ones.[103] By virtue of the traditional political domain of governance, governance is all about using power and holding accountability, to ensure the decision-makers make reliable decisions.

Many scholars therefore seek to bring political understanding into corporate governance. For example, in recent years, some scholars have paved a way to introduce a political term—"global governance" into corporate analysis. They note that in a globalised world, corporations do not merely act as rule takers but also possess a constitutional interest,[104] and business firms have emerged as significant political players in the global society.[105] In turn, global governance also could help to create preconditions for the corporations' success in the long term.[106] It appears that the political approach aligns with certain arguments regarding the governance of major institutions in our society, highlighting the importance of due process, substantive debate, and the implementation of formal voting referenda.[107]

Moreover, there are scholars advocating a "power model" which draws on organisational and management theory. For instance, Dallas emphasises the political nature of decision-making within large corporations, viewing each company as an organic institution with its own internal structure and processes that affect the control of the company.[108] Based on the power model, Moore and Petrin define "corporate governance" as "concerned—first and foremost—with the problem of power" by

---

[100] Jamali (n 99) 229.

[101] Bottomley (n 21) 38.

[102] Phillip Blumberg, 'The Politicalization of the Corporation' (1971) 51 *BuL Rev.* 425, 462.

[103] Stevenson Jr (n 20) 40.

[104] Viktor J Vanberg, 'Corporate Social Responsibility and the "Game of Catallaxy": The Perspective of Constitutional Economics' (2007) 18 *Constitutional Political Economy* 199.

[105] Andreas Georg Scherer and Guido Palazzo, 'The New Political Role of Business in a Globalized World: A Review of a New Perspective on CSR and Its Implications for the Firm, Governance, and Democracy' (2011) 48 *Journal of Management Studies* 899, 900.

[106] Nick Lin-Hi and Igor Blumberg, 'The Relationship between Corporate Governance, Global Governance, and Sustainable Profits: Lessons Learned from BP' (2011) 11 *Corporate Governance: The International Journal of Business in Society* 571, 577.

[107] John Pound, 'The Rise of the Political Model of Corporate Governance and Corporate Control' (1993) 68 *NYUL Rev.* 1003, 1009.

[108] Lynne L Dallas, 'Two Models of Corporate Governance: Beyond Berle and Means' (1988) 22 *U. Mich. JL Reform* 19, 25–26.

stressing the term "governance" which is normally comprehended within the "traditional political domain".[109] In particular, they provide an academic definition of corporate governance, describing it as an investigation into the causes and consequences of the allocation of decision-making power within large, socially significant business organisations.[110] Gourevitch and Shinn also state that corporate governance structures are fundamentally a reflection of political choices and decisions.[111] That is because legal protections and market structure derive from decisions made in the political process.[112] Unger observes that modern society seems to be "a constellation of governments".[113] His observation inspires some scholars to approach the second sense of companies that views them as comparable to political institutions. Based on these ideas, Bottomley has developed his corporate constitutionalism framework—"a corporate species of political theory"[114] which will be analysed in detail in the following chapters.

What can be concluded here is that different theoretical frameworks reveal and address different angles about corporations. And what is clear from the survey of the above literature study is that "corporate governance" tends to be a contested and debatable term, both practically and theoretically.Depending on scholars' different cultural contexts, intellectual backgrounds, interests and theoretical viewpoints,[115]governance theory is "generally not robust or well-rooted",[116]possessing a "plurality of meanings and forms".[117] Although its plurality produces controversies and debates, it broadens our view and encourages critical thinking towards issues in corporate governance.

The theoretical study of this book shifts from the private and contractual observation to the public and political relevance of the company. From the corporate contractual aspects, the orthodox corporate contractual paradigm in corporate governance is rooted in a tradition that narrowly defines corporations as mechanisms to mitigate the conflicts between the shareholders and managers. Thus, Bottomley critiques economic contractualism for offering a framework that either disregards

---

[109] Marc Moore and Martin Petrin, *Corporate Governance: Law, Regulation and Theory* (Macmillan International Higher Education 2017) 4.

[110] Ibid.

[111] Peter Alexis Gourevitch and James Shinn, *Political Power and Corporate Control: The New Global Politics of Corporate Governance* (Princeton University Press 2005) 3. They explain that "Corporate governance systems reflect policy choices. They are shaped by a mixture of laws, rules, regulations, and the degree of their enforcement. These laws define the obligations of managers, the rights and duties of owners, the claims of shareholders, and the powers of boards."

[112] Ibid. Gourevitch and Shinn explain the political process including: "laws passed, laws enforced, regulations applied, courts sheltered from corruption—all deeply political variables."

[113] Roberto Mangabeira Unger, *Law in Modern Society* (Simon and Schuster 1977) 193.

[114] Bottomley (n 21) 40.

[115] Turnbull (n 70) 184.

[116] Thomas Clarke, 'Research on Corporate Governance' (1998) 6 *Corporate Governance* 57, 63.

[117] Maria Bonnafous-Boucher, 'Some Philosophical Issues in Corporate Governance: The Role of Property in Stakeholder Theory' (2005) 5 Corporate Governance: *The International Journal of Business in Society* 34, 35.

or downplays the company as an analytical construct, instead concentrating on the roles of managers and shareholders.[118] Essentially, as Horn states, such tradition has concealed the underlying power imbalances within the political economy of the corporation.[119] Under the contractual arrangement, what the current corporate governance mechanism is trying to achieve, in the name of solving the agency problem, is to align the interests of the managers with the shareholders. By giving managers the shareholder-like interests, for example, allowing managers to have shares, corporate contractual models of corporations hope they could think like shareholders. However, instead of aligning managers' and shareholders' interests, that may lead to a contrary way of conduct. In reality, we can see shareholders are more and more distant from corporate operations, and play minimal roles in decision making, especially in large public companies. Meanwhile the managers, holding increasingly discretionary power, are more likely to choose short-term strategies to improve share prices instead of concentrating on the corporate longer-term value.

Seeing all these problems in the current corporate governance system, there should be an alternative analytical approach to respond to these issues. With Unger's thinking as a starting point, Bottomley argues for a broadly political framework which is complementary to the existing contractual-based framework. The key concept of Bottomley's theory suggests that there exists a "constitution" which establishes and defines the governance structure of a political institution, thereby contributing to the definition of the institution itself.[120] And unlike the contract, a constitution is more than just an agreement. It is the basis of the allocation and exercise of power with the polity of corporation. Within the corporate constitutional framework, corporate governance encompasses two key dimensions: the internal dimension, which relates to practices such as monitoring, steering, and influencing organisational relations and issues within the corporation; and the external dimension, which refers to the control mechanisms imposed from outside the corporation.[121]

1.4.3 Tracing Bottomley's Theoretical Development

There is an evolving process of Bottomley's ideas on corporate constitutionalism from 1997 to 2021. If tracing his works or arguments on corporate constitutionalism in these phases, the clear chain along a developing line could be his thinking on shareholders' role in corporate governance. What sparked off the corporate constitutional framework was the decision of one Australian case in 1995, *Gambotto v WCP Ltd* which was related to minority shareholders' protection.[122] In this case,

[118] Bottomley (n 16) 287.

[119] Laura Horn, 'Corporate Governance in Crisis? The Politics of EU Corporate Governance Regulation' (2012) 18 *European Law Journal* 83, 84.

[120] Bottomley (n 21) 49.

[121] Horn (n 119) 91.

[122] *Gambotto v WCP Ltd* [1995] 182 CLR 432.

the Australian High Court upheld the minority shareholder's claim that the majority shareholders cannot compulsorily buy his shares in the company. This court decision ignited fierce debates and critiques from the scholars that persisted a law and economics framework. This ready-made and well-developed law and economics model supplied these criticisms with a complete conceptual framework that can be used to respond quickly to the decision. However, other corporate scholars, including Bottomley himself, were incapable of mounting a response; even they felt that this decision could contribute to great development of corporate jurisprudence.

Starting from this minority shareholder protection case, Bottomley therefore attempted to develop an alternative conceptual framework of corporate governance—corporate constitutionalism.[123] He then first introduced "corporate constitutionalism" in his essay named *From Contractualism to Constitutionalism: A Framework for Corporate Governance* published in 1997. Since then, he developed the ideas on corporate constitutionalism in a journal essay—*The Birds, the Beasts, and the Bat: Developing a Constitutionalist Theory of Corporate Regulation* (1999) and a book—*The Constitutional Corporation, Rethinking Corporate Governance* (2007). Through these three works, Bottomley has gradually established a comprehensive conceptual evaluative framework which is alternative to corporate contractualism. His corporate constitutionalism still accepts the "shareholder primacy" doctrine, but in a slightly different way. Instead of treating shareholders as purely rentiers, he intends to grant to shareholder members a role in corporate governance and to highlight the value of the shareholders' voice in controlling a corporation. By establishing an *accountability-deliberation-contestability* mechanism of internal control, one of his main goals is to encourage shareholders' participation in corporate operation. And the contestability mechanism also concerns minority shareholder protection issues. Thus, from his standpoint, shareholder primacy does not only mean to ensure shareholders' interests, but also ensure their members' status and engagement in running a company well.

His most recent book, *The Responsible Shareholder* (2021), although not a sequel of the former book, presents arguments on shareholders' central role and the principles of accountability, deliberation and contestability within the corporate governance mechanism which seem to be spawned from his former works around corporate constitutionalism. His updated ideas on shareholders' responsibility which entail a discussion about corporate collapses in the UK and Australia will also enlighten this book to analyse the relevant issues in Carillion case.

1.5 Conclusion

This chapter has outlined the central goal of this book: to investigate whether Carillion Plc could have been saved had the corporate constitutionalism theory, as proposed by Bottomley, been applied to its internal and external governance mechanisms.

[123] Bottomley (n 21).

The literature reviewed in this chapter traces the development of the UK's corporate governance system, highlighting the dominance of corporate contractualism while also addressing alternative theories that critique this prevailing model. Given the ongoing corporate failures and scandals in the UK and beyond, it is clear that deeper reflection is needed on the core practices, regulatory oversight, and theoretical foundations of governance.

As Dine's statement suggests, the choice of theoretical framework fundamentally shapes our understanding of state intervention and corporate interests. Contractual theories, particularly economic contractualism, are fundamentally anti-regulatory, relying on market forces to dictate corporate behaviour, and they view corporate interests as the sum of individual profit-seeking actions, focusing on shareholder wealth accumulation. Despite the dominance of economic contractualism in contemporary corporate governance, alternative frameworks are essential to expand our understanding of corporate behaviour and governance.[124] The director primacy model, team production theory, stakeholder theory, and political frameworks all present important alternatives to the shareholder-centric, contract-based paradigm. This book adopts corporate constitutionalism's political perspective as a new lens through which to reconsider corporate governance.

Why not rely on other theories? First, these alternative theories often fail to clarify the appropriate role of the state or government in regulating corporate affairs. Corporate constitutionalism provides a clearer understanding of the interplay between public regulatory mechanisms and the private ordering of business. It helps define how public power should be appropriately applied in relation to corporate governance, while also highlighting the role corporations must play in their internal governance.

Second, corporate constitutionalism offers a framework that shifts our attention to a power-related corporate structure to define the nature of relations inside the corporation. Corporations themselves are powerful entities which are not entirely private, as their business conducts may have important social consequences. This book observes that the stakeholder theory also takes in this point so that it calls for corporate social responsibility. However, stakeholder theory has some limitations. According to Brown and Forster, "responsibility" in the stakeholder theory context is limited to firm-specific stakeholders and to create values for them,[125] rather than societal needs.[126] Another major limitation explained by Villiers is that it fails to clarify how the potential interests between different parties may be accommodated and balanced in the conduct of business affairs.[127] And more importantly, as revealed by Wicks et al., the stakeholder concept has been shaped by such metaphors as:

[124] Bottomley (n 21) 12.

[125] Jill A Brown and William R Forster, 'CSR and Stakeholder Theory: A Tale of Adam Smith' (2013) 112 *Journal of Business Ethics* 301, 302.

[126] Charlotte Villiers, 'Corporate Governance, Responsibility and Compassion: Why We Should Care' in *Shaping the Corporate Landscape Towards Corporate Reform and Enterprise Diversity*, Eds. Boeger and Villiers, (Hart Publishing, 2018) Chapter 8, 155.

[127] Charlotte Villiers, *Corporate Reporting and Company Law* (Cambridge University Press 2006) 96.

"corporations are autonomous entities",[128] "conflict and competition best describe how firms should be managed",[129] "strategy formulation should be objective",[130] and "power and authority should be embedded in strict hierarchies".[131] These metaphors are essentially "individualistic and masculine".[132] In comparison, the constitutional ideas have capacity to direct the attention to integrate individuals together, rather than just separating them.

Third, this constitutionalism framework changes the way in which we look at corporations and corporate relations. That is, (a) it suggests a possibility that a collective purpose is constituted when corporations are formed rather than viewing corporations as only an aggregation of individual actors; (b) shareholders are regarded as active members rather than passive investors who are far away from business sectors; (c) a corporation has its public dimensions in addition to its private business; (d) a significant part of corporations involves complex structures and processes of decision-making. The outcomes of decision-making should be "accountable, deliberate and contestable".[133]

Fourth, this framework points out the double roles of the corporate participants, that each participant in a corporation is both a member of a collective set of corporate interests and simultaneously maintains their own individual or personal interests.[134]

This analysis does not aim to favour one theory over another but rather seeks to further the academic conversation by expanding the largely underexplored area of corporate constitutionalism. It is also important to note the scope of this inquiry. While this book focuses on corporate governance, particularly through the lens of corporate constitutionalism, it does not attempt to address every aspect of Carillion's failure. The company's involvement in public–private partnerships and public procurement, while a significant factor, will only be briefly discussed, as these topics fall outside the primary scope of this book.

---

[128] Andrew C Wicks, Daniel R Gilbert Jr and R Edward Freeman, 'A Feminist Reinterpretation of the Stakeholder Concept' (1994) *Business Ethics Quarterly* 475, 479.

[129] Ibid., 480.

[130] Ibid., 481.

[131] Ibid., 482.

[132] Villiers (n 126) 155.

[133] Bottomley (n 16).

[134] Bottomley (n 21) 66.

Part I Theoretical Foundations and Paradigm Comparison

Chapter 2
Corporate Contractualism

2.1 Introduction

This chapter seeks to lay a theoretical foundation of the book through an analysis of corporate contractualism. This chapter starts with a description of the key features of the UK's company law and corporate governance framework and then explains its evolution and development and practice from the perspective of the theory of corporate contractualism. It approaches as follows: Sect. 2.2 starts by asking "what is corporate governance" and then describes what it looks like in the UK. Then Sect. 2.3 looks at the historical tendency of corporate contractualism and shows how this theory has influenced the development of corporate governance framework. Section 2.4 examines two models under the corporate contractual paradigm and evaluates the roles of key corporate actors, including the managers, shareholders, auditors and regulators in the corporate operation within the corporate contractualism framework. Section 2.5 will give a critique on contractualism and consider how contractual theories might contribute to corporate failure. The concluding section sets out to finalise the main points and give an initial evaluation of the constitutional approach which may provide a conceptual alternative in the corporate governance arrangement.

2.2 Corporate Governance in the UK

2.2.1 What is Corporate Governance?

What is corporate governance? The most commonly adopted definition of corporate governance in the UK was offered by the 1992 Cadbury Report which stated that "corporate governance is the system by which companies are directed and

Y. Yang, *Corporate Collapse and Corporate Governance*, CSR, Sustainability, Ethics & Governance, https://doi.org/10.1007/978-981-96-9666-6_2

controlled."[1] However, "corporate governance" is a contested system with no overarching concept and scope: depending on scholars' different cultural contexts, intellectual backgrounds, interests and theoretical viewpoints,[2] governance theory is "generally not robust or well-rooted",[3] possessing a "plurality of meanings and forms".[4] Corporate governance is also a "multi-layered topic" that has attained great practical importance: it could be a formalistic system embracing a burgeoning body of consultation documents and codes; or it could be a system with the combination of hard law and soft law in the corporate arena; or it could also be an open-ended subject of legal-academic enquiry which concerns extra-legal questions within a broader social context.[5] As Solomon asserted, this is a dynamic term which has grown and changed in various ways.[6] Far greater clarification and cognition have been achieved as the disciplines of corporate governance both in academic research and policymaking have been evolving and developing rapidly during past 30 years.

Moore borrows the understanding from state law on "governance" which conventionally refers to the counterbalance of the authority of powerful political decision makers, or otherwise the acquisition of legitimacy from whose interests are affected by the power.[7] Building on the concept of public governance, corporate governance can be seen as the societal challenge of holding influential decision-makers in large economic organisations accountable for their actions, thereby legitimising

---

[1] *Report of the Committee on the Financial Aspects of Corporate Governance—Cadbury Report* (Gee and Co. Ltd., London, 1992) Para. 2.5.

[2] Shann Turnbull, 'Corporate Governance: Its Scope, Concerns and Theories' (1997) 5 *Corporate Governance: An International Review* 180, 184.

[3] Thomas Clarke, 'Research on Corporate Governance' (1998) 6 *Corporate Governance* 57, 63.

[4] Maria Bonnafous-Boucher, 'Some Philosophical Issues in Corporate Governance: The Role of Property in Stakeholder Theory' (2005) 5 *Corporate Governance: The International Journal of Business in Society* 34, 35.

[5] Nick Lin-Hi and Igor Blumberg, 'The Relationship between Corporate Governance, Global Governance, and Sustainable Profits: Lessons Learned from BP' (2011) 11 *Corporate Governance: The International Journal of Business in Society* 571, 575.

See also Kose John and Lemma W Senbet, 'Corporate Governance and Board Effectiveness' (1998) 22 *Journal of banking & Finance* 371, 372.

Different scholars have proposed a 'multi-layered topic' in corporate governance. For instance, Clarke focuses on re-conceptualisation of corporate governance theory after the Enron experience. See from Thomas Clarke, 'Accounting for Enron: Shareholder Value and Stakeholder Interests' (2005) 13 *Corporate Governance: An International Review* 598.

Daily et al. concentrate on the determination of the broad uses to which organisational resources will be deployed and the resolution of conflicts among the myriad participants in organisations. See from Catherine M Daily, Dan R Dalton and Albert A Cannella, 'Corporate Governance: Decades of Dialogue and Data' (2003) 28 *The Academy of Management Review* 371.

Turnbull also analyses the scope, concerns and theories of corporate governance. See from Shann Turnbull, 'Corporate Governance: Its Scope, Concerns and Theories' (1997) 5 *Corporate Governance: An International Review* 180.

[6] Jill Solomon, *Corporate Governance and Accountability* (John Wiley & Sons 2020) 4.

[7] Marc Moore, *Corporate Governance in the Shadow of the State* (Bloomsbury Publishing 2013) 25.

their ongoing control and use of power.[8] Consequently, the study of corporate governance is essentially an investigation into the causes and outcomes of the distribution of decision-making power within large, socially important business organisations.[9] Moore's definition detaches from the mainstream of thought that views corporate governance as purely private orderings and he develops the conceptual framework to include a public arena. He clearly highlights three key words—*power, accountability and legitimacy* as the intrinsic components of corporate governance which reveal the public character of governance of corporations.

Bottomley's perception also emphasises the public attribution of corporate governance. From his standpoint, corporate governance serves as an organising motif for identifying the role, composition, and responsibilities of the board of directors, as well as the role and rights of shareholders, and the position of other non-decision-makers, including auditors and other stakeholders, whether individually, in groups, or collectively, while also examining the ways in which all these corporate actors interact within a company.[10] The fundamental theme of all these arguments, as Bottomley revealed, is essentially about the legitimacy of corporate power,[11] or the board of directors' full managerial power and the supplemented specific grants of power.[12] But what is different with Moore's definition constituted by power, accountability, legitimacy, Bottomley also stresses the importance of the principles of *deliberation and contestability*, besides *accountability* for corporate internal control. Thus, *power, legitimacy, accountability, deliberation, contestability* are the key words of Bottomley's conception of corporate governance.

Although it is not this book' intention to be involved in the debates about the definition of corporate governance, a clear understanding of this term could help approach the following context. For this book, corporate governance is a subject of power. From this power lens, in metaphorical words, a corporation is an ecosystem in which every corporate actor is tied together and contributes to the operation of the whole system. It is only a power-balanced corporate ecosystem that can realise its long-term sustainability. Drawing from the public-value-oriented definitions as stated by Moore and Bottomley, this book perceives that corporate governance is designed to contribute to power legitimacy and power balance within this ecosystem: the allocation and the continuing possession of managerial power should be legitimised and balanced by a system of checks and balances (corresponding to accountability in Moore's thinking, or accountability, deliberation, contestability in Bottomley's statement). The values of power, legitimacy, and checks and balances play throughout the whole book as the key parameters to examine and evaluate corporate contractualism

[8] Ibid., 26.

[9] Marc Moore and Martin Petrin, *Corporate Governance: Law, Regulation and Theory* (Palgrave 2017) 4.

[10] Ibid.

[11] Ibid.

[12] Stephen Bottomley, 'From Contractualism to Constitutionalism: A Framework for Corporate Governance' (1997) 19 *Sydney L. Rev.* 277, 279.

and corporate constitutionalism. This book argues that the failure of legitimising and balancing corporate power is an immediate reason for corporate collapses.

2.2.2 Description of the Company Law and Corporate Governance System—The Key Features

In the UK, a contractual conception is predominant in viewing the interactions and interplays among corporate actors with the aim to maximise individual advantage. But the "contract" of corporate context is not totally equal to the contracts as understood in the content of contract law. Rather, "corporate contractualism" refers to the ideological pattern or a paradigm that contributes to exploring the nature of corporations. A corporate contractual paradigm sets the underlying logic of how we understand the corporation, the methodology for scholars to investigate corporate conducts, and the role of the corporation as a whole domain for societal relations. Corporate contractualism has established a complete, longstanding normative framework of UK's corporate governance. Companies, in the eyes of contractarians are in voluntary, private relations with the overriding goal of "shareholder value maximisation". Corporate contractualism presents a whole picture in which the shareholder sits at the core of the ecosystem associated with the company and the directors by private, flexible and negotiable bargaining. Moreover, in the logic of contractarians, external regulatory intervention is essentially incompatible with the doctrine of contracting in a free market. In terms of the existing double tracks of corporate rules—the company law, consisting of statute and a body of common law, and the soft corporate governance rules, these corporate laws are regarded as the "survival value" of an "endogenous" market evolution.[13] The prevailing legal regulatory structure of corporations has therefore largely been designed in the reflection of corporate contractual ideology.

As to the company law, it focuses mainly on the relationship between the directors and the shareholders as well as the relationship between the company and the shareholders and that between the shareholders. It also refers to the procedures for meetings, voting rights, use of corporate assets, distribution of profits/dividends, duties of directors, transparency requirements, mergers and acquisitions, and change of contractual terms. In terms of the corporate governance system, it concentrates on the agency relationship and monitoring of managers by the shareholders. It is largely self-regulatory, based on a comply-or-explain approach and supplemented by other codes (such as the Stewardship Codes and Takeover Codes) and requirements. These soft rules mostly focus on protecting shareholders from dishonest or neglectful managers. Some element of stakeholder value has begun to get established in recent versions of Corporate Governance Codes and this perhaps changes

[13] Marc Moore, 'Private Ordering and Public Policy: The Paradoxical Foundations of Corporate Contractarianism' (2014) 34 *Oxford Journal of Legal Studies* 693, 697.

the dynamics and the relationships that shareholders and managers have with each other and with others.

Within a corporate contractual paradigm, company law and corporate governance in the UK have constructed a system that is traditionally market-disciplined and non-interventionist with the primary goal of serving the companies' economic interests. And that companies' interests are always interpreted as for the best interests of shareholders. Consequently, the performance metrics applied to judge directors' behaviours largely revolve around the economic returns of investment. Although there is an enlightened shareholder value approach of the law to think about stakeholders' benefits and directors are encouraged to take account of the long-term operation of companies, shareholders are still the priority to be considered in the governance of companies. Thus, the corporate contractualist theory is evident in shaping a shareholder-primacy-oriented, free-market-based, profit-maximisation-pursued facilitative corporate regulatory framework.

This section has provided a brief description of the key features of UK's corporate regulatory framework in the reflection of corporate contractualism. It gives us a general understanding and initial impression on what UK's corporate governance looks like under corporate contractual ideology. The following sections will gradually dig deeper to explore how this ideology has developed and acted in the corporate arena.

2.3 Historical Approach of Corporate Contractualism

Paradoxically, tracing through the historical development of the UK Company Law, contractualism runs directly counter to the flow of historical tendency, according to Ireland's investigation.[14] In the mid-1830s, a de-contractualisation movement had occurred along with the rise of railway companies. However, the late-twentieth-century contractarian assertion of reducing corporations to a nexus of contracts could be seen as a recurrence of the old agency and contractual principles in the late eighteenth and early nineteenth centuries when company law was seen as the adjunct to partnership law.[15]

The UK "company law" we call today was developed on a partnership base which was applied to joint stock companies. In the first "company law" work—Charles Wordsworth's book, joint stock companies were seen as "voluntary and contractual affairs",[16] without regard to the modern doctrine of separate legal personality.[17]

---

[14] Paddy Ireland, 'Property and Contract in Contemporary Corporate Theory' (2003) 23 *Legal Studies* 453, 457.

[15] Ibid.

[16] Ibid., 458.

[17] Charles Favell Forth Wordsworth, *The Law Relating to Railway, Bank, Insurance, Mining and Other Joint-Stock Companies: With an Appendix, Containing Statutes, Cases at Law and in Equity,*

Shareholders within these joint stock companies were regarded as partners or co-owners of the corporate assets and directors were appointed as shareholders' agents. Resembling the modern contractualism, the relationships within companies and with outside parties were viewed as contractual relations.

During the 1830s, the introduction of limited liability, the fully paid-up and freely transferable shares changed the economic and legal structure of companies and gradually eliminated the contractual conceptions in company law. The erosion of the contractual base also reconceptualised the role of directors as the agent of the company, rather than the agent of shareholders. With the development of the doctrine of *ultra vires* and the restrictions of shareholders' collective power in the general meeting, managing power was steadily transferred from shareholders to the board of directors.[18] As a result, shareholdings held by these pure rentiers turned to embody "no-obligation, no-responsibility, personality-poor" features.[19] Against this backdrop, the courts and legislature moved away from the old contractual model. For example, *Colman* V *Eastern Counties Railway* [1846] and the later *Ashbury Railway Carriage & Iron Co* v *Riche* [1875] abandoned the contractual principles of the law of partnership.[20] And company law was not a part of partnership law, but was instead an independent, distinctive and autonomous company law that had been constructed.[21]

By the end of the nineteenth century, and then the development of Berle and Means's contribution in building the fundamentalism of separation of ownership and control,[22] and the increasing externality of shareholders, companies were deemed as "autonomous, property-owning legal persons" and shares more likely had the feature of the property of rights in rem.[23] Shareholders' ineffectiveness of control, lack of enough information on the company leads to the question about shareholders as the rational recipients of corporate residual resources, and leads to a worry that any dividend paid to shareholders could not benefit the business operations which would cause a waste of resources for the company.[24] In the meantime, the professional managers who gained the ultimate corporate control established a solid decision-making primacy status in the company.

Moreover, with the burgeoning expansion of joint stock companies, the collective investment of the middle class led to highly capitalised oligopolies which made it

---

Resolutions of the Houses of Parliament as to Railway and Other Bills, Forms of Deeds, &c (Henry Butterworth 1837).

[18] Ireland (n 15) 468.

[19] Ibid.

[20] *Colman* v *Eastern Counties Railway Company* [1846] C157; *Ashbury Railway Carriage and Iron Co* v *Riche* [1875] LR 7 HL 653.

[21] Ireland (n 15) 471.

[22] Adolf Berle and Gardiner Means, *The Modern Corporation and Private Property* (London: Macmillan 1932).

[23] Paddy Ireland, 'Capitalism without the Capitalist: The Joint Stock Company Share and the Emergence of the Modern Doctrine of Separate Corporate Personality' (1996) 17 *The Journal of Legal History* 41. See also from Ireland (n 15) 462.

[24] Berle and Means (n 23).

possible to get rid of the constraints of traditional product market competition and reduce companies' dependence on outside capital providers. In this sense, companies acquired the decision-making discretion to invest in key industries, automobile manufacture and societally important utilities, for example.[25] As a result, they appeared to be analogous to statist institutions which became more and more imperative in conforming public-service expectations.[26] It is thus manifested that, by the mid to late twentieth century, companies in the Anglo-American world held and exercised quasi-public power in parallel with the function of the state.

However, by the late twentieth century—a time when the state-centric ideology transformed into the market-centred and deregulated neo-liberalism,[27] neo-classical legal formalism played a very key role in Anglo-American corporate law sector. Contractualism was initially an invention of American-founded economists—Chicago scholars in particular, with the mission to tackle with the post-Second World War stagnation of economic in the western world.[28] The contractarian conception had its origins in a renewed interest by economists in the internal mechanism of the company and provided quite different perspectives towards it.[29]

Coase's seminal article—*The nature of the firm* published in 1937 is regarded as a landmark of the contractarian movement. However, unlike Coase's statement that the firm is "a realm beyond contracts and the market",[30] the subsequent scholars insist on attempting to make the deviation or opposite. Alchian and Demsetz, for example, deny that the firm is characterised by power, authority or disciplinary actions, instead emphasising the role of agreement in the team production process. The firm is viewed as a highly specialised surrogate market, lacking any power of fiat, authority, or disciplinary actions that would differ in the slightest from ordinary market contracting.[31] In their words, the actions in the firm are no different with ordinary market voluntary exchanges between two people.[32]

Even furthering Alchian's and Demsetz's objection to the Coasian concept of the firm, the term "nexus of contracts" was first formulated by Jensen and Meckling in *The Theory of the Firm: Managerial Behaviour, Agency Costs, and Ownership Structure*. They argue that the firm is essentially formed by contractual relations, including the relations with employees, suppliers, customers, creditors, etc.[33] Most organisations, including firms, are just "legal fictions" constituted by a nexus of

---

[25] Moore (n 7) 58.

[26] Ibid., 60.

[27] Moore (n 14) 698.

[28] After the Second World War, during the period of 1945–1960s, the western world did some massive effort to rebuild welfare states. However, the economy in 1970s appeared to slow down.

[29] Christopher A Riley, 'Contracting out of Company Law: Section 459 of the Companies Act 1985 and the Role of the Courts' (1992) 55 *The Modern Law Review* 782, 783.

[30] Ireland (n 15) 475.

[31] Armen A Alchian and Harold Demsetz, 'Production, Information Costs, and Economic Organization' (1972) 62 *The American Economic Review* 777, 777.

[32] Ibid., 777–778.

[33] Michael C Jensen and William H Meckling, 'Theory of the Firm: Managerial Behavior, Agency Costs and Ownership Structure' (1976) 3 *Journal of Financial Economics* 305, 310.

contractual relations among individuals.[34] Eisenberg explains the meaning of "nexus of contract" as "nexus of reciprocal arrangements".[35] By the 1990s, Easterbrook and Fischel play a leading role in bringing contractual thinking into the corporate law. In their work, *The Economic Structure of Corporate Law*, they dismiss the personality of corporations and emphasise the congruity of the interests between shareholders and the corporation.[36] For them, the doctrine of separate corporate personality is a matter of convenience rather than an actual reality.[37] When considering the relationship within the directors and shareholders, they attempt to introduce a concept of implicit contractual obligation to define the directors' duty to shareholders. Simply, bearing the resemblance to the old-days contractual theory of company law, the market-fundamentalist supporters depict corporations as essentially contractual collections without moral footing and hierarchy. These contractarians strip corporations' personality and existence and reconnect the shareholders with corporate assets and managers.

Contractarians have already reinvigorated the idea of the corporation as subject to the orthodox market governance mechanism as opposed to bureaucratic state control. Thus, companies, long seen as entities of power with vertical hierarchies, were reconceived by economists as purely a "nexus of contracts" amongst individuals.[38] As revealed by Ireland, the claim of the existence and effectiveness of this market, along with the strong correlation between corporate managerial efficiency and the market price of a corporation's shares, forms one of the foundational principles of contractualism.[39] This statement identifies the fundamental ideology of contractualism which highly relies on an efficient market control—corporations' managerial behaviours would be directly and precisely reflected in their share prices of the market.

With the widespread expansion of the US-initiated contractualism and coupled with the insufficiency of viable UK-based counter theories, the UK company law retreated to its old agency, contractual and partnership-based eighteenth-century predecessor. Meanwhile, faithful in the efficacy of the market, products of voluntary and contractual exchanges, contractualism was consistent with the 1970s privatisation and deregulation of Thatcherism politic-economy which led to the rise of a "contract state" or an era of "contracting out the delivery of public services".[40] Thatcher's "New Right" government redefined the relationships between the government and private sectors that by utilising free market or market-mimicking methods

---

[34] Ibid.

[35] Melvin Eisenberg, 'The Conception That the Corporation Is a Nexus of Contracts, and the Dual Nature of the Firm' (1998) 24 J. *Corp. L.* 819, 822.

[36] Frank H Easterbrook and Daniel R Fischel, *The Economic Structure of Corporate Law* (Harvard University Press 1996) 34.

[37] Ibid., 12.

[38] Riley (n 30) 783.

[39] Ireland (n 15) 482.

[40] Karen Wong, 'The Collapse of Carillion: Regulatory Failure in the Contract State' (2019) 4 *LSE Law Review* 1.

(such as privatisation and quasi-privatisation),[41] their relations turned from regulations to contracts. Harnessing private bodies for public departments will help bring in experiences and resources and improve competitive abilities for public sectors. The contractual culture from the top down ensured corporate contractualism increasingly merged into the UK corporate law scholarship and government policy making. After more than 50 years' spreading and developing, the ideology of the free market and contractarianism have already constructed a solid framework in the legislation, the courts of law, agencies with market-regulatory responsibilities, and academia.

2.4 Corporate Governance Under Contractualism

An analogy has always been made between the state governance and the corporate governance in that they all refer to the governance of "power"—public power and private power respectively. Governance stems from liberalism's tenet that all power, no matter public power or private power, should be constrained or subjected to checks and balances. In a western-style liberal democratic society, public power is legitimated by two elements: a system of democratic government and the Rule of Law.[42] Regarding the former element, originating from Montesquieu's call for a separation of powers, administrative power is legitimated from the assurance of the legislature which itself gains authority from a system of representative democracy. Meanwhile, the Rule of Law which is a principle of institutional morality intrinsic to any constitutional democracy, is characterised by four key features: legality, certainty, equality, and access to justice and rights. These elements ensure that laws are applied consistently and fairly, providing a framework within which individuals and entities can operate with the assurance that their rights will be protected and their actions will be governed by clear and just legal principles.[43] The Rule of Law imposes the constraints and checks on the wield of the state power. In private power, individuals are empowered by their ownership of property. It is claimed that the justification of individual's power in a liberal world could be their ownership of the property and the constraint of the competitive market. The private power is distributed in the hands of each owner so that it cannot be a threat to liberty. The competitive market plays the same role of the Rule of Law that could limit and control that private power.

However, the increase in the size and capital of corporations seems to undermine the private power legitimacy framework. In other words, business companies centralise authority to manage the capital aggregated from their investors. The power gathered by corporate directors and managers thus poses a problem of legitimacy. The

---

[41] Christopher Hood, 'A Public Management for All Seasons?' (1991) 69 *Public Administration* 3. Citing from Wong (n 41).

[42] Mary Stokes, 'Company Law and Legal Theory' (1986) *Legal Theory and Common Law* 155, 157.

[43] Jeffrey Jowell, Dawn Oliver, and Colm O'Cinneide, *The Changing Constitution (Eighth Edition)* (Oxford University Press) 13.

principle of limited liability enables a collectivisation of large amounts of privately invested capital in big companies which lead to a problem of monopoly in an uncompetitive market. Additionally, the doctrine of the separation of ownership and control also leads to a so-called agency problem implying a risk that the managers will pursue their interests to the sacrifice of shareholders' interests. Again, in the real world, because of the imperfect market's inability to regulate powerful companies, a potentially increased and unlimited power would be concentrated in the hands of the managers who get the ultimate control of the company. This unchecked power may lead to risks not only relating to internal agency cost, but also to external social problems; a private decision made by socially significant corporations would have public results. The impact of private power therefore is expanded to a wider societal dimension by corporate actors exerting their abilities of political lobbying and influencing the policy-making process, as opposed to being encapsulated within an inner dimension filled with "contractual or quasi-contractual control relationships".[44]

The underlying theme of corporate governance is essentially to solve the problem of the legitimacy of such corporate power. In other words, owing to the failure of the traditional tenet in justifying increasingly converged private corporate power, the corporate governance framework takes a very key role in legitimising the continuous possession and exertion of corporate discretionary power. "Contractualism" is deemed as a theoretical root for the prevailing understanding of corporations in the UK.[45] What the UK legal form adopts therefore is a contractual paradigm that has been embedded deeply into the company law and corporate governance system to legitimate management's substantial power. As Mary Stokes observed, the conception of the company explicitly adopted by the legal model is clearly the contractual one. By embracing a contractual view of the company, the legal model justifies the centralised authority of the board of directors to manage the company based on the contractual agreement of the company's owners.[46]

Just as the term implies, contractualism develops a complete framework based on the concept of "contract". Nevertheless, contractualism derives from a two-pattern basis—the traditional legal model and the law and economics one. These two ways share a similar contractual foundation arguing that the essence of companies is reflected in the different contractual relationships of corporate participators, but they differ substantially from each other and tend to be not well reconciled in certain aspects. The following sections set out to investigate how could a double-strand contractual approach engender a normative and paradigmatic, but also paradoxical, framework to secure corporate managerial power legitimacy.

---

[44] Scott Bowman, *Modern Corporation and American Political Thought: Law, Power, and Ideology* (Penn State Press 2010) 1. Citing from Marc Moore, 'Understanding the Modern Company through the Lens of Quasi-Public Power' (2015) *University of Cambridge Faculty of Law Research Paper* 7.

[45] Ireland (n 15) 456.

[46] Stokes (n 43) 163.

2.4.1 The Legal Model

In a legal model, each company is regarded as an artificial legal person (*Salomon v A Salomon & Co Ltd*) which is distinct from its shareholders and directors.[47] The contractual nature of these three sets of relationships among the corporate entity, its shareholders and its directors is clearly defined and embodied in the corporate constitution.

The corporate constitution is seen as a contractual arrangement in nature that is situated at the heart of a corporation's internal power control. As noted by Gower et al., a remarkable character of the UK company law is the extent to which it leaves substantive regulations of the internal matters, central to the business's operation, to the corporate constitution, in particular its articles of association.[48] As the primary document of a company, the corporate constitution—including any internal governance rules established therein—is vested with the formal status of a contractual relationship binding together a company and its members or shareholders. On the contractual effect of the articles of association, in *Oakbank Oil Co v Crum*, Lord Selborne LC stated that, each party is presumed to have familiarised themselves with the terms of the written contract set out in the articles of association… They are also, in law, deemed to have understood the terms of the contract according to their correct meaning. Therefore, they must accept the consequences, whatever they may be, of the contract they have entered into.[49] This statement clearly defines the contractual attribution of articles of association and the relationships that are connected by it.

In statutes, the term "corporate constitution" is defined in Section 17 of the Companies Act 2006 as including the articles of association and any resolutions or agreements referred to in Chapter 3 of the Act.[50] Section 33 of the Companies Act 2006

---

[47] *Salomon v A Salomon & Co Ltd* [1896] UKHL 1.

[48] PL Davies and others, *Gower's principles of modern company law (Tenth edition)*, (Sweet & Maxwell) 218.

[49] *Oakbank Oil Co (Ltd) v Crum* [1882] 8 App. Cas. 65 (HL).

[50] Section 17: "unless the context otherwise requires, references in the Companies Acts to a company's constitution include—(a) the company's articles, and (b) any resolutions and agreements to which Chapter 3 applies (see Section 29)." Basically, ordinary and special resolution are the most important categories of resolutions in practice.

Section 29: Resolutions and agreements affecting a company's constitution: "(1) This Chapter applies to—(a) any special resolution; (b) any resolution or agreement agreed to by all the members of a company that, if not so agreed to, would not have been effective for its purpose unless passed as a special resolution; (c) any resolution or agreement agreed to by all the members of a class of shareholders that, if not so agreed to, would not have been effective for its purpose unless passed by some particular majority or otherwise in some particular manner; (d) any resolution or agreement that effectively binds all members of a class of shareholders though not agreed to by all those members; (e) any other resolution or agreement to which this Chapter applies by virtue of any enactment.

(2) References in subsection (1) to a member of a company, or of a class of members of a company, do not include the company itself where it is such a member by virtue only of its holding shares as treasury shares."

(the predecessor is Section 14 of the Companies Act 1985) makes a direct articulation of the relationship between members and the company, with rather peculiar contractual status.[51] Section 33 made a near restatement of Section 14 CA1985. It expressly endows a multi-party contractual relationship between the company and its members like many other contracts established in a private commercial world that are enforceable by the parties on legal grounds.

2.4.1.1 Company and Shareholders

The corporate constitution could be treated as a binding contract between the company and its members.Their contractual relationship has been clarified not only by the statutes, but also by the UK common law, for example in the leading case of *Hickman v Kent or Romney Marsh Sheepbreeders' Association.*[52] However, the corporate contract is actually treated as more than a private bargain.[53] As Lord Greene MR asserted, Section 14 (1) CA 1985 has historically been a matter of significant debate, and it is likely to continue provoking substantial controversy in the future.[54] The "controversy" in this field seems to remain still. The corporate contract has its distinctive features—it could be seen as a statutory contract embedded with both privity and publicity. As to privity, it establishes contracts between private parties—the company and members; while as to publicity, it is also a kind of public document which represents a statement of the company's internal rules that may be of concern to the external persons who are willing to engage in corporate affairs.[55] Thus, the logic of contract law can only be applied in certain circumstances in the corporate arena. The court seems to be also reluctant to apply contract law doctrines into a statutory contract. For example, in the case of *Bratton Seymour Service Ltd v Oxborough*, Steyn LJ stated that the statutory contract "was not defensible on the grounds of misrepresentation, common law mistake, mistake in equity, undue influence or duress".[56] In other words, not all the conditions of contract law could be applied in the corporate context.

---

[51] Section 14 (1) Companies Act 1985: Subject to the provisions of this Act, the memorandum and articles, when registered, bind the company and its members to the same extent as if they respectively had been signed and sealed by each member, and contained covenants on the part of each member to observe all the provisions of the memorandum and articles.

Section 33 (1) Companies Act 2006: The provisions of a company's constitution bind the company and its members to the same extent as if there were covenants on the part of the company and of each member to observe those provisions.

[52] *Hickman v Kent or Romney Marsh Sheepbreeders' Association* [1915] 1 Ch 881; see also *Rayfield v Hands* [1960] Ch 1; *Pender v Lushington* [1877] 6 Ch D 70.

[53] Davies and others (n 49) 221.

[54] *Beattie v E and F Beattie Ltd* [1938] Ch 708.

[55] Davies and others (n 49) 221.

[56] *Bratton Seymour Service Ltd v Oxborough* [1992] BCLC 693.

2.4.1.2 Company and Directors

The connection between the company and its directors is also seen as residing in contractual relationships, or in a fiduciary relationship to be more precise. In general, fiduciary duties can be formulated as three distinct rules: directors owe a duty of care and skill; a duty of loyalty; a duty to act bona fire in the best interest of the company and not for any improper purpose. The duties that the directors owe to the company have been codified in statute and defined in the case law and principles. Directors' statutory duties are clarified in the Sections 171–177 of Companies Act 2006 which include "duty to act within powers; duty to promote the success of the company; duty to exercise independent judgement; duty to exercise reasonable care skill and diligence; duty to avoid conflicts of interest, duty not to accept benefits from third parties; and duty to declare interest in proposed transaction or arrangement".[57] Beside these statutory duties, directors must also comply with the common law duties, although there may be some overlaps between the former duties. Directors should also follow the duty to act in good faith in accordance with the best interests of the company (a subjective test),[58] the duty to exercise power within company's constitution and act for a proper purpose,[59] the duty to avoid conflicts of interest,[60] and the duty not to make unauthorised profits.[61]

However, what should be highlighted here is that although the company law and common law principles have clarified that the directors owe a fiduciary duty to the company and their behaviours should therefore be in line with the best interests of the company, the company's best interests are usually assessed by reference to or directly interpreted as shareholders' interests in practice.

2.4.1.3 Shareholders and Directors

In the legal model, corporate power could be exerted by two mechanisms of the corporation—meetings of shareholders and meetings of directors. Typically, a corporate constitution ensures the power of the meetings of shareholders to appoint directors. As determined by the Court of Appeal in the case of *Automatic Self-cleansing Filter Syndicate Co Ltd v Cunninghame*,[62] the relationship between the board and

---

[57] Companies Act 2006 Sections 171–177.

[58] *Dawson International Plc v Coats Paton Plc* [1989] BCLC.

[59] *Howard Smith Ltd v Ampol Petroleum Ltd* [1974] AC 821.

[60] *Regal (Hastings) v Gulliver* [1967] 1 AC 134; *Island Export Finance Ltd v Umunna* [1986] BCLC 460; *CMS Dolphin Ltd v Simonet* [2001] BCLC 315; *Foster Bryant Surveying Ltd v Bryant* [2007] IRLR 425 CA.

[61] *Murad v Al-Saraj* [2005] All ER (D) 503.

[62] *Automatic Self-Cleansing Filter Syndicate Co Ltd v Cunninghame* [1906] 2 Ch 34; see also *Quin & Axtens Ltd v Salmon* [1909] AC 442.

the shareholders is of a contractual nature, founded upon the articles of association which prescribe the extent of the managerial powers delegated to the board.[63] This essentially reveals the typical division of power between these two groups of people—the board of directors has the exclusive authority to manage the company's business, while the shareholders could direct the directors by special resolutions on specified actions.[64]

The effect of this power division is that shareholders seem to be formally excluded from certain important corporate decisions, although the UK company law reserves decisions on some forms of significant matters for the meeting of the shareholders or a class of shareholders.[65] Shareholders' residual power of management could arise in the circumstances where the board is unable to operate (*Foster v Foster*),[66] or is deadlocked or for all practical purposes has ceased to exist (*Barron v Potter*).[67] The law also asserts that the annual general meeting must be held within six months of the financial year end (Companies Act 2006, s336 (1)). Nevertheless, to a large extent, the directors enjoy great autonomy of decision-making. In the case of *John Shaw & Sons (Salford) Ltd v Shaw*, Greer LJ ensured the exclusive management power of directors—If managerial powers are conferred upon the directors, it is they, and only they, who are entitled to exercise such powers. The general body of shareholders may influence the directors' use of these powers solely through formal mechanisms—either by amending the articles of association or, where the opportunity presents itself, by declining to re-elect directors whose conduct they oppose. Shareholders cannot directly appropriate powers allocated to the board, just as the board cannot encroach upon powers reserved for shareholders under the articles.[68] Thus, a corporate-constitution-based power separation constructs a clear boundary of the activities between shareholders and directors.

2.4.1.4 Legitimacy in the Legal Model

In summary, in the legal model of the corporate contractual framework, according to Dine, a company comes into existence when two or more parties come together to make a pact to carry on commercial activity, and it is this very agreement, the pact, that gives birth to the company.[69] This model thus views the legitimisation of the corporate power as originating from the private contractual activities of its members. We can clearly see that there are two strategies to legitimate directors' discretionary power

---

[63] Brenda Hannigan, *Company Law* (Oxford University Press, USA 2015) 183.

[64] A special resolution is used in some significant occasions for the corporation, such as constitutional changes, capital changes, corporation winding up.

[65] Leslie Kosmin QC and Catherine Roberts, *Company Meetings and Resolutions: Law, Practice, and Procedure* (2013) OUP Catalogue. Citing from Hannigan (n 64) 418.

[66] *Foster v Foster* [1916] 1 Ch. 532.

[67] *Barron v Potter* [1914] 1 Ch. 895.

[68] *John Shaw & Sons (Salford) Ltd v Shaw* [1935] 2 KB 113.

[69] Janet Dine, *The Governance of Corporate Groups*, vol 1 (Cambridge University Press 2000) 3.

to manage the corporation. First, in the traditional legal model, directors are viewed as the agents of the company.[70] Their power could be constrained by shareholders who hold the power to revoke or dismiss directors' administrative power. Although shareholders cannot directly control the day-to-day business of a company, the mutual agreement on the division of internal power between shareholders and directors could limit management's allocative power. The courts can also help to ensure the system of indirect control will be enforceable. Second, the imposition of fiduciary duty is a further method to restrain directors from pursuing their own interest to the sacrifice of the company and shareholders. The logic is borrowed from the relationship of trustees that directors are under a duty to act on behalf of or for the best of their trust settlor—the company. And if directors breach their duties, the court can also be brought in although the role of the court is limited by the business judgement rule. Thus, by utilising these two forms of contractual relationships, directors' discretional management power could be controlled and legitimated.

Clearly, in the legal model, since shareholders retain control over the company's constitution, the British approach may be understood as embodying the view that shareholders are the ultimate source of managerial authority. Under this model, directors derive their powers through a process of delegation by the shareholders, albeit a formal and structured delegation, which for as long as it remains in effect, positions the directors as the principal decision-making body acting on behalf of the company.[71] Shareholders thus appear to have a key role in legitimating the manager's power. In turn, it strengthens the vital status of shareholders in corporate governance mechanisms. In Ireland's words, corporate contractual theories provide an "ideological defence" for shareholders' priority.[72]

Moreover, it also has a further effect of classifying corporate affairs into the private sphere, and company law is consequently categorised as being situated within the private law arena. In this sense, the justification of the state's external intervention on corporate conducts has been considerably lessened.[73] Influenced by the power of freedom of contract, the rise of legal formation, and perhaps, on occasion, a sympathy for these agencies of economic growth, the courts often embrace the mantle of legal abstentionism rather than acting as a "watchdog".[74]

2.4.2 The Law and Economics Model

The other strand of corporate contractualism is the law and economics model which has prevailed since the 1970s. The literature and historical study in Chapter 1 and

---

[70] *Isle of Wight Rly v Tahourdin* [1883] 25 Ch.D 320.

[71] Davies and others (n 49) 218.

[72] Ireland (n 15) 482.

[73] Dine (n 70) 4.

[74] Gerry R Rubin and David Sugarman, *Law, Economy and Society, 1750–1914: Essays in the History of English Law* (Professional Books/Butterworths 1984) 12–13.

this chapter respectively have tracked the theoretical development and assessed the different approaches of the legal and economics scholarship—the agency theory and the transaction cost theory. This section seeks to investigate the extent to which this underlying discipline and ideology underpins the UK's company law system and corporate practices. In general, the law and economics model of corporate contractualism holds that the company is a network of a series of bargains between the individuals, namely shareholders, managers, creditors, workers, customers and others that involve in the corporate activities, as opposed to a separate legal entity as advocated by the traditional legal model. Within such a totally private sector that is regulated by contract both internally and externally, there is no reason for the state public power to intervene. But this does not mean it totally refuses the existence of company law. In terms of the company law and other corporate regulatory regimes, contractarians seek to rationalise these rules as the dynamic product of a market-evolutionary process involving investors, firms, and regulators.[75] Instead of detracting from the endogenous market-based ordering, the utility of regulatory law is to reduce the transaction costs between private bargains and to facilitate business by establishing "off-the-rack legal rules that mimic what investor and their agents would typically contract to do".[76]

Compared with the traditional legal model that insists on the separations of ownership and control between shareholders and managers, the economic-oriented model just simplifies the company as an ownerless network of contracts as there is nothing that can be owned.[77] The corporate structure is the outcome of dynamic processes of contracting and bargains, rather than a "given" based on a priori ground.[78] In this sense, shareholders are not supposed to behave like an owner of the company. Between shareholders and managers, and between other forms of relationships of corporate participants, there is nothing more than contracts. To motivate managers' behaviours that align shareholders' interests, offering the management group share options, generous bonus payment and other incentives are often the common choices of this contractual model.

In the UK, corporate practices to a large extent have accepted such a market-oriented or economic-oriented approach to shareholders' role and executive remuneration. It is reported that eight out of ten UK's biggest corporations by market capitalisation have two huge passive fund investors—BlackRock and Vanguard—as their major shareholders.[79] For those passive funds who own shares in tens of thousands of worldwide companies, they are more like "pieces of market infrastructure"

---

[75] Moore (n 14) 709.

[76] Dine (n 70) 8.

[77] Eugene F Fama, 'Agency Problems and the Theory of the Firm' (1980) 88 *Journal of Political Economy* 288, 290. Frank H Easterbrook and Daniel R Fischel, 'Voting in Corporate Law' (1983) 26 *The Journal of Law and Economics* 395, 396. Citing from John E Parkinson, 'The Contractual Theory of the Company and the Protection of Non-Shareholder Interests', *Corporate and Commercial Law: Modern Developments* (Lloyds of London Press 1996) 123.

[78] Parkinson (n 78) 123.

[79] 'Passive Investment and Ownerless Companies' *Financial Times* (11 March 2018), https://www.ft.com/content/0a23ddac-23b3-11e8-ae48-60d3531b7d11, accessed 18 April 2024.

instead of owners that often take a supervisory role in corporate governance.[80] In this regard, the relations between shareholders and managers have indeed changed as opposed to the conception of ownership and control separation. It is also a belief of corporate practices that generous executive remuneration payments would incentivise management to create greater values for shareholders by aligning those two groups' interests more tightly.[81] Since the 1980s, the top executives' remuneration in the UK has grown rapidly; much faster than the growth of national average earnings. According to Pepper and Willman's statistics, in 2000 the FTSE100 CEO's ratio of median total payment to UK's average national earnings was 59:1; while in 2015 the statistic increased to 161:1.[82] And it is reported that in 2020, the median CEO payment was 86 times the median earnings of a full-time worker in the UK.[83]

Moreover, naturally rejecting regulatory interference the from the state, the law and economics model tends to change the relationship between the private and public sectors as well. Corporate contractualism has established a strong ideology that it is the modern condition markets, particularly the market for corporate control that installs an appropriate apparatus of checks and balances to managers' freedom of activities.[84] The successive UK governments are also the contributor of such commercial setting. The government, rather than acting as a regulator to business conducts, resembles a customer or partner of these companies. Many public bodies, namely Whitehall, the local government and the NHS, spend over £100bn on public procurement annually.[85] And through private finance initiatives (PFI) or Public Private Partnership (PPP), the government seeks to transfer market risks from the public to the private sector. In this sense, the public sector can be involved in corporate affairs as a non-interventionist contractual character. But on the other side, their regulatory role has been greatly diluted.

Corporate contractualism has nurtured a business environment in the UK that is keen on efficiency and profit maximisation. It builds on a system that regards these economic values as the decisive metrics to judge managers' performance on investment. To some extent, this has driven up the UK's economic growth and provided shareholders and directors with considerable wealth and income. The UK's corporate

---

80 Ibid.

81 Terence Tse and others, 'Are We Falling Asleep at the Switch, Again? Some Propositions for Executive Compensation' (2014) 7 *International Journal of Trade and Global Markets* 53. Citing from Charlotte Villiers, 'Executive Pay: A Socially-Oriented Distributive Justice Framework' (2016) 37 *The Company Lawyer* 139.

82 'UK Intra-Firm Inequality: Stock-Based Pay for CEOs and Outsourcing of Lower Paid Jobs' (*LSE Business Review*, 7 December 2020), https://blogs.lse.ac.uk/businessreview/2020/12/07/uk-intra-firm-inequality-stock-based-pay-for-ceos-and-outsourcing-of-lower-paid-jobs/, accessed 18 April 2024.

83 High Pay Centre, 'CEO Pay Survey 2021: Median FTSE 100 CEO Now Paid £2.69 Million • High Pay Centre' (*High Pay Centre*, 18 August 2021), https://highpaycentre.org/ceo-pay-survey-2021-median-ftse-100-ceo-now-paid-2-69-million/, accessed 18 April 2024.

84 Parkinson (n 78) 122.

85 'Carillion-Two-Years-on. Pdf' 2, https://www.instituteforgovernment.org.uk/sites/default/files/publications/carillion-two-years-on.pdf, accessed 14 November 2024.

law system has been known worldwide for its efficiency, practicality and freedom that has influenced many countries on their corporate arrangements.[86]

To sum up, under the law and economics model, corporate relations are private and voluntary in nature and are "regulated both internally and externally by contract".[87] Internally it is regarded as an aggregation of individuals which comprises contractual relations between shareholders *inter se*, and between shareholders and directors.[88] Externally, the contractual approaches follow a weak external regulatory mechanism. The general assertion of the external mechanism could be that the authority of the sovereign over the corporation is neither greater nor lesser than its authority over any other private agreement among contracting parties.[89] Corporate contractarians views corporate governance rules as the endogenous outcomes of private bargaining, so that the legal rules should be limited and only be a choice to reduce the transaction costs. Thus, by invoking the idea of the freedom of contract the law and economics model legitimates the directors' discretionary power. It reassures the allocation of power vested in company would not be a threat to a liberal democracy society because it is a free choice by private individuals.

2.4.3 Summary

"Corporate contractualism" is deemed to be a theoretical root of the prevailing understanding on corporations in the UK. The corporate contractual paradigm possesses two models—the traditional legal model and the law and economics model. Companies in the eyes of contractarians are in voluntary, private relations with the overriding goal of shareholder value maximisation. The contractual paradigm establishes a strong ideology in shareholder primacy and free private ordering with opposition to state's interference. Although these two models together provide a contractual bedrock for the UK's corporate governance system, they tend not to be very compatible with each other. The conflicts between the traditional legal model and the law and economics model appear to lead to a paradoxical ideological underpinning of UK's corporate governance system.

Both the legal model and the law and economics model are based on a contractual conception of corporations, but the later one presents corporations as an accumulation of contracts in stark contrast to the legal model which views corporation as a real entity. In addition, the term "contract" itself as an economic idea does not

---

[86] Department for Business, Energy & Industrial Strategy, *Corporate Governance Reform (Green Paper*, November 2016), https://assets.publishing.service.gov.uk/government/uploads/system/uploads/attachment_data/file/584013/corporate-governance-reform-green-paper.pdf, accessed 10 October 2023.

[87] Stokes (n 43) 162.

[88] Stephen Bottomley, 'Taking Corporations Seriously: Some Considerations for Corporate Regulation' (1990) 19 *Federal Law Review* 203, 208.

[89] A. Conrad, 'Constitutional Rights of the Corporate Person' (1982) 91 *The Yale Law Journal* 1641, 1648.

necessarily correspond with the above legal idea. In economics, "contract" refers to voluntary, consensual and private relations of exchange between individuals.[90] According to the economists Easterbrook and Fischel, "contract means voluntary and unanimous agreement among affected parties".[91] As to contractarians therefore, the firm consists of a nexus of contracts so that persons within the contractual relationships of the corporation should be free to make any reciprocal arrangements, with no constraints of mandatory legal rules.[92] Moreover, even incomplete contract theory recognises the complex and long-duration contracts, the contractarian scholars do not view the company as an independent entity that itself may refer to the problem of power arrangement, governance and others. By contrast, in law, "contract" means a legally enforceable promise.[93] The legal concept focuses on the legal obligations and the legal enforceability of the obligations setting in the contract.[94] The contractual freedom is limited by some mandatory rules. Additionally, the company is a separate legal "person" with its own property and legal rights. In contrast, under the law and economics model, "contract" is more likely to represent the adaptive, flexible and voluntary nature of the arrangements and orderings between corporate participants.

However, on the other hand, both models have some points in common that help establish a normative and paradigmatic framework of contractualism in corporate governance. First, the UK legal model of corporate governance is generally portrayed as being shareholder-centric. The agency theory persists and continues to be well accepted as offering justification for the exclusivity of shareholders' interest over all other corporate participants. Second, according to company law in common-law jurisdictions, two groups of people—directors and their managers, and shareholders populate the corporation and play a main role in decision making. Although the law delegates power to shareholders to dismiss the directors, and imposes the fiduciary duties upon the directors, as to contractarians, such legal rules simply reflect a standard to govern the relationship between the shareholders and the directors with the objective of reducing the transaction costs caused in the private bargains. The law, especially mandatory rules, should keep a distance from the private business affairs. Third, as stated by Stokes, the contractual paradigm the contractual paradigm does not explicitly address the legitimacy of corporate power in relation to society at large.[95] Treated as a purely private organisation, the political orientation of the company is to some extent obfuscated. The popular conception of the company as a contractualised organisation should therefore be understood as part of an ideological project to de-politicalise the company and retranslate corporate activity as the manifestation of individual choice.[96]

---

[90] Peta Spender and Stephen Bottomley, 'How to Do Things with Contractarianism: Michael Whincop's Contribution to Corporate Law Scholarship' (2004) 13 *Griffith Law Review* 9, 12.

[91] Easterbrook and Fischel (n 37) 15.

[92] Eisenberg (n 36) 824.

[93] Ibid., 822.

[94] Ibid. See also, Bottomley (n 10) 19.

[95] Stokes (n 43) 162.

[96] Lorraine Talbot, *Critical Company Law* (Routledge 2015) 185.

2.5 Critique Towards Corporate Contractualism

As stated above, although approached in various ways, the contractual paradigm largely establishes a strong ideology in private orderings, shareholder primacy, and a presumption against the state's interference. This section will provide a critique of this paradigm.

The above discussion has pointed out the conflicts between the traditional legal model and the law and economics model in terms of the concept of "contract". From this book's standpoint, a corporate contract cannot be equated with the contract that is formulated in the contract law. In a general sense, a valid and enforceable contract should include three core elements—agreement (offer and acceptance), intention to create legal relations, and consideration. Other elements such as capacity to contract, consent, legality and certainty of terms should also be considered to form a valid contract. Contracts are mostly divided into bilateral and unilateral contracts. For an ordinary contract, it is defensible on the grounds of misrepresentation, mistake, duress, undue influence, illegality in court. As an important sector of private law, legal rules on private contract are perceived as a "structural vessel" in which the participants remain free to give their own willingness by literal or notional private bargains.[97] It is commonly accepted that law should keep its distance from the events of individuals or private organisations.

However, "contract" in the corporate context discussed here does not mean ordinary contracts as understood in the content of contract law. Rather, this term refers to the ideological pattern that contributes to exploring the nature of company (publicly-held company in this book). What the contract in the corporate context borrows from the ordinary contract could be the privity of contract, principles of freedom of contract and the laissez faire doctrine which help establish a private ordering of the company. Pertinently, for example, by utilising the logic of privity of contract, shareholders could enjoy the quality of structural exclusivity—they are entitled to be viewed as the ultimate beneficiary exclusive from non-contractual party, such as an employee in the company. Or by applying principles of freedom of contract and the laissez faire doctrine into the normative framework of corporate governance, companies are portrayed to be subject to the "invisible hand" as opposed to the "visible hand" of state and external regulatory control.

The use of contract law principles results in two key outcomes: first, it excludes the interests of those considered non-contracting parties, and second, it excludes the non-corporate interests of the contracting parties themselves.[98] Therefore, under UK company law, one of the most vital effects of statutory contract should be the exclusion of non-contract parties from the enclosed realm of the internal governance mechanism. The contractual model restricts the corporate role to the protection of shareholders' interest and disregards other contractual relations in a company. UK company law has historically concentrated upon the shareholder primacy model of corporate governance which is justified by the assertion that shareholders' interests

[97] Moore (n 7) 56.

[98] Bottomley (n 10) 25.

converge with those of the company. In the traditional legal model of the company, when the law says that directors are bound to promote the "interests" or "success" of "the company", this is usually interpreted to promote the interests of shareholders.[99] The common law also holds the view that the interests of the company in practical terms are equated with those of the shareholders, specifically present and future ones (*Gaiman v National Association for Mental Health*).[100] According to *Brady v Brady*, "the interests of the company, as an artificial person, cannot be distinguished from the interests of the persons who are interested in it".[101] In this respect, as Stokes asserted, the objective is to structure the internal organization of the company in such a way that, while the directors, as managers of the company, are granted substantial discretionary power to operate the company efficiently, they are still obligated to exercise that power in the best interests of the company's owners. This approach ensures that the directors have the flexibility to manage the company effectively, while maintaining accountability to the shareholders or owners, aligning the directors' actions with the ownership's expectations and interests.[102]

On the subsequent reformulation of directors' duties, an important debate took place about whether to retain a shareholder primacy model or a pluralist model (a stakeholder approach). In this pluralist model, shareholders' interest will not necessarily be prioritised, rather a balance is sought between shareholders and other groups who may be "affected by an organisation or may in turn bring influence to bear".[103] However, the present UK Company Law tends in practice not to accept this viewpoint on companies, maybe on the grounds that it failed to accommodate and balance the interests of all the groups and failed to provide a safe enforcement mechanism.[104]

The present model of UK Company Law tends to give an alternative approach which links the interests of shareholders and stakeholders by connecting long-term shareholder value to corporate sustainability and social responsibility.[105] Section 172 is an attempt for UK Company Law to "enlighten" companies into taking a long-term and more sustainable approach, but still attaining shareholder value—introducing a new concept of "enlightened shareholder value". With shareholders' interests remaining prioritised, this new model takes other parties' interests (such as employees, supplies and the community) into consideration. It reveals that the boards as a matter of law should take a responsibility to accommodate a more pluralist

---

[99] Paddy Ireland, 'Corporate Schizophrenia: The Institutional Origins of Corporate Social Irresponsibility' in *Shaping the Corporate Landscape Towards Corporate Reform and Enterprise Diversity*, Eds. Boeger and Villiers, (Hart Publishing, 2018) 16.

[100] *Gaiman v National Association for Mental Health* [1971] Ch at 330.

[101] *Brady v Brady* [1998] BCLC 20 at 40.

[102] Stokes (n 43) 166.

[103] David Wheeler and Maria Sillanpa, 'Including the Stakeholders: The Business Case' (1998) 31 *Long Range Planning* 201, 205.

[104] Charlotte Villiers, *Corporate Reporting and Company Law* (Cambridge University Press 2006) 96. See also Georgina Tsagas, 'Section 172 of the Companies Act 2006: Desperate Times Call for Soft Law Measures' in *Shaping the Corporate Landscape Towards Corporate Reform and Enterprise Diversity*, Eds. Boeger and Villiers, (Hart Publishing 2018) 134.

[105] Villiers (n 105) 96.

set of interests in their pursuit of shareholder value.[106] Tsagas suggests that this new approach to management decision-making tends to be a compromise between two opposing positions—the law *vs* economics on the purpose of the company.[107] Namely, that directors on the legal perspective should legally owe the duties to the company; and owe duties to their shareholders through free market and competition pressures on the economic side.[108]

However, although Section 172 accepts a more pluralist approach, this "enlightened shareholder value" has essentially left the UK's shareholder-centred corporate governance system intact.[109] Also the problem "to what extent the interests of the company and the interests of the shareholders overlap" remains unclear. Section 172 appears to be problematic in enforceability and accountability as well.[110] The contractual paradigm essentially enticed managerial executives to join in excessive risk-taking activities and to offload long-term payouts of such risk-taking to public corporations, employees and states.[111] Additionally, under this framework, the corporate culture neoliberal, self-interested framework, manifesting as a hierarchical, profit-driven capitalist system with patriarchal tendencies.[112] Even if the managerial hierarchy, as described in Jaques' research, is the most "efficient", the "hardiest", the "most natural" structure encouraging "energy", "creativity", "productivity", and "morale",[113] this hierarchy creates an individualistic culture,[114] which gives rise to the "caution with others, competitive, confrontational, and often combative behaviours".[115]

In addition, the authority on the rule that whether members are bound by corporate contract is unclear. Although there is some clarity on who can sue to enforce the articles, there is still however some controversy regarding to the right of one member to sue another.[116] In the case of *Wood v Odessa Waterworks*, Stirling J gave a clear statement that the articles of association constitute a contract "not merely between the

---

[106] Beate Sjåfjell, 'Dismantling the Legal Myth of Shareholder Primacy: The Corporation as a Sustainable Market Actor' in *Shaping the Corporate Landscape Towards Corporate Reform and Enterprise Diversity*, Eds. Boeger and Villiers, (Hart Publishing, 2018) 79.

[107] Tsagas (n 105) 134.

[108] Ibid.

[109] Tsagas (n 105).

[110] Ibid., 137.

[111] Lynn Stout, *The Shareholder Value Myth: How Putting Shareholders First Harms Investors, Corporations, and the Public* (Berrett-Koehler Publishers 2012).

[112] Charlotte Villiers, 'Corporate Governance, Responsibility and Compassion: Why We Should Care' in *Shaping the Corporate Landscape Towards Corporate Reform and Enterprise Diversity, Eds.* Boeger and Villiers, (Hart Publishing 2018) Chapter 8, 153.

[113] Elliott Jaques, 'In Praise of Hierarchy' (1991) *Markets, Hierarchies and Networks: The Coordination of Social Life* 48, 48.

[114] Kathleen A Lahey and Sarah W Salter, 'Corporate Law in Legal Theory and Legal Scholarship: From Classicism to Feminism' (1985) 23 *Osgoode Hall LJ* 543, 555.

[115] John Dobson and Judith White, 'Toward the Feminine Firm: An Extension to Thomas White' (1995) *Business Ethics Quarterly* 463, 466.

[116] Dignam and Lowry, *Company Law* (8th edn, OUP 2014) 159.

shareholders and the company, but between each individual shareholder and every other".[117] The case of *Rayfield v Hands* also holds a similar fairly categorical opinion. However, in the case *Salmon v Quin & Axtens,* Farwell LJ, manifested that the court is unlikely to enforce the contract between individual shareholders in most cases.[118] In *Welton v Saffrey,* Lord Herschell denied the existence of the contractual status between individual members. And as Lord Davey stated, "But such contracts, whether made by all or some only of the shareholders, would create personal obligations, or an exception personalise against themselves only, and would not become a regulation of the company, or be binding on the transferees of the parties to it, or upon new or non-assenting shareholders".[119]

The discussion here on whether the constitution is enforceable between members could be in relation to the traditional logic of UK company law on the nature of a company. Borrowed from Talbot's words, If members were typically able to directly enforce the contract against each other, it would reinforce the contractual theory of the company. In such a case, the company would be viewed as a collection of enforceable contracts, with its separate legal identity being a mere fiction, and the members' relationships resembling those in a partnership. Conversely, if the contract could only be enforced by a member against the company, and vice versa, it would strengthen the argument that the company's distinct legal personality is not merely a legal fiction.[120] Although the above cases do not give a coherent rule on it, what we can see clearly here is that cases that admit members are bound *inter se* are exclusively related to small companies.[121]

In small companies, shareholders are connected and are more likely to be co-owners of the companies' assets. There is often a conceptual dissonance when the principles are applied to small, private companies: the company and shareholders are always intuitively closely connected, partnership-founded.[122] These companies undoubtedly bear some resemblance to the nexus of contracts, and the contractual conceptualisation may indeed have an analytic value. The partnership-like solutions of the above cases may be appropriate to solve the disputes. However, when applied to corporate governance area, these quasi-partnership relations between members seem to be inapposite. Unlike small private ones, the contractual basis of the relations between shareholders appears to be eroded in the publicly-held companies by virtue of the principle of limited liability and the externalisation of shareholders. Principles established in the content of small private companies have no utility in large public companies. Therefore, in this circumstance, any right of shareholders given by the articles should only be enforced by or against a member through the company itself.

Thus, although Section 33 has constructed contractual relationships between the company and its members, the court has affirmed the corporate contracts in a quite

---

117 *Wood v Odessa Waterworks Co* [1889] 42 Ch D 636.

118 *Quin & Axtens Ltd v Salmon* [1909] AC 442.

119 *Welton v Saffrey* [1897] AC 29.

120 Talbot (n 97) 182.

121 Ibid.

122 Ireland (n 15) 479.

limited and conflict fashion. The statutory contract "derives not from a bargain struck between the parties but from the terms of the statute", according to Steyne LJ.[123] Although controversy around the effect of statutory contract remains, what is clear here is that in case law, far from the members *inter se* emerging as equal contracting partners in publicly-held companies, the enforcement of their rights must be through the company. Then back to Talbot's assertion stated above, the contract was only enforceable by a member against the company and vice versa within large public companies, the distinct legal personality of the company was not a legal fiction. We may conclude that there is no credence in seeing public companies as a nexus of enforceable contracts from the traditional logic of UK company law, the case law especially. Moreover, even though there is a contractual relationship between company and its members, far from being private ordering contract, this statutory contract is strictly limited and protected by law.

Thus, this leads to a further question of corporate contractualism—the traditional logic of the UK corporate governance law seems to be less readily reconciled with the free ordering contractarian paradigm. There is a conflict in the nature of the company between the legal model and the law and economics model. Moore offers a deep analysis on the paradoxical basis of the corporate contractualism. According to him, the UK corporate legal model adopts a contractual paradigm, where the fundamental allocation of governance rights, the initial terms of contractual negotiations, and the subsequent distribution of soft law rights are primarily dictated by mandatory rules.[124] By evaluating the traditional logic of the UK company law from relevant cases, it can be seen that the supposedly "private" contractual document of corporate constitution is essentially based on a public statutory bedrock.

Following the above analysis, this book now returns to a main question of concern—does the corporate contractual paradigm really legitimate or justify the business discretionary power? Defining corporations as purely private bodies, corporate contractualism attributes the legitimacy of corporate managerial power in purely private spheres. As evaluated by Eisenberg, the legitimacy of corporate power in the economic model of the corporation is founded on three main principles. First, there is a belief that placing control over the factors of production and distribution in the hands of privately appointed corporate managers, who are accountable for their performance and act in the interests of those who own the corporation, leads to a more efficient use of economic resources than alternative economic systems. Second, it is assumed that corporate managers are genuinely accountable for their actions. Third, it is believed that shareholders, as the owners of the corporation, possess the ultimate right to control it. However, this right is often disputed, given that share ownership is typically short-term and derivative, with shareholders buying and selling stock on the market rather than directly contributing capital to the corporation. This position is difficult to reconcile.[125]

---

[123] *Bratton Seymour Service Ltd v Oxborough* [1992] BCLC 693.

[124] Moore (n 14) 697.

[125] Melvin Aron Eisenberg, 'Corporate Legitimacy, Conduct, and Governance—Two Models of the Corporation' (1983) 17 *Creighton Law Review* 1, 5.

To summarise, the legitimation of corporate power in corporate contractualism relies on two parties—managers and shareholders. For managers, it is assumed that they should be responsible for their behaviours; while for shareholders, they have the exclusive rights to control managers' performance. From this book' standpoint, these economics assumptions obviously fail to legitimate the managerial power. First, as acknowledged above, modern large companies are more likely to be "ownerless" nowadays in so far as shareholders are not willing to and not be able to efficiently control the company. In practice, shareholders, who are remote from the daily business, are a dispersed group with limited influence on the matters of substance. Hannigan asserts that the division of power between directors and shareholders is predominantly in favour of the board, at the expense of shareholders.[126] In Bottomley's words, the board of directors is a decision-making organ that holds relatively autonomic power from the general meeting of shareholders.[127] As companies grow in size, shareholdings are increasingly highly dispersed. Shareholders individually do not own a significant and influential proportion of shareholding and cannot gain sufficient information to perform properly in monitoring and supervising the management's powers. Passive shareholders, including institutional shareholders, hardly give a substantive control over the managers in publicly held companies and therefore are incapable of fully limiting and checking directors' power. Moreover, the fiduciary duties of the directors to act in the best interest of shareholders is also fundamentally flawed. It is said that shareholders' interest is equated with profit-maximisation. However, this norm appears to struggle to set a hard guideline for directors to distinguish what is shareholders' interest. What we could learn from recent corporate failures in the UK is that, instead of taking shareholders' interests as priority, directors and managers sought to exploit the corporate interests for their own benefit. The Carillion case could also be an example demonstrating that the enforcement of the statutes when directors break their duties is inefficient and delayed.

2.6 Conclusion

From the dimension of power-legitimacy, this chapter gives an overall understanding on the corporate contractualism of the UK corporate governance. However, this book argues that the contractual paradigm has failed to keep a balanced power-legitimacy corporate ecosystem with its inability to cope with complex relationships inside and outside of the company. It can be stated that the company is more than a private phenomenon; and the interactions cannot be purely attributed to private orderings. The theoretical fundamentalism of corporate governance is important to construct the frameworks and ideology of how corporate governance practices being operated.

---

[126] Hannigan (n 64) 184.

[127] Bottomley (n 10) 21.

A fundamental change of the prevalent understanding on the normative UK corporate governance framework is required.

The contractual approach, having a paradoxical basis, leads to a simple understanding of the corporate internal interrelations, a narrow interpretation of the goals of the company and unchecked power vested in the hands of directors. The practices of public companies are supported by a contractarian theory of the corporate form in which investors and, by extension, short-term profit, are privileged over other interests *e.g.*, labour, prudent pension fund governance, fair treatment of suppliers etc.

A company is not the aggregation of bilateral or multilateral contractual relations, rather it is a complicated entity involving interplays with the regulatory mechanism, government, the community, citizens and members inside of it. This entity itself holds great power that makes impacts internally and externally. According to Parkinson, companies hold the power to make decisions that have significant social implications, as their private choices often lead to public outcomes. This type of power necessitates justification and forms the foundation for the argument that companies should be obligated to operate in the public interest.[128] Also as employers, companies also play as income redistribution mechanisms that are important in bringing government industrial policies into effect.[129] Companies may also wield significant economic and political power and they have the capacity to impact the policy and regulation making processes and such complex power extends to influencing the lives of individuals.[130]

Attempts should be made to erase the dysfunctional features of the corporate governance system. Following the power considerations on companies, Bottomley strives to borrow the political idea and incorporate it into his constitutionalism framework. Bottomley suggests that companies should be seen not only as economic entities but also as political institutions, asserting that "corporations are polities in their own right".[131] In his broader framework, Bottomley introduces the concept of "corporate constitutionalism," arguing that companies are political institutions not just because they participate in social power dynamics, but also because they are systems in which power, authority, rights, obligations, duties, expectations, benefits, and disadvantages are distributed and exercised.[132]

For him, a constitutional framework helps to understand the evolving complexity of the relationship between individual members and the collective group. It acknowledges that this relationship is a continuous process of negotiating and redefining power dynamics based on established procedures, rather than adhering to fixed ideas of how those relationships should be structured.[133] Compared to the weak external

---

128 JE Parkinson, *Corporate Power and Responsibility: Issues in the Theory of Company Law* (Clarendon; 2002) 10.

129 Bottomley (n 89) 215.

130 Charlotte Villiers, 'Corporate Law, Corporate Power and Corporate Social Responsibility' (2008) *Perspectives on Corporate Social Responsibility* 85.

131 Bottomley (n 13) 292.

132 Ibid., 291.

133 Bottomley (n 10) 50.

regulatory mechanism of contractualism, Bottomley's constitutionalism develops a mechanism within which this book can examine the interplay between the state and the corporation. Constitutionalism supports the maintenance of confidence in the market and the protection of relevant groups (creditors, employees, the community and so forth) who may require external intervention and, possibly, an investigation of the conduct of business.

This book anticipates that by virtue of Bottomley's political thinking, a different approach could be given to rethink the legitimacy of discretionary business power and the UK's corporate governance as a whole in the context of corporate constitutionalism framework. The following chapter will explore in depth the corporate constitutional framework.

Chapter 3
Corporate Constitutionalism

3.1 Introduction

The last chapter analysed the legitimate processes of corporate power from the profoundly accepted corporate contractual paradigm. Intertwined with the "shareholder primacy" principle, the contractual paradigm of corporate governance whether in the traditional legal model or the law and economics model sought to present the corporate order predominantly in private terms. This two-strand corporate contractualism paradigm attributed the legitimation of corporations' discretion power to shareholders and the free-style marketplace. It assumed that corporations would be subject to constraint by the invisible hand of the market, and managerial discretionary power could be effectively limited in the contractual normative pattern. However, it is clear to see that the contractual paradigm fell into the trap of paradoxical and dysfunctional situations. Both models of contractual norms failed in legitimating corporations' immanent power depending on shareholders and the ineffective market. As a result, the UK has built a relatively non-interventionist corporate governance system that is keen on the economic values of efficiency, profit maximisation.

Thus, in view of the investigation of last chapter, the following chapters of this book seek to find an alternative way—the political approach to assess corporate governance and Carillion's failure. Clearly there is a large theoretical gap in that the "polity" of the corporation is an under-explored area of corporate governance beyond the existing law, the economic theory, and the theory of management of corporate enterprise.[1] As Eells observed, although the corporation's economic roles have been extensively discussed, there remains limited understanding of its nature as a largely autonomous entity with its own internal structures of power and authority.[2] However, we can feel that there may be a connection between the establishment of a power-balanced corporate ecosystem and the political approach of corporate

[1] Richard Eells, *The Meaning of Modern Business: An Introduction to the Philosophy of Large Corporate Enterprise* (Columbia University Press 1960) 94.

[2] Ibid., 12.

Y. Yang, *Corporate Collapse and Corporate Governance*, CSR, Sustainability, Ethics & Governance, https://doi.org/10.1007/978-981-96-9666-6_3

governance. As Latham revealed that any fully developed political understanding of the corporation should recognise it as a structured mechanism designed for the accumulation, exercise, and management of power.[3] The power-legitimacy theme of corporate governance is political in nature. Corporations themselves are polities—the power held by a corporation could be as much as, and as strong as, the power wielded by a state. This chapter therefore turns to the political view of corporations, seeks to evaluate corporate constitutionalism and to explore the possibility of this alternative framework as a basis for starting a new direction for solving corporate governance issues. It argues that corporations have dual meanings—the public dimension interrelated with the external society and the private dimension linked with power relations within the corporate entity.

The corporate constitutionalism concept, developed by Stephen Bottomley, could enable this book to pursue the possibilities opened up by the language of constitutional and political theory to re-conceptualise the legal thinking on corporate governance and to ensure democratic processes in the corporations. A corporate constitutionalism framework is coherent with the system of political governance in a society. It respects the complexity and reality of corporations and creates interactions between state regulation and the company, between the public character and the private character of a company, and between corporate participants within a company. By borrowing from the political constitutional framework on constraining state power, corporate constitutionalism could provide a distinct justification framework of corporate governance for legitimating, checking and balancing the corporate managerial powers.

The structure of this chapter is as follows: it begins with the justification for embedding political thinking into the corporate area. In this section, the initial and important issue is to justify the application of political understandings on corporations in the UK. Then Sect. 3.3 will elaborate upon how the political wisdom might be applied to corporate governance. This section will also analyse how the political understandings might differ from corporate contractual understandings. Section 3.4 will explore how corporate managerial power could be legitimised within a political context and how the corporate constitutionalism framework could contribute to a power legitimised order of corporate governance. Section 3.5 seeks to give a general description of what might become the key features of company law and corporate governance under the corporate constitutionalism model. The final section will provide a critique of corporate constitutionalism and end with a prediction of how this political framework could be developed and applied in dealing with Carillion's problems.

[3] Earl Latham, 'The Body Politic of the Corporation', *The Corporation in Modern Society* (Harvard University Press 2013) 220.

3.2 The Justifications of Political Understandings on Corporations in the UK

In contrast to the well-developed corporate contractual paradigm, political perspectives on corporations remain insufficiently examined and under-theorised. As some have noted, this may be due in part to the fact that classical political thinkers like Plato, Aristotle, Locke, and Rousseau did not confront the corporate form, and our awareness of the corporation as a political entity has only emerged in more recent times. Consequently, we are still far from formulating a comprehensive theory that explains how political forces shape corporate behaviour.[4] As Stevenson revealed with regard to the issue of legitimation and constraint of large business corporations' power, no amount of theoretical rationalisation has resorted to the political forces, compared with the economic forces which have played and are playing a crucial role in corporate activities. And utilising political eyes on corporations has never been a well-accepted way. There is no shortage of critiques towards this political approach. Eisenberg for example, questions the relevance of the political model being applied to large corporations. For him, the economic model better reveals its "functional advantage" and "accepted conception of institutional competence and legitimacy" of big publicly held companies than the political models which rely on the principles appropriate to a democratic nation.[5] More importantly, he denies the political model would be workable in the United States. As the US's ally, the UK shares similar conceptual understandings on corporations to a large extent. We may wonder: if the political model cannot be feasible in the US as stated by Eisenberg, would it be workable in the UK? Thus, the political understandings on corporations in the modern day should be justified from two aspects at least: first, would the political understandings on corporations be justifiable? Second, would these understandings be workable in the UK?

3.2.1 Would the Political Understandings on Corporations Be Justifiable?

Corporations in the modern time not only perform as a pure private sector, but also play as a quasi-governmental aspect for the whole society. Over a century ago, Maitland drew a simple yet powerful analogy, suggesting that the State and the Corporation are both species of the same genus composed of organised groups of individuals. He observed that within such collective structures, people are inclined to assign actions, intentions, rights, and responsibilities not just to individuals, but

[4] Russell B Stevenson Jr, 'The Corporation as a Political Institution' (1979) 8 *Hofstra L. Rev.* 39, 41.

[5] Melvin Aron Eisenberg, 'Corporate Legitimacy, Conduct, and Governance—Two Models of the Corporation' 17 *Creighton Law Review* 20, 17.

to the collective "group-units" themselves.[6] This judgment is also verified by Mary Stokes' argument of viewing these powerful players as a "miniature state".[7] Like the state, corporations lead to a powerful unity of resources, acts, capitals, workforce and so on. Corporations, especially giant listed companies in modern society, have crucial economic and financial roles, but their behaviours as polities should not be ignored. In other words, the domination of large corporations is not purely a matter of market reach, but also extends to political, social, religion arenas etc.

Thus, the justification of using political and constitutional thinking in corporate governance can find its origin from the perspective of corporate powers. As to the definition of "power", there are various responses to it. According to the early Weberian conception, power refers to the likelihood that an individual within a social relationship can assert their own will, even in the face of opposition.[8] Pfeffer perceives power as "a relationship among social actors in which one social actor, A, can get another social actor, B, to do something that B would not otherwise have done".[9] Additionally, based on and critiqued upon Dahl's one dimension of power, and Bachrach and Baratz's two dimensional power, Lukes advances the concept of "three-dimensional power", where the first dimension centres on observable behaviour in decision-making processes. This form of power is exercised in situations involving visible conflicts of interest, typically manifested through expressed policy preferences and active political engagement.[10]The two-dimensional view of power gives a critique on the behavioural focused definition of power. It is also a major advance over the one-dimensional definition which brings the analysis of the power of controlling the processes and agenda into discussion. The three-dimensional view of power reveals a deeper form of influence that operates by shaping individuals' perceptions, cognitions, and preferences in such a way that they come to accept their roles within the existing social order, thereby preventing them from even recognising potential grievances.[11] To express it succinctly, the three-level power separately refers to the most straightforward and easily-observed decision-making power; the latent power that occurs in the non-decision-makings; and the most subtle power in the underlying ideology. The latter two dimensions of power identify that power can be wielded unobservably through the processes of deciding what can/cannot be taken into account in decisions and controlling how people think respectively.

The remarkable ascent of corporations seems to reflect a progressive convergence between the state and society, as well as a blurring of the boundaries between the

[6] Frederic Maitland (Trans & Intro), "Introduction" to Otto Gierke, *Political Theories of the Middle Age* (1913) ix. Citing from Stephen Bottomley, *The Constitutional Corporation: Rethinking Corporate Governance* (Ashgate Publishing, Ltd 2007) 37.

[7] Mary Stokes, 'Company Law and Legal Theory' (1986) *Legal Theory and Common Law* 155, 180.

[8] Max Weber, *The Theory of Social and Economic Organization* (Simon and Schuster 2009).

[9] Jeffrey Pfeffer, *Power in Organizations* (Ballinger Pub Co 1981) 3.

[10] Steven Lukes, *Power: A Radical View* (Macmillan International Higher Education 2004) 19.

[11] Ibid., 28.

public and private spheres.[12] Today, corporations must perceive their powers and be understood within the social fabric.[13] Eells attributes this idea to a philosophical framework which examines the relationships between corporations and their deeper social foundations. He recognises that with immanent and transitive power from individuals to corporate ownership, the actions and functions of business are not isolated and are tied to the framework of a greater society.[14] In addition, large corporations' decisions essentially have social and political impacts so that they should cater to a wider range of non-economic needs.[15] Davis also notes that the causes of corporate power are not only allocated internally but also externally ranging from the economic to the social and to the political aspect and vice versa.[16]

This book therefore perceives that Luke's three dimensions of power have been obviously reflected in the corporate setting both internally and externally. Internally, corporations' core decision-making organs of directors' meeting and shareholders' meeting are the most direct manifestation of exercising power. These decision-making processes are normally open-discussed and recorded, and corporate participants gain access relatively easily. But corporate power can still be utilised when business affairs are deliberately excluded from open discussion by certain processes or structures. Unlike the first layer which only concentrates on the apparent issues that are arranged onto a discussion agenda, the second layer of corporate power realises the subtler way of using power. In this sense, the powerful group can also determine what can be included in discussions and how the discussions may be presented and controlled—they can decide the boundary and scope of corporate actors' information. For the third layer, within the corporation, the power may be created as a featured corporate culture or naturally accepted rules, thus the power can be exerted in an un-observed way.

In addition, corporate power also has external influences. First, decisions of companies have a direct effect on the public settings. Carillion Plc, as the biggest suppliers of public sector services in the UK could be a good example. Its every decision on the way of conducting business, even more private decisions on nominating directors would impact its societal supply chains. Carillion's sudden collapse in January 2018 plunged the society and market into turmoil. One of its public projects—the new royal Liverpool hospital was originally planned to be completed in 2017. But building work was halted after Carillion's collapse. It is estimated that it will not open until at least 2022 and will cost another £300 m to complete, this cost and long delay severely impacting on the local economy and the local environment and community. Second, corporate power can also decide what may be included in a public-related discussion. Drawing from the example of dealing with pollution

[12] Roberto Unger, *Law in Modern Society* (Simon and Schuster 1976) 193.

[13] Eells (n 1) 12.

[14] Ibid., 7.

[15] Ibid., 4.

[16] Elisabet Garriga and Domènec Melé, 'Corporate Social Responsibility Theories: Mapping the Territory' (2004) 53 *Journal of Business Ethics* 51, 75. Keith Davis, 'Understanding the Social Responsibility Puzzle' (1967) 10 *Business Horizons* 45.

problems in Gary and East Chicago, discussed in Luke's book, in order to sustain the US Steel's reputation, the government of Gary kept out disclosure of pollution problems and only started to take action in 1962, while East Chicago, with similar environmental issues, took measures as early as 1949.[17] In this case, the US Steel was actually using a silent power that forced the policy makers to exclude certain issues from the agenda. In terms of the third level of power, companies also have the ability to shape and model how people think and the underlying logic of how society is running. Large-scale enterprises possess a significant capacity to influence not only the markets in which they operate,[18] such as through resource extraction, financialisation, and infrastructure management, but also the processes by which laws and regulatory systems are formulated and developed. Crouch observed that a major corporation may hold such a dominant position within its markets that it can actively shape the terms under which those markets operate, relying on its organisational capabilities to formulate strategies that entrench its market power.[19] In this regard, this silent power inevitably sets the boundary of the market and the legal rules within which people manage their behaviours. For instance, the acceptance of corporate contractualism also means approving such kind of ideology, consequences and the status quo of society running.

From the perspective of corporate power, this discussion shows that corporations actually possess a quasi-governmental power or a power that is even beyond that of state power. Thus, some transnational companies can "regime shop" so that they may choose the regions where the regulatory framework is relatively weak and companies therefore get more autonomy;[20] and some large-scale companies are also adept at integrating complicated vertical and horizontal resources through their corporate vehicles and supply chains to mitigate their liabilities, such as tax and tort. Thus, the political understandings on corporations can be justifiable since corporations themselves are political institutions with their own formations.[21] "With their own formations" means that the polity of corporations cannot be understood curtly from the operational processes and organisational patterns of the state. Rather, corporations possess their own sets of function and values as political entities. The state and the corporate polity are vested in the same genus and share the wisdom of political understandings, but they are not same. Thus, in a word, as a state-like entity with enormous power in hand, corporations, especially the large ones, are in no doubt that they can be understood from a political perspective with their own special features.

[17] Lukes (n 10) 42–43.

[18] Ciarán O'Kelly, 'Corporate Governance and Resentment', *European Group of Public Administration: Annual Conference* (2019).

[19] Colin Crouch, *The Strange Non-Death of Neo-Liberalism* (Polity 2011) 49.

[20] Colin Crouch, 'The Global Firm: The Problem of the Giant Firm in Democratic Capitalism', *The Oxford handbook of business and government* (Oxford University Press 2010) 155–156.

[21] Stephen Bottomley, 'From Contractualism to Constitutionalism: A Framework for Corporate Governance' (1997) 19 *Sydney Law Review* 277, 291.

3.2.2 Would the Political Understandings on Corporations Be Workable in the UK?

According to Eisenberg's formulation, the corporation as a political institution is one in which legitimacy derives from democratic participation by the groups most directly affected by its operations. Each of these groups is understood to have its own objective, and management is tasked with mediating among these differing goals. The board of directors, ideally composed of or including representatives from these constituency groups, is responsible for ensuring that their respective interests are fairly addressed.[22]

Eisenberg's skepticism about the political model applied in the US stemmed from the concern that new investors would be hesitant to invest capital in corporations controlled by groups whose interests in corporate profitability were either diluted, as seen with labor, or virtually nonexistent, as with consumers.[23] To be clear, unlike the economic model with a single clear purpose—corporate profit and shareholders' interest, corporations are characterised with multiple objectives under the political model. Alongside making profits for shareholders, corporations are also responsible for offering work, decent wages and working conditions for labour; supplying safe, good-quality, acceptable priced products for the customer; maintaining good image in the community and so on. As a result, Eisenberg considers that corporations under the political conception seem to take on so many burdens rendering them far less attractive to investors who view business profit as a priority. This statement may have been rational to some extent in the US forty years ago, but it seems to be unconvincing in the modern days of the UK.

It is evident that the existing legal model in the UK does not preclude the concerns of the stakeholders. The present model of UK Company Law tends to give an approach to connect long-term shareholder value to sustainability and social responsibility. Although Section 172 Companies Act 2006 still attains shareholder value as the primary consideration which introduces a new concept of "enlightened shareholder value", it is undeniable that this section is an attempt for UK Company Law to "enlighten" companies into taking a long-term and more sustainable approach. It is indeed in the shareholders' interests over the long term which is the point of enlightened self-interest that Section 172 seeks to encourage. Furthermore, cultural diversity and engagement with stakeholders in corporations have been paid more and more attention by shareholders and corporations since 2017.[24] Stakeholders' participation is seen as crucial to a company's success in the long run. This tangible change has been updated into the newest 2018 UK Corporate Governance Code which significantly elevates the position of stakeholders in corporate governance. According to provision 5 of the latest code, "the board should understand the views

---

[22] Eisenberg (n 5) 3.

[23] Ibid., 17.

[24] 'How the 2018 UK Corporate Governance Code and New Legislation Impacts Premium Companies | EY UK', https://www.ey.com/en_uk/assurance/how-the-2018-uk-corporate-governance-code-and-new-legislation-impacts-premium-companies, accessed 11 January 2024.

of the company's other key stakeholders and describe in the annual report how their interests and the matters set out in Section 172 of the Companies Act 2006 have been considered in board discussions and decision-making".[25] Thus, within the corporate governance mechanism in the United Kingdom, stakeholders do have a contribution to make their interests matter, rather than an obstacle for investment.

In addition, it is safe to argue that the political understandings on corporations would be workable in the UK because British corporate governance scholarship has profoundly investigated the political implications of the existing legal model. Moore specifically highlights that the legal-doctrinal foundation of UK corporate governance is fundamentally anchored in a mandatory, irreversible, and publicly formal statutory framework.[26] It follows that the corporate governance mechanism in the UK is a publicly driven process which depends on the political democratic forces inherently. This recent theoretical change in the UK reveals that corporate governance rules should not be locked in by the orthodox economic theorising. On the contrary, it is highly necessary to encourage a broader scope of cognitive diversity on the "rightful democratic objectives" of UK corporate governance law.[27]

In summary, political understandings of corporations could be justifiable and workable based on the fertile theoretical and practical ground of UK corporate governance. Corporations should rightfully be perceived as quasi-government entities with the allocations of internal decision-making power, the extending corporate external power which at the same time are impacted by the power of the society. These processes of power exercises entail the political determinations and consensus to manifest a desirable democratic corporate governance framework.

3.3 From Political Constitutionalism to Corporate Constitutionalism in the UK

Political theory should influence companies.[28] But what is the bridge between the political wisdom and corporate governance? Or how may we transfer national political logic to the corporate arena? The answer for this book is "the constitution"—a doctrine of constraining government power which is also related to the polity of corporations. As Bottomley demonstrates, through its constitution, a corporation could mediate the public and the private. However, what should be noted here is that,

---

[25] '2018 UK Corporate Governance Code', https://www.frc.org.uk/getattachment/88bd8c45-50ea-4841-95b0-d2f4f48069a2/2018-UK-Corporate-Governance-Code-FINAL.PDF, accessed 13 November 2023.

[26] Marc Moore, 'Private Ordering and Public Policy: The Paradoxical Foundations of Corporate Contractarianism' (2014) 34 *Oxford Journal of Legal Studies* 693, 720.

[27] Ibid., 728.

[28] Bottomley (n 21) 292.

"political theory must be adapted, not simply adopted".[29] It means that the differences between the state and corporations are undeniable. The theoretical transition should proceed with the full consideration of corporations' special formations—entities possessed of both public and private formulations. This section thus intends to illustrate this transition between politics and corporations by borrowing Bottomley's label of "corporate constitutionalism".

But what is important to mention initially here is that political constitutionalism is a pivotal and deeply-analysed subject. Political constitutions are a mirror of a specific nation or society. The formation, structure and even the definition of constitution as a political word may vary with relation to different countries. It is thus not this thesis' intention and it is impossible to give a detailed and comprehensive elucidation of this political constitutionalism subject. For the study of political constitutionalism, to a large extent, this book seeks to avoid the analysis of experience of a specific country or region, rather it seeks to take the key features of political constitutionalism as the general ideological and theoretical context in which corporate governance is situated and to which issues of corporate governance are required to refer.

3.3.1 Political Constitutionalism

Liberalism appears to be recognised as the ideological foundation of the modern western political philosophy.[30] As to the understanding of this word, Honderich states that liberalism is characterised by its emphasis on the civil and political rights of individuals. Liberals argue for a significant domain of personal freedom, within which the state should refrain from interference, except when it is required to prevent harm to others.[31] The following study of political constitutionalism is based on such individual-based liberal ideology.

One of the key features of a constitution in political life is that it plays an integrating role that bonds individual constituents as a group. Within the representative model of modern liberal democratic government, the decisions of elected persons have a public effect on the whole community. Those small numbers of individuals thus can exercise a state power.[32] Constitutions within a system of representative government serve as both political documents and as instruments that establish the structural framework for institutions.[33] According to Wolin, the role of a constitution extends beyond merely establishing a structure of power and authority; it also shapes individuals in particular ways. He argues that a constitution proposes a distinctive identity and

[29] Ibid.

[30] Pierre Yves Gomez and Harry Korine, *Entrepreneurs and Democracy a Political Theory of Corporate Governance* (Cambridge University Press 2008) 2.

[31] Ted Honderich, *The Oxford Companion to Philosophy* (Oxford University Press USA—OSO 2005) 996.

[32] Bottomley (n 21) 294.

[33] Bottomley (n 21) 278.

envisions individuals in their collective capacity. Wolin describes the constitution as having a circular nature: it is constituted by the collectivity, and the actions performed under it, in turn, help to constitute the collectivity.[34] In other words, constitutions have an aggregative capacity that can unite individuals together.

Second, the principles of constitution, together with more general doctrines about the relationship between power and authority have been implemented as specialised procedural safeguards against irresponsible exercise of power by any official group. Whether written or unwritten, constitution is a term related to equilibrium, or checks and balances.[35] Specifically, in the British context, Griffith defines this term in a rigorously non-evaluative manner, asserting that "the constitution is no more and no less than what happens".[36] According to King, in the political context, a "constitution" can be understood as the collection of fundamental rules and broadly accepted understandings within a given country that regulate both the relationships among its governing institutions and the interactions between those institutions and the citizenry.[37] For King, constitutionalism as a normative political doctrine rests upon three core pillars. The first is that a central purpose of any constitution should be to protect individuals and organisations from arbitrary and intrusive actions by the state; the second pillar specifically cares about preventing the organisation of the state to misuse its power; the third one concerns the relationships between the citizens and the state.[38] A proper sense of the constitution cannot be simply be viewed merely as a disorganised collection of laws, institutions, customs, conventions, and commonly held understandings. Rather, it ought to exhibit a degree of overall coherence and internal logic.[39] Thus, through processes and structures, political constitution could give an ordered power-balanced framework of the society. The possibilities of the misuse of power could be reduced by separating governmental power: legislative power is separated from the executive power, and those both kinds of power should be independent of the judiciary power. In general, as Bottomley concludes, the key features of a constitution lie in its role in constituting a political system. It defines how decision-making power is distributed within the polity, or how such distribution is to be determined, sets out the procedures that must be followed for decisions to be regarded as legitimate, and delineates the rights, duties and obligations afforded to members of the polity.[40]

As discussed above, liberal political perceptions on constitution have been dedicated to pursuit of a stable political structure or framework to make sure the autonomy of its constituent members. Gomez and Korine consider the nature of power from the

---

[34] Sheldon S Wolin, 'Collective Identity and Constitutional Power' in G Bryner and D Thompson (eds), *The Constitution and the Regulation of Society* (1988) 94.

[35] J.A.G. Griffith, 'The Political Constitution' (1979) 42 *The Modern Law Review* 1, 1.

[36] Ibid., 19.

[37] Anthony King, *The British Constitution* (Oxford University Press 2007) 3.

[38] Ibid., 12–13.

[39] Ibid., 14.

[40] Stephen Bottomley, 'The Birds, the Beasts, and the Bat: Developing a Constitutionalist Theory of Corporate Regulation' (1999) 27 *Federal Law Review* 243, 259.

perspective of political philosophy. They believe that corporations and their governance were in the reflection of liberal thinking.[41] Historically, from the beginning of capitalism, each country's system of corporate governance has been established to be compatible with the specific political governance.[42] The corporations and their governance are not beyond this liberal inquiry; rather they are still under the extensive liberal shadow. As Eells observed, once the corporation came to be regarded as a constitutional person, it became entitled to the rights and protections ordinarily granted to individual citizens under both procedural and substantive guarantees. At the same time, it also assumed corresponding duties and responsibilities, not only towards private individuals but also in relation to the broader public interest. Eells contended that a proper appreciation of the constitutional and philosophical underpinnings of such freedoms is essential if business leaders are to respond in ways that are both practically effective and ethically justifiable.[43] It thus could be argued that corporations on the one hand are actors within the national constitutional arrangements in which the state takes a charge; and on the other hand, corporations are constitutional settings in themselves. Corporate constitutionalism should work the same way with the political constitutionalism in establishing an ordered power balanced framework within the liberal reflection—an entire power-legitimacy framework of corporate governance.

3.3.2 Varieties of Economies on Which Corporate Constitutionalism is Based

Constitutions in different countries or regions may be used in different ways. As the same, constitutions in various corporations and even various types of capitalism might be presented in different ways. Gomez and Korine elaborate on this distinction by examining the historical evolution of capitalism. They observe that historical research has demonstrated how, from the origins of capitalism, each country has developed its own institutions and regulatory frameworks. These have led to systems of corporate governance that reflect and align with the prevailing systems of political governance within each nation, covering areas such as incorporation laws, business rights and regulations, and the governance of stock markets and trading practices.[44] In addition, towards the varieties of capitalism, Hall and Soskice develop a distinction between liberal market economies and coordinated market economies. For them, in liberal market economies in which the UK is situated, corporate endeavours are coordinated mainly by hierarchies and competitive market actions; while for the latter one in which Germany is situated, coordination strategically depends more heavily

[41] Gomez and Korine (n 30).

[42] Paul Frentrop, *A History of Corporate Governance, 1602–2002* (Deminor 2003). See also, Masahiko Aoki and others, *Toward a Comparative Institutional Analysis* (MIT press 2001).

[43] Eells (n 1) 11.

[44] Gomez and Korine (n 30) 4.

on non-market relations to bond their activities with others and to build their core competitiveness.[45]

Different varieties of economy may be reflected in their corporate governance arrangements. For corporations in coordinated market economies, they rely on the dense networks between the managers and their counterparts, third parties, their corporate reputations and highly-skilled workers to ensure the corporate operation. Within this structure of the market which discourages hostile takeovers, corporations are insensitive to the external finance. And by encouraging inter-firm cooperation, corporations pursue effective production tactics depending on the coordinated relationships. The state and stakeholders are important in the decision-making processes of the corporate governance framework. The supervisory boardroom in which employees get the opportunity to be represented in the two tiers of boardroom ensures the equal rights of constituencies within a corporation to a large extent. Other companies also get the chance to be represented on the supervisory boards and are typically engaged closely with their partner corporations in joint research as well.[46] All these actors are coordinated to construct a company's competencies.

However, corporate governance in the UK is consistent with the credo of the modern free market economy. Capitalism in the UK is distinguished by its reliance on the market and external finance. Unlike firms in coordinated markets economies, the continuing survival of corporations in liberal market economies are contingent to the terms on which finance market is required. The financial systems for corporate governance force corporations to be attentive to current monetary flows and their share price on equity markets in order to avoid hostile mergers and acquisitions. As stated by Hall and Soskice, the markets for corporate governance drive firms to focus on the publicly measurable aspects of their performance that impact share prices, such as current profitability.[47] In terms of the internal governance structure within such economies, shareholders who possess exclusive governance rights are central in disciplining the directors and in endowing discretionary administrative power to their agencies.

This book focuses on understanding corporate constitutionalism within the liberal economy. Bottomley, who initially brings forward the "corporate constitutionalism" proposition has established a general conceptual framework that can fit into the UK's free-market founded liberal economy. He thus reconstitutes the corporation into the image of political government. According to Bottomley, corporations are essentially "political entities" in their own formations,[48] that can be described as "corporate government".[49] In Bottomley's research, the political constitutional theory

[45] Peter A Hall and David Soskice, *Varieties of Capitalism: The Institutional Foundations of Comparative Advantage* (Oxford University Press) 8.

[46] Ibid., 23.

[47] Ibid., 29.

[48] Bottomley (n 21) 291.

[49] Richard Eells, *The Government of Corporations* (Free Press 1962) 11.

gives a "rhetorical", "methodological" and "normative" inspiration to his corporate constitutionalism framework.[50]

3.3.3 Corporate Constitutionalism

In terms of the definition of constitution in the corporate arena, company lawyers usually regard it as the internal rules of one company. The corporate constitution in a contractual pattern (the memorandum and articles of association) investigated in Chapter 2 has given a narrow meaning with "contract" or "agreement". However, in Bottomley's theory, a corporate constitution is likely to be broader than just a contract. Unlike the contractual definition where certain substantive goals and interests are to be pursued, corporate political advocates view the constitution in corporations as a framework within which the members can identify preferences and make decisions. The contexts of the corporate constitution are not pre-dated goals; rather the contexts entail the basic rules on corporate powers, and the arrangements of corporate structure and procedure or "matters of institutional design" (including the allocation of decision-making, the terms for directors, and the like).[51] In reality, companies, especially large companies, have corporate constitutions that are somewhere in between public and private arrangements. In addition to the memorandum and articles of association, Bottomley views the provisions in the company law and relative judicial or administrative interpretations and relative common law doctrines which deal with decision-making structures and processes within companies, and those which regulate members' rights to request or convene a special general meeting as a part of the corporate constitution.[52] In this way, company law values could be profoundly infused into every company. Thus, in general, corporate constitutions within Bottomley's political way of understanding have two sources—the corporations' own constitution, and the relative statutes or judicially created standards which cannot be changed directly by the corporate constituents. Moreover, by virtue of the constitutions of public law, the format of corporate constitutions may not be restricted to formal written ones. Bottomley proposes that the codes of conduct retaining the best practices on corporate governance (such as designating independent non-executive directors, separating the roles of the head of companies, concerning the behaviours of audit committees) could be an example of informal corporate constitutions.[53]

---

[50] Bottomley (n 21) 293. Bottomley has explained that: "rhetorical" means he use the constitutionalism to "import liberal political theory in general rather than any particular species of that theory; "methodological" means "in order to discuss individuals one must look first at their communities and their communal relationships"; "normative" means constitutionalism "provides a benchmark against which to evaluate the structures and processes of particular governance systems".

[51] Richard Bellamy and Dario Castiglione, 'Constitutionalism and Democracy-Political Theory and the American Constitution' (1997) 27 *British Journal of Political Science* 595, 602.

[52] Bottomley (n 40) 260.

[53] Ibid., 261.

So, what are the connections between constitutionalism in a political context and that in the corporate sphere? Or how will the political constitutional wisdom be connected with the corporate constitutionalism framework?

First, corporate constitutionalism is rooted in the established political values. According to Bottomley, the concept of corporate constitutionalism is informed by several political theories, including liberal constitutionalism (which emphasises individual rights and interests), communitarianism (which acknowledges the importance of the group alongside individual members), and republicanism (which highlights governance aimed at promoting the common good).[54] These political thoughts set the foundation for the very essential value orientation of corporate constitutionalism. The corporate constitutionalism framework therefore respects the interplay between the public orderings and the private rules of corporate issues. It deems that, via the legal system, the public strength and constraints (including the law, the government power, and the societal influence) can be imposed on corporate activity. The republican message assumes that the state has an irreplaceable role in defending and enhancing public values; meanwhile the state regulation must and will be beneficial for society as a whole.[55] As a result, the general idea behind corporate constitutionalism is to "develop a framework within which we can understand the interplay between state and corporate contributions to the governance of, and governance within, corporations".[56]

Second, the corporate constitutionalist framework incorporates both corporate and public political inputs. It aligns with the distribution of powers both within and outside the corporation, thereby defining the corporation as an economic, social, and political entity.[57] Additionally, it occupies a position between the public and private dimensions of the corporation. In the public political context, constitutionalism plays a role in mediating the public and private aspects within a state. Similarly, corporate constitutionalism entails both external and internal aspects with relation to a corporations' three layers of powers. As observed above, a companies' external power exerts a great influence on the society and a company is impacted by the society at the same time; while the internal power cares about how the company has been structured and who have the decision-making roles within the company. Correspondingly, the double meaning of corporate constitutionalism on the one hand refers to the connections between the corporation and the state or the society; and on the other hand, it handles certain relationships inside a company.

The third connection could be, by virtue of a constitution's integrating role, to reconsider the roles of corporate actors. The constituent members hold double roles—on the one side they are personal individuals holding private rights in the company, while on the other side they collectively behave as one whole, representing the overall interests of the company. It is not a fundamental requirement of a constitutionalist

[54] Stephen Bottomley, *The Constitutional Corporation: Rethinking Corporate Governance* (Ashgate Publishing, Ltd 2007) 55.

[55] Bottomley (n 40) 255.

[56] Bottomley (n 54) 56.

[57] Ibid., 59.

theory that the interests of the individual should always take precedence over those of the collective;[58] rather, the corporate constitutionalist framework aims to maintain a balance between the collective and the individual by considering the shifting complexity of the relationship between individuals within the corporation and the entire group. Thus, the corporate activities are not just the simple sum of individual actions, instead, corporate life involves complicated power interactions and systems of checks and balances that could vary over time and from one institution to another.

Fourth, the political wisdom helps to redefine the structure and processes of decision-making in corporations. Decisions in corporations range from corporate business projects, financing, investment to employment, pension funds, bonus pays and to future development and so on. Corporations are not simple as purely contractual allocations, instead they are complex entities assembled with continuous processes of negotiating and power playing. Contracts signed by corporations are not just one-off contracts, instead they have an evolutionary dimension. Decision-making is the central part of corporations. Issues of structure and process are to be considered primarily in decision-making. The internal decision-making processes should be power-balanced and elaborated by a system of *accountability-deliberation-contestability*.

An effective corporate *accountability* structure should involve a plurality of checks and balances and multiple separation of decision-making powers which are not restricted to the formal division of power between shareholders and directors, but also pay attention to the roles of independent non-executive directors, independent chairpersons, external/internal auditors and institutional shareholders. The multi-level separation of powers thus is to guarantee the diffusion of corporate decision-making powers of the whole company. Moreover, for *deliberative* decision-making, the corporate constitutionalist framework aims to guarantee that different levels of corporate decisions are open and genuine. Decisions should be made based on considerations of all relevant arguments rather than mere allocation of members' votes.[59]The third part of the corporate constitutionalist framework—*contestability*—requires that the corporation tracks the interests and ideas of its members/shareholders, and so those interests must be brought to the attention of the decision-makers.

In summary, a similar reflection for a corporate constitution could be made in reference to King's three-pillar statement of political constitution discussed above: first, one of the main purposes of any institution's constitution should be to ensure that any individuals related to corporate actions are protected against arbitrary and instructive action by the corporation; the second pillar specifically cares about preventing the corporation from misusing its power; the third one concerns the relationships between the corporation and its constituent members, and the relationships between the corporation and the external actors, the government, stakeholders etc.

58 Bottomley (n 21) 295.

59 Bottomley (n 21) 312.

Additionally, what can be seen clearly here is that, in contrast with corporate contractualism, there are four important conceptual shifts of corporate constitutionalism: first, corporate constitutionalism respects the complexity of corporations—that they are not purely the assemblance of contracts, but entities with hierarchy, people interactions, power plays and so on. This framework is thus concerned more about the balance between the coordination interactions and private-ordered individual actions within a company. This framework is also inclusive in integrating both a political insight of corporate law and a respect for the economic markets. Second, it is important for corporate constitutionalism to note that how decisions are made is as important as the outcomes that they achieve. The processes and structure of decision-making therefore are the key matters of this framework which will be analysed in depth in the following section. Third, this framework gives a critical insight towards the role of shareholders. According to Bottomley, the role of shareholders should be as members or participants in a collective enterprise rather than purely as rentiers. When we think about shareholders as investors, we give priority to their economic role and to their status as owners of property. But when thinking about shareholders as members, this framework highlights their role as participants sharing the identification, responsibility and obligation. Fourth, there is a deep thinking on companies' public dimension and their interplay with the state. This framework admits both the internal and external dimensions of corporations. For the external part, the corporations are related to society and the state. Thus, by expanding the content and formation of corporate constitutions, via the legal system, corporations are protected and constrained by the external frames.

3.4 A Checked and Balanced Power-Legitimacy Ecosystem of Corporate Governance Under Bottomley's Corporate Constitutionalism?

As revealed in Chapter 2, the three fundamental elements of governing a corporation—power, legitimacy and checks and balances mechanisms are disordered in the contractual paradigm of corporate governance. In other words, purely private and contractual understandings fail to legitimise corporations and their managers' discretionary powers. At the same time, corporate contractualism is inefficient in holding the managers' actions accountable. This chapter sheds light on a different dimension of corporations—to view them as political entities. From the above discussion, we can accept that political understandings are justifiable in developing a normative paradigm in UK's corporate area, especially the emergence of Bottomley's novel idea in establishing a corporate constitutional framework. His political-oriented framework in the corporate arena provides an alternative opportunity to build a checked and balanced power-legitimacy ecosystem of corporate governance. This section will therefore expand his framework to a broader theoretical issue and assess how may the political understandings, with the corporate constitutionalist approach as a bridge, be workable in establishing a feasible checked and balanced power-legitimacy corporate governance ecosystem.

3.4.1 *The Parameter of a Checked and Balanced Power-Legitimacy Ecosystem of Corporate Governance*

What are the metrics to evaluate an ordered power-legitimacy? In Chapter 2, corporate contractualism appears to pay attention to the profit capacity and the efficiency of a corporation. However, the answer from the corporate constitutionalism perspective would be distinct from the economic one.

From a political dimension, there is an emphasis on the democracy technique that expands its influence from the political aspect to the business sphere. Technically, democracy is a tool of the state to give an efficient means of collective actions by utilising procedures and structures.[60] It is asserted that those who are affected by the political decisions should give their voice to the process of decision-making. The democratic theory of state governance in establishing the proper purpose of government, processes and structure of constraining power, checks and balances, decision-making processes, and in upbuilding a constitutional framework of a state also play a vital role in the corporate arena. It can state that corporate powers may be recognised as acceptable authorities only if those powers originate from fully democratic processes. Gomez and Korine argue that, in the modern mindset, democracy is seen as nothing more than a technique of government—one among several—serving as a means to legitimise the governing powers and the decisions they make.[61] Thus, applying a similar definition to corporate democracy, it could be described as "nothing more than a technique of the polity of the corporation—one among several—a manner of legitimating corporate powers and the decisions they reach."

Although this democratic idea has no obvious presence within the UK company law scholarship according to Stokes, it indeed offers the guiding rules for a list of proposals for arranging representatives of employees, consumers, environmentalists, and the neighbouring community on the boards of companies.[62] Moreover, as stated by Moore, with the intrinsic involvement of the active-interventionist (as opposed to passive-instrumentalist) state in core corporate governance law-making processes, there emerges the corresponding need to legitimise prevailing regulatory outcomes in corporate governance by reference to the political criteria of democratic consensus, rather than the market-liberal notion of unanimity based on the (arguably now defunct) logic of mutual quasi-contractual agreement.[63]

---

[60] Gomez and Korine (n 30) 9.

[61] Ibid., 48.

[62] Stokes (n 7) 187.

[63] Moore (n 26) 726.

According to Davis,[64] one of the first scholars to explore the societal impacts of corporate power, corporations, as societal institutions, must use their powers responsibly. In order to manage the power, Davis has proposed two principles—the social power equation, which holds that the social responsibilities of businessmen arise from the amount of social power they possess; and the iron law of responsibility, which asserts that failure to use power responsibly will lead to its eventual loss.[65] For Davis, this equation of power-responsibility is required to be understood by corporations and the business leaders that, on the one hand corporate leaders should use their powers to maintain their business status in society; and on the other hand they should use their powers properly and responsibly. In this respect, he refuses the extreme ideas on total responsibility of business and the radical free market.[66] Therefore, corporations as political entities with their own formulations entail both the economic and political considerations. Both the economic and political portions are equally important to corporations.

For this thesis, it therefore could be argued that the parameter to evaluate an ordered power-accountability-legitimacy ecosystem of corporate governance is keeping the balance between corporate democracy and corporate economic capacity. In other words, if one corporate governance system could realise the equilibrium of corporate democracy and corporation's business interests, we could say the system is in a checked and balanced power-legitimacy order.

It follows that there may be a radical change in the existing corporate governance norms. The present corporate governance system is rooted in the shareholder-democracy-standard legal model. In this model, the legitimacy of managerial power is grounded in the oversight exercised by shareholders through the corporate electoral system. That power could, in principle, be fully legitimised if the electoral system were brought to a more effective or perfected state.[67] Clearly the exponents of shareholder democracy heavily depend on the stability of shareholders' suffrage to decrease the incidence of corporate invasions of the public good.[68] Stevenson views this reliance as an ironic phenomenon in that corporate governance in this sense is actually deviating from the modern notion of the separation of ownership and control.[69] It is the shareholder activists who are passionate about the old wisdom of shareholder control that prove the corporate electoral machinery is fashioned into the tool for increasing corporate accountability when that old wisdom seemed to have expired because of Berle and Means' near-fatal blow.

---

[64] Notably, Garriga and Melé views Davis's idea as "corporate constitutionalism". This book admits that Davis as the one of the first scholars researched in power relations of corporations, his ideas of "corporate constitutionalism" may provide a basis for Bottomley's "corporate constitutionalism" or "corporate constitutionalism framework". But the term "corporate constitutionalism" stated in this book always refer to Bottomley's statement.

[65] Davis (n 16) 48.

[66] Garriga and Melé (n 16) 76.

[67] Stevenson Jr (n 4) 42. See also Frank D Emerson and Franklin C Latcham, *Shareholder Democracy: A Broader Outlook for Corporations* (Press of Western Reserve University 1954).

[68] Stevenson Jr (n 4) 43.

[69] Ibid.

However, the democratic approach for this book pursues assimilation of a broader context in which not only the shareholders, but also all the corporate participants, including the internal constituents (worker, shareholders, the boardroom, managers) and all the other stakeholders should be included for the corporate decision-making processes and structure. Corporate governance for this book is thus inherently a publicly driven system where its intrinsic logic, regulatory arrangement, and structure construction are relying on democratic ideology or democratic force. Thus, the parameter, the balance between corporate democracy and business performance, is key to establishing an order to the corporate governance system.

3.4.2 Could a Corporate Constitutionalism Framework Contribute to a Checked and Balanced Power-Legitimacy Ecosystem of Corporate Governance?

How can we assure that those who possess great powers will exercise those powers responsibly and efficiently (which, in the democratic context, implies accountably)? More and more corporate scholars have recognised the dramatic social consequences of companies' choices: private decisions are made that carry significant public implications.[70] As Parkinson evaluated that, the holding of such power necessitates a clear justification and forms the foundation for the view that companies ought to operate in accordance with the public interest.[71] Business behaviours essentially generate a requirement for legitimacy and rationalisation of that power.[72]

The legitimacy of corporate power seems to have long been an important subject under political philosophers' discussion. Gomez and Korine highlight that a central concern in corporate governance theory, both historically and presently, has been the legitimacy of power.[73] In addressing the question of what legitimises power within a corporation, they offer insights into the nature of power, drawing from political philosophy to explore its fundamental justification.[74] Gomez and Korine give a

---

[70] John Galbraith, 'On the Economic Image of Corporate Enterprise' (1973) *Corporate Power in America* 3, 6. The author sets an example to illustrate the social consequence of a company's decision: "General Motors sets the prices for its cars (and, in conjunction with the other automobile companies, for all cars) with public effect. And it negotiates wage contracts with public effect. And it designs cars and incorporates or rejects safety features with public effect. And it decides on engine design and emissions with public effect. And it persuades the public to its designs with public effect. And it powerfully influences highway construction with public effect. The public decisions of General Motors in the course of any year are far more consequential than those of any state legislature. So with other large firms.

[71] JE Parkinson, *Corporate Power and Responsibility: Issues in the Theory of Company Law* (Oxford University Press) 10.

[72] Eells (n 1) 5.

[73] Gomez and Korine (n 30) 5.

[74] Ibid., 1.

thought on the nature of power from the political philosophy understandings. In their book—*Entrepreneurs and Democracy, a Political Theory of Corporate Governance*, they thus seek to find out the legitimacy of corporate power within the western liberal political context. Based on the liberal political model, they illustrate two opposite forces—"the entrepreneurial force of direction" which intends to be directed towards collective activities in corporations and "the social fragmentation" which intends to protect individual liberty from the possible threat from the former collective force. The two authors perceive that it is the dialectical equilibrium between these two forms of forces that set the basis of legitimation of corporate power.[75] Or in other words, an acceptable corporate governance framework is established on the dynamic counterbalance between these two opposite forces.

In addition, Stokes integrates a wider societal argument into the discussion on the rationale for business corporations' behaviours and functions. She finds that there is an approach of corporatist view of the company that obliterates the differences between the state and society and between the public and private.[76] In this different normative vision compared to the contractual paradigm, the power of corporate managers could be legitimated from two sides: the power is legitimated by providing benefits for the public good *vis-à-vis* society; and within the company, the power is legitimated by helping "formulate, articulate and execute the common purpose of shareholders, creditors, employees, and the community".[77]

The above analyses of the legitimacy of corporate power form the skeleton of political thoughts on corporations, and they also set the ideological foundation of an ordered corporate governance system. However, those theoretical ideas towards the legitimacy of corporate power seem to be trapped in a purely theoretical layer; we could hardly see how could these wisdoms be really applied in practice. In this regard, Moore has identified the challenge of creating suitable institutional conditions that enable each corporation to reach the optimal level of managerial accountability relevant at the micro (i.e., individual firm) level.[78] Only through the establishment of a balanced managerial accountability system at the micro level can corporate governance law ensure the legitimacy and long-term viability of discretionary administrative power in complex private sector organisations.[79]

Bottomley's theory of corporate constitutionalism seems to provide an opportunity to embed power, checks and balances, and legitimacy, the three basic components of corporate governance,[80] to a practical and micro level. Instead of using economic criteria, such as efficiency, as the sole measure for deciding what constitutes "good"

---

[75] Ibid., 8.

[76] Stokes (n 7) 182.

[77] Ibid., 183.

[78] Marc Moore, *Corporate Governance in the Shadow of the State* (Bloomsbury Publishing 2013) 39.

[79] Ibid.

[80] Ibid., 26.

corporate governance, Bottomley examines whether ideas of accountability, deliberation and contestability may provide a valuable framework for assessing corporate structures and process and for encouraging greater shareholder participation.

Based on political understandings, the framework of corporate constitutionalism respects the complex reality of companies so that we can establish a framework in a company that connects the role of the state regulation and the company; connects the public dimension and private dimension of a company; and connects the corporate participants within a company. By seeing the corporation as a body politic, its internal organisational life captures all different kinds of complex interplays, not only the simple individual actions.[81] Moreover, this lens allows us to evaluate corporate governance by both political and economic perspectives. Although corporate constitutionalism is discussed as within a political context, it does not mean that political understandings necessarily exclude economic contractual thinking. As stated above, one of the conceptual shifts of corporate constitutionalism is that it opens up a possibility for stakeholders and the state to let corporations be responsive to political, as well as economic, thoughts. It means that the corporate constitutionalist framework does not deny the economic oriented evaluation parameter; rather both the political and economic elements should be considered in operating a corporation.

Thus, back to the initial question—could a corporate constitutionalism framework contribute to an ordered power-legitimacy ecosystem of corporate governance? The answer for this book is positive. What emerges from the corporate constitutionalism framework is a democratic-oriented and inclusive portrait of corporate governance arrangement which appears to be compatible with the parameter of an ordered power-legitimacy ecosystem of corporate governance to a large extent.

3.5 A Description of What Might Become the Key Features of Company Law and Corporate Governance Under the Corporate Constitutionalism Model

Based on the above brief description on corporate constitutionalism, this section seeks to give a brief outline of what a corporate constitutionalist model of company law and corporate governance would include so that we can be clear about the potential consequences of the theory for the development and shape of the framework.

The underlying ideology of corporate constitutionalism seeks to ensure a democratic public value of building a corporate governance structure, rather than using profit maximisation and efficiency as the only key metrics. It draws from some political thoughts that have been summarised as the main principles of "accountability, deliberation and contestability" to measure whether the company's corporate governance mechanism is reasonable, reliable and sustainable. Unlike corporate contractualism that emphasises the ultimate results or the substantial justice, these principles

[81] Philip Selznick, *The Moral Commonwealth: Social Theory and the Promise of Community* (University of California Press 1994) 242.

are be used to ensure the processes and structures of corporate governance, or the procedural justice of the legal framework.

Moreover, although the corporate constitutional framework still sustains a shareholder-primacy model and encourages shareholders' participation into corporate governance, it does not mean shareholders have an exclusive right in legitimating corporate power or that shareholders' interests would be the only matter for directors to concern. Section 172, as an enlightened-shareholder–value approach could be seen as a starting point of company law to take other corporate actors' interests into consideration of corporate decision making, but this is still not enough of the legal power to protect the public or to protect a broader range of stakeholders under the concept of corporate constitutionalism. Company law and the entire corporate governance system are not designed to provide the private off-the-peg legal rules, rather their public and supervisory functions should be confirmed and ensured. The public values of the legal framework are ensured by the enforcement of these legal rules. However, the relatively non-interventionist character of the legal framework seems to be equipped with a weak enforcement mechanism. Carillion could be presented as a good example. Although the Second Joint Report has clearly concluded that Carillion's directors have breached their duties, four years after Carillion's meltdown, the law still has hardly sanctioned them. The existing legal framework tends to have been accustomed to giving non-intervention to the commercial world so that when something is wrong, they seem to be reluctant to and inefficient in exercising their regulatory power.

Additionally, the legitimacy of corporate power should be confirmed by different sets of strength—internally, directors, shareholders, auditors, workers and so forth; externally, the checks and balances of the state, the society and other public measures. For the internal element of corporate governance, the corporate constitution is the fundamental source of corporate power that is not limited to the concept of contract but is a public-oriented framework that embraces a broader context, as stated above. Within the corporation, these corporate constituents should construct a balanced power network with shareholders sitting at the centre. Shareholders are the "members" of the company, and their participation is important to a sustainable corporate governance mechanism, rather than just playing as pure inessential rentiers. Regarding this network, it should be designed by the law to balance the expansionary managerial power by virtue of the different strengths of shareholders, auditors, workers, whistleblowers and others under the requirements of accountability (responsibility), deliberation (communication and sufficient information) and contestability (challenge) of corporate constitutionalism. Meanwhile, external intervention is vital in strengthening the status and interests of non-shareholder corporate participators. The role of the state in company law and corporate governance is a significant part of corporate constitutionalism but should be in a deconcentrated position.

The above description presents a general understanding of what might become the key features of company law and corporate governance if we apply a corporate constitutionalism model into the corporate governance system. These ideas provide a direction for the following chapters in evaluating corporate constitutionalism in the corporate arena and this will continue to be critically evaluated in Chapters 6 and 7.

3.6 Critique and Conclusion

This chapter gives an overview of political understandings, especially Bottomley's analysis on corporations. The initial thinking of corporate constitutionalism here opens up a new perspective on establishing a corporate governance framework from political wisdoms. The great strength of this framework is that it re-assesses the shareholder primacy model and precisely points out new expectations on shareholders' participation and responsibilities in dealing with corporate problems. And it sets a new evaluative basis to corporate governance issues by highlighting accountability, deliberation and contestability principles. Corporate constitutionalism provides a new roadmap for the way that corporate governance system and scholarships can respond to corporate failures.

However, a few questions of this framework also remain. In many respects, the approach of developing a corporate constitutionalism is still a work-in-process. Currently, corporate constitutionalism still adheres to the shareholder primacy tradition. In Bottomley's viewpoint, he worries that a stakeholder approach would depart too far from the existing shareholder-primacy based corporate law system which may have tremendous resistance of the prevailing mindset. What he advocates is initiating a small step of corporate-constitutionalism-oriented reform from the shareholder primacy model. In this sense, Bottomley perceives that deliberation does not always demand complete and direct involvement from all individuals impacted by the decision.[82] Stakeholders' need may however be voiced by the shareholders who are given more expectations and responsibilities under corporate constitutional framework.[83] Notably, Bottomley urges that concerns about CSR issues must be founded on the renewal of the shareholder role.[84] However, this pursuit of shareholder primacy may lead to certain issues. As Chayes argued, it is unrealistic to depend on the shareholder constituency to hold corporate power accountable through the exercise of the franchise. Shareholder democracy, as it is termed, is misguided because shareholders are not the governed within the corporation whose consent should be sought, even though they nominally possess decision-making power.[85] Thus, a crucial and unresolved question remains regarding how stakeholders, particularly workers who are often the direct and immediate victims of corporate scandals, should be positioned within this shareholder-primacy corporate constitutional framework.

Second, tensions between corporate values and outside values will persist.[86] The framework has instilled the role of the state into the corporate governance mechanism, but in this case, the tensions between the private and the public aspect of corporations may be more severe. Third, as stated above, corporate constitutionalism draws widely

---

[82] Bottomley (n 54) 72.

[83] Ibid., 175.

[84] Ibid., 178.

[85] Abram Chayes, 'The Modern Corporation and the Rule of Law' (1959) *The Corporation in Modern Society* 40.

[86] William W Bratton, 'Public Values and Corporate Fiduciary Law' (1991) 44 *Rutgers L. Rev.* 675, 698.

from the political understandings, including liberal constitutionalism, communitarianism and republicanism. The UK is itself rooted in the liberal values which may conflict with the diversified values of corporate constitutionalism.

Acknowledging such problems with the corporate constitutionalism framework, this book argues that, although it is not perfect, the value of Bottomley's corporate constitutionalism framework is that the principles and political ideology offered by it provide an evaluative exercise through which corporate practices and the legal regulations could be assessed.[87] The above analysis on corporate constitutionalism sought to construct a general power-accountability-legitimacy framework by integrating political understandings into corporate area. However, no single set of political arrangements is uniquely mandated by constitutionalism.[88] Regarding to the special context of different institutions, political organisations may be constituted in various ways. Constitutions in corporate area thus also preserve the exclusive feature of one specific company.

The above political analysis has offered a brief description of corporate constitutionalism and the following chapters will explore these points in greater detail about this political framework. The next chapter will contrast and compare corporate contractualism and corporate constitutionalism to elucidate a better understanding of the differences and similarities between these two corporate frameworks.

---

[87] Bottomley (n 54) 69.

[88] Gordon J Schochet, 'Introduction: Constitutionalism, Liberalism, and the Study of Politics' (1979) 20 *Nomos: the American Society for Political and Legal Philosophy* 1, 11.

Chapter 4
Corporate Contractualism vs Corporate Constitutionalism—A Comparative Evaluation

4.1 Introduction

Via critical elaboration and analysis, Chapters 2 and 3 together set a theoretical basis for this book. To clarify further the differences between corporate contractualism and corporate constitutionalism before moving on to a hypothetical application of corporate constitutionalism in the context of Carillion's case study, this chapter will compare and contrast these two theoretical frameworks. Corporate contractualism has, for a long time, provided corporate academia and Anglo-American company law with a theoretical framework by which to embed the neo-classic economic ideas into corporate governance. Bottomley's corporate constitutionalism, however, turns the spotlight onto the political side and reminds us to think outside the contractual and economic box. By conducting this compare-and-contrast approach, this chapter may more easily identify which changes Bottomley's corporate constitutionalism might bring to the corporate world, both practically and theoretically.

Corporate contractualism and corporate constitutionalism are distinct paradigms. Both theories have significant differences in their logic origins, methodologies, ideas towards the arrangements and relations of the internal corporation, and ideas towards the relationships between corporations and the state. Nevertheless, although using various theoretical underpinnings, Bottomley regards these as two complementary theoretical frameworks that may share some standpoints.

The compare-and-contrast approach is a meaningful technique for this book to reveal the shifts from a contractual to a constitutional perspective, and to highlight the main features of the later theory. It is precisely because of the characteristic features of corporate constitutionalism that it is possible to explore a different way to prevent Carillion-style corporate scandals. The following sections will be divided into two main parts, focusing on these theories' key differences and similarities separately. The contrast part will concentrate on four different aspects—their logical roots and developmental threads, their methodologies, the internal corporate arrangements (including the corporate constitution, internal relationships among corporate

Y. Yang, *Corporate Collapse and Corporate Governance*, CSR, Sustainability, Ethics & Governance, https://doi.org/10.1007/978-981-96-9666-6_4

members, shareholders' status, the legitimacy of corporate power and decision-making), and the external relations with the state and regulation; while the compare part will identify and assess their connections and similarities of their arrangements in corporate governance.

4.2 Corporate Constitutionalism vs Corporate Contractualism

What is a corporation? The question referring to the corporate ontology still has not generated a clear answer since the origin of modern Anglo-American Company Law in the late eighteenth and early nineteenth centuries. During the past few hundreds of years, different theories gave various answers to the question "what is a corporation?". For example, the concession theory, which was prominent in the early nineteenth century, proffered that the corporation is an artificial entity whose existence is granted by the state;[1] the natural entity theory developed in the last decades of nineteenth century viewed a corporation as a natural creation of private initiative and market forces.[2] In the middle of the twentieth century, the development of the neo-classic economic, headed by the Chicago school of economics, led to the rise of corporate contractarian theory (or corporate contractualism). Developed by Easterbrook and Fischel, who fit the economic thinking into the legal frame, the thought of law and economics set the spiritual connotation and the basis of modern Anglo-American Company Law. However, the frequent occurrence of big corporate scandals, from Enron in the US to the BHS and Carillion failures in the UK, raises deep concerns and serious criticism around the prevalent ways of corporate understanding. Corporate constitutionalism, a distinct theoretical framework constructed by Stephen Bottomley, looks at corporations from a political dimension and embeds the political ideas into the analysis of corporate governance. In contrast with corporate contractualism, corporate constitutionalism appears to be an under-researched area, and its literatures seem to lack full-scale and systematic examination on this perspective. But Bottomley's work provides a strong potential to explore a distinct corporate governance paradigm that may eradicate the corporate scandal traps resulting from corporate contractarian defects. This section seeks to contrast these two theoretical frameworks.

[1] Stephen Bottomley, *The Constitutional Corporation: Rethinking Corporate Governance* (Ashgate Publishing, Ltd 2007) 41.

[2] David Millon, 'Theories of the Corporation' (1990) 39 *Duke Law Journal* 201.

4.2.1 Logical Roots and Development Paths

What is primary for this part is to burrow deep down into the logical roots and to figure out their development trends that contributed to the construction of these distinct corporate contractual/constitutional paradigms. Their roots determine the genes of these separate paradigms. By examining and contrasting the theoretical roots and the following development paths, this book might unearth the core values of both paradigms which will make it easier for the following chapters to explain why different paradigms may lead to the differences in corporate governance arrangements, business conduct, relationships with the state, attitudes towards regulatory regime and then to consider whether an alternative paradigm of corporate governance could prevent a Carillion-style collapse.

4.2.1.1 Corporate Constitutionalism

The foundation of corporate constitutionalism is deeply rooted in political and constitutional wisdom. Drawing inspiration from various political scholars, including Hobbes, Mills, Maitland, Unger, Eells, Pettit, and so forth, who initially brought political thoughts into corporations, Bottomley's corporate constitutionalism sits within the domain of classic political philosophy, in particular with regard to issues of the legitimacy of power, democratic ideal, purpose of the government, and structure and processes of decision-making. Bottomley concludes by viewing corporations as systems of government with the underlying theme of "the legitimacy of corporate managerial power".[3] His theory of corporate constitutionalism provides an evaluative framework by which to assess corporate structures and processes and to consider whether the corporate government embodies and upholds the values of accountability, deliberation and contestability.[4]

Bottomley finds the historical root of the mutual relationship between political constitutional language and corporate law from the early European canon law in the Middle Ages.[5] During this period, the model of Roman-Canonist theory of corporations had been widely accepted in the political theories of constructing the Church and the State.[6] Especially between the late eleventh and twelfth centuries, according to Berman, corporate law had a great impact on the development of constitutional structures of the European church.[7] Drawing from corporate law, the church, as a corporate legal entity, granted jurisdiction to individual ecclesiastical officers (such as the pope, bishops, and abbots), with the law of corporations shaping the scope and

[3] Bottomley (n 1) 10.

[4] Ibid., 16.

[5] Ibid., 37.

[6] Otto Von Gierke and Bernard Freyd, *The Development of Political Theory* (Routledge 2018) 241.

[7] Harold Berman, *Law and Revolution. The Formation of the Western Legal Tradition* (Harvard University Press 1983) 215.

boundaries of the jurisdiction conferred.[8] On the other side, the law of corporations also accommodated a considerable use of the political representative concept in the Middle Ages. According to Gevurtz, the corporate board of directors was originated from the political concept of representation which held the ruler as a representative of the community and the majority representing the will of all.[9] For Gevurtz, corporate governance through a representative board, in collaboration with a chief executive officer (or "governor" as referred to in early corporate charters), mirrors the political practices and ideas prevalent in Western Europe during the late Middle Ages.[10] Bottomley nevertheless stands on a critical point and finds out that, unlike parliamentary systems of public government, corporations have their own formations and specialties. In his eyes, a board of directors cannot be simply treated as analogous to "parliamentary systems of public government" because they do not represent specific constituencies and they need not to be elected from the shareholders, rather they take on duties for the entire corporation.[11]

As noted in Chapter 3, the observation of the "corporation as a political entity" is derived from traditional political scholarship. And it is this scholarship that justifies Bottomley's initial motivation of resorting to political theories to evaluate corporations. Hobbes, in his 1651 work, *Leviathan,* views corporations as "lesser commonwealths" which share identity with the state in their characteristic as "public systems" or a "body politic".[12] Hamilton extends the Hobbesian concept by suggesting that corporations are, to some degree, "greater commonwealths". They function as a form of industry governance, possessing their own constitution, statutes, administrative and judicial processes, and managers responsible for enforcing industry laws.[13] Latham identifies five elements of corporations to clarify why corporations can be described as bodies politic: "an authoritative allocation of principal functions; a symbolic system for the ratification of collective decisions; an operating system of command; a system of rewards and punishments; and institutions for the enforcement of the common rules".[14] The concept of the "corporation as a body politic" is reflected in the significant political and societal influence of corporations. These "private governments", with their own political systems, can, in certain cases, extend beyond the private sphere to exert control over the "public government".[15] Likewise,

---

[8] Ibid.

[9] Franklin A Gevurtz, 'The Historical and Political Origins of the Corporate Board of Directors' (2004) 33 *Hofstra L. Rev.* 89, 129.

See also from Gierke and Freyd (n 6) 241.

[10] Gevurtz (n 9) 129.

[11] Bottomley (n 1) 38.

[12] Thomas Hobbes, *Leviathan or The Matter, Forme and Power of a Commonwealth Ecclesiasticall and Civil* (Oxford: Clarendon Press 1651) 218.

[13] Walton Hale Hamilton, *The Politics of Industry*, vol. 8 (New York: Alfred A. Knopf, Inc. 1957) 7.

[14] Earl Latham, 'The Body Politic of the Corporation', *The Corporation in Modern Society* (Harvard University Press 2013) 220.

[15] Charles E. Merriam, *Public and Private Government* (New Haven: Yale University Press, 1944) 7–8.

Dimock also notes that business firms, like governmental organisations, are inherently engaged in the allocation of power and influence within society.[16] According to one more recent scholar—Stevenson, corporations can be seen as both political and economic institutions, and are subject to analysis from both political and economic perspectives.[17]

Thus, modern society is more likely to be an aggregation of government, instead of a constellation of individuals under one single government.[18] As to all the above founders who give an initial corporate political conception, each corporation is a body politic which presents the same pattern of government. Like a government, corporations, especially large public corporations, are not simply players in societal relations, but they also entail a concentration of power. In Bottomley's words, corporations, whether closely held or large public entities, serve as platforms where power, authority, rights, obligations, duties, expectations, benefits, and disadvantages are distributed and exercised. These dynamics occur through relationships that can involve conflict, control, competition, or cooperation, either actively or passively, and collectively or individually.[19]

However, that corporate power—including the boardroom's decision-making power and the power held by the corporation as a whole, in Bottomley's view, is not legitimated within the corporate contractual paradigm. Chapter 2 holds the same viewpoint towards the problem of legitimacy of corporate power in the context of corporate contractualism. Directors of large corporations need a more comprehensive doctrine than just legal and economic theory to justify the powers they exercise.[20] In this regard, Bottomley resorts to political terms to re-conceptualise corporate legal structures.

For Bottomley, "political theory must be adapted, not simply adopted".[21] Rather than limiting his ideas to one political theory, his corporate constitutionalism framework refers to extensive influential political thoughts which form the basis of the consensus on modern democratic society. The corporate constitutional arrangement complies with the basic modern democratic ideal—those who are largely affected by the decisions of political and social institutions ought to be involved in the decision-making process.[22] Drawing on Plamenatz's concept of political theory as a structured inquiry into the purpose of government, as well as the questions raised by Kukathas and Pettit regarding what the state should aim to achieve, how it should be organised,

[16] Marshall Edward Dimock, *Business and Government, vol. 4* (The Business of Government 1949) 47.

[17] Russell B Stevenson Jr, 'The Corporation as a Political Institution' (1979) 8 *Hofstra L. Rev.* 39, 39.

[18] Roberto Mangabeira Unger, *Law in Modern Society—Toward a Criticism of Social Theory* (Simon and Schuster 1976) 193.

[19] Bottomley (n 1) 37.

[20] Richard Eells, *The Government of Corporations* (Free Press 1962) 11.

[21] Bottomley (n 1) 40.

[22] Mary Stokes, 'Company Law and Legal Theory' (1986) *Legal Theory and Common Law* 155, 180.

and what rights it holds over its citizens,[23] Bottomley raises a few parallel questions—"what is the purpose of a corporation? How should corporations be organised? What claims do corporations have over their members?" Unlike the contractual ideas viewing corporations as contract-based institutions, Bottomley digs deeper to identify the complex interplays of "power and authority, rights and obligations, duties and expectations, benefits and disadvantages" of the corporate governance mechanism. These complex interplays are presented both inside and outside of a corporation. As Eisenberg emphasised, political constitutionalism aims to reconcile the public and the private of social and political life.[24] The adaptation of political constitutionalism into corporate settings thus needs to play the same role to mediate the public and private interests and values of corporations. Corporations therefore should be understood from the internal dimension—each corporate participator is oriented to pursue personal interests, but their behaviours should not impair the common good; and from the external dimension—the company as whole can obtain its private business interests but should not in the sacrifice of the public.

What is also notable is that corporate constitutionalism cares about shareholders' participation in the corporation. To highlight shareholders' key role in corporate governance, shareholders are regarded as "members" of corporations within the corporate constitutional framework. As Mill pointed out, political machinery does not function on its own. It must be operated by people, including ordinary individuals. It requires not just their passive consent, but their active involvement, and must be tailored to the abilities and characteristics of those who are available.[25] These classical political wisdoms set the keynote of the corporate constitutional framework which all transformed, presented and developed into Bottomley's view on the daily running of corporations.

However, although Bottomley has assimilated various political ideals in his constitutional paradigm, as the term implied, corporate constitutionalism essentially concentrates on the constitutional theory. Bottomley seeks to explore a particular approach within the extensive domain of political theory. In terms of the specific theories relating to political constitutionalism, Bottomley mainly discusses three theories—a liberal democratic vision of constitutional theory, republican theory, and deliberative theory. But he draws on a republican and deliberation-oriented constitutional approach which is concerned more about the role of state regulation and the common good in decision-making processes of corporate constitutionalism paradigm.[26] The state's regulation is an important element in legitimating corporate power, but it should be situated at a decentralised position.

---

[23] Chandran Kukathas and Philip Pettit, *Rawls—A Theory of Justice and Its Critics* (Polity Press 1990) 1.

[24] Melvin Aron Eisenberg, 'The Legal Roles of Shareholders and Management in Modern Corporate Decisionmaking' (1969) 57 *Calif. L. Rev.* 1, 4.

[25] John Stuart Mill, *Considerations on Representative Government* (Floating Press 2009) 11.

[26] Bottomley (n 1) 16. As Bottomley noted, although there is no clear demarcation between liberal, deliberative, and republican theories, in order to distinguish constitutional approach from contractual patterns, he tends to lean heavily on republican and deliberative theories.

To summarise, this part examines the processes of establishing corporate constitutionalism. It is clear to see that using political ideas to analyse corporate issues is not novel, but by adapting, instead of simply adopting, Bottomley importantly creates an integrated paradigm that tends to be quite distinct from corporate contractualism. Rooted in political ideals on democracy, legitimacy of power, the growing path of corporate constitutionalism is developed from the basic ideas of viewing corporations as body politics which identifies the possibility of a combination of political ideal and corporate issues. In order to focus on the structures and processes of corporate decision-making, rather than purely the economic result of corporate conducts, Bottomley draws on a republican-deliberative-oriented constitutional approach, although he notifies that there is no clear cut among liberal, republican and deliberative approaches of constitutional theory. In a nutshell, corporate constitutionalism can be applied to criticise typical corporations and the rules surrounding them. And the speculative processes of Chapters 7 and 8 will indeed attempt to turn corporations to a corporate constitutionalist approach.

4.2.1.2 Corporate Contractualism

Unlike corporate constitutionalism, rooted in republican and deliberation-oriented political thoughts, corporate contractualism has inherently originated from the fundamentalism of "freedom of contract". Although Chapter 2 observed that two strands of corporate contractualism—the traditional legal model and the law and economics model—seem not to be very compatible or reconciled in the UK company law scholarly literature, they indeed share the same logical root of "freedom of contract" as they developed. To be clear, the literature review in Chapter 1 and the historical part of Chapter 2 have already revealed the intellectual movements of corporate contractualism, this part is not going to repeat this approach, but to simply draw the development lines for the purpose of this contrast exercise.

As revealed in Atiyah's book, *The Rise and Fall of Freedom of Contract,* which traces the conceptual movements of the English "freedom of contract" ideal from around 1770 to 1970, two stages of economics—Adam Smith's and his successors' classical economics which flourished between 1776 and 1870,[27] and neo-classical economics which was prosperous in the 1970s, seemed to have a great influence on the major intellectual twist of corporate contractualism.

It has been suggested that, since the beginning of the nineteenth century, the academic thinking that influenced lawyers and judges, as well as the development of common law, was generally the thinking of classical economists.[28] The "freedom of contract" was recognised as a sacred spirit in determining the relationships between contracting parties. According to a remarkable judicial statement by Sir George Jessel at this stage, "if there is one thing which more than another public policy requires it is that men of full age and competent understanding shall have the utmost

[27] PS Atiyah, *The Rise and Fall of Freedom of Contract* (Clarendon Press, 1979) 292.

[28] Ibid., 294.

liberty of contracting, and that their contracts when entered into freely and voluntarily shall be held sacred and shall be enforced by Courts of justice. Therefore you have this paramount public policy to consider—that you are not lightly to interfere with this freedom of contract."[29] In correspondence with the inveteracy of "freedom of contract" spirit, the joint stock companies in that era were regarded as voluntary and contractual affairs.[30] In the initial period (late 18th and early nineteenth centuries) of the UK "company law", the law consequently was treated as a pure adjunct to partnership law. At this time, British industry in the hands of individual entrepreneurs was highly fragmented and competitive.

However, from the last 30 to 40 years of the nineteenth century, the UK began to enter a stage of institutional growth. Taking advantage of limited liability of incorporations and a wave of mergers and acquisitions, shareholders started to be detached and marginalised from corporate affairs, and more and more concentrated large corporations emerged, especially in the railways, insurance, mining, banking and manufacturing industries.[31] The sheer growth of the size of corporations had a direct impact on the corporate contractual relationships. In parallel with Coase's arguments on firms, Atiyah recognised that, the fewer the institutions, the fewer the contractual relationships needed between them; and the larger the units, the greater the administrative structure within those units. Within an institution, relations are maintained through administrative methods rather than contractual ones.[32] Moreover, together with the factors of the separation of ownership and control which led to the deficiency of shareholders' control on businesses, the increase of middle-class savings in companies which caused capital oligopolies in main industrial sectors, and the changes of the nature of shareholdings from a source of financial funds with strong personal identities to pure rentier shareholding, corporate intellectuals moved on to a stage that departed from the orthodox economic thinking to a broader field of political-economy analysis.

Nevertheless, the second intellectual movement of "freedom of contract" from 1870 to 1970, which was carried forward by neo-classical economic scholarships provided an opportunity for orthodox economic analysis to come back onto the stage. Particularly, over the course of the late 30 years of the twentieth century, corporate contractualism—developed initially by the US Chicago School of economics, started to become an increasingly imperative ideological paradigm of corporate governance. Corporate contractualism, according to Moore, served as a vital "antidote" to the modern business corporation's increasing intellectual detachment from traditional economic analysis over the past several decades.[33] In other words, the corporate

---

29 *Printing & Numerical Registering Co. v. Sampson*, L.R. 19 Eq. 462 [1875], at 465. See also from Gerald Fridman, 'Freedom of Contract' (1967) 2 *Ottawa L. Rev.* 1, 1.

30 Paddy Ireland, 'Property and Contract in Contemporary Corporate Theory' (2003) 23 *Legal Studies* 453, 458.

31 Atiyah (n 27) 596–597.

32 Ibid., 601.

33 Marc Moore, *Corporate Governance in the Shadow of the State* (Bloomsbury Publishing 2013) 58.

contractual paradigm provided an opportunity for the economic ideology to return to the central stage of understanding modern corporations.

Three main branches of corporate contractualism—transaction cost theory, agency theory, and incomplete contract theory, catering to the Hayekian assertion on the spontaneous order of society,[34] stick to the vision on the voluntary, private and contractual nature of companies, regardless of their great changes in social and legal status comparing to joint stock companies over previous decades. Despite simplifying the nature of companies, the purported "privity" of contract within the contractual paradigm also called for restrictions on regulators and the state in setting and enforcing rules in business sectors. It has been suggested that freedom of contract, or at least the freedom to exchange, was considered a valuable freedom, similar to other freedoms, and prima facie, of worth.[35] In this regard, corporate contractualism successfully reinvigorates the classical "invisible hand" of the free market as opposed to the "visible hand" of state governance within Anglo-American corporate governance mechanisms.

4.2.1.3 Summary

From the above, undeniably, corporate contractualism to a large extent is a paradigmatic arrangement for the law and economics. The law and economics theories always lie at the heart of UK company law and corporate governance. To date, the present pervasive references for corporate scholars and even policy makers still remain rooted in contractualism. Although we cannot say political theories have no role in the construction of corporate governance mechanisms, the gleam of corporate political thought is only shining in the shadow of the economic thought. In contrast with corporate contractualism which ultimately gains a widespread success in corporate study and policy making within Anglo-American jurisdictions, corporate constitutionalism remains a rather weak and under-developed thought in corporate governance, even though many social scientists were indeed aware of corporate powers and corporations' quasi-governmental dimension by the mid-to-late twentieth century.

For much of the past century, the UK Company Law academic contour has developed from a private, facilitative, de-regulatory logical root. The dominant perception in the UK therefore locates Company Law in the private law sphere which is inherently opposed to the meddling reach of the public and state control. Along with the private law logic, legal rules on corporations are more likely to be a "structural vessel" in which contractual parties are able to pour "substantive content" by the contractors' own will.[36] The corporate constitutional paradigm, however, seeks to assimilate public law ideology into corporate governance study, especially thinking

---

[34] Friedrich A Hayek, 'The Corporation in a Democratic Society: In Whose Interest Ought It and Will It Be Run' in *Management and Corporations* 1985, Eds. Anshen and Bach, (Greenwood 1975).

[35] Atiyah (n 27) 614.

[36] Moore (n 33) 56.

that is related to issues of the legitimacy of power, democratic ideal, purpose of the government, and processes of decision-making. According to Moore, in contrast with the private law doctrine which accepts free bargains among business parties within that structural vessel, the public law logic inherently governs and influences the results of corporate activities by imposing externally established standards or norms, beyond the actual or presumed preferences of contractors or business partners.[37] Indeed, unlike the corporate contractual paradigm which is antagonistic towards public power interventions, the corporate constitutional paradigm opens a gate for state control on corporate issues.

4.2.2 Methodologies

This book views methodology as the path for scholars to get access to reliable and valid research findings. According to Bottomley, corporate constitutionalism and corporate contractualism are two complementary frameworks that draw upon distinct paradigms.[38] The contrast of the methodologies of corporate contractualism and corporate constitutionalism has a double meaning: the first is to investigate the overall approach that Bottomley has adopted to construct a wholly different paradigm in corporate governance; the second is based on the thesis' belief that different methodologies drive different trains of thoughts on corporations. The contrast of the two paradigm's methodologies thus helps to further identify the specific processes used to contribute to these different thoughts.

According to Bottomley, the contract-based models are the "paradigmatic arrangement for economic analysis" within which other perspectives on corporate governance are ruled out.[39] In general, the methodological differences between corporate contractualism and corporate constitutionalism tend to correspond to the differences between "economics" and "politics". By referring to Kukathas and Pettit's explanations, their inherent distinctions can be summarised across three aspects: the economic-rooted corporate contractualism is concerned more about personal and private interests, while the political-founded corporate constitutionalism recognises the common, collective interests; in order to achieve their preferred interests, contract-oriented models seek to bargain with other interest-related or contract parties within the market to the exclusion of the non-contracting ones, while political models seem to create an equal environment for all relevant interest groups to debate to find out a "best answer".[40] Through these different processes, corporate contractualism seeks to protect the largest interests in isolation, while corporate constitutionalism pursues a

[37] Ibid.

[38] Bottomley (n 1) 33.

[39] Bottomley (n 1) 31–32.

[40] Kukathas and Pettit (n 23) 32–33.

result that is for the common good. In this regard, contract-based approaches to corporations and corporate law are predominantly focused on private matters.[41] Corporate law, based on a contractual foundation, is therefore generally viewed as a body of rules that facilitates private and voluntary agreements. However, what should also be recognised is that in the processes of the political approach being institutionalised, relevant parties are prevented from arguing by referring to specific personal issues that deviate from the common concern.[42] There is therefore less space for members to personalise their own interests, instead they are required to make concessions for the public interests.

To be more specific, corporate constitutionalism reconceptualises the corporation as a body politic and applies a constitutionalist framework to corporate decisions-making structures and processes. The methodology of corporate constitutionalism is an approach that accesses an evaluative framework in assessing corporate structures and processes of decision making by reference to certain political-rooted values and principles. In this regard, Bottomley's ideas on three principles—accountability, deliberation and contestability—set the basic standards and benchmarks for people, both inside or outside the company, to understand and evaluate corporate structures and processes in real corporate practices. This is a pragmatic-oriented evaluative framework that is devoted to avoiding the corporate constitutional paradigm entering into inconclusive debates about corporate ontological dilemma and to present a framework that is alternative to the explanatory theory of the corporations and corporate law in the corporate contractual paradigm. It is also the evaluative function of corporate constitutionalism that provides an opportunity for the following chapters to understand and assess Carillion's behaviours from a different perspective.

In contrast, unlike the corporate constitutional paradigm focusing on the structure and processes of business conduct, corporate contractualism establishes a result-oriented explanatory framework which tends to explain the origins, development tendency and future prediction of corporate law and corporate form.[43] In this respect, it leads to the consequence that corporate actions and decisions are primarily judged by whether they achieve the pre-established goals rather than being understood from the impacts on the rights or interests of persons who are involved in business conducting processes. Moreover, corporate contractualism relies on the methodology of individualism, stressing the exclusivity of individuals' actions in understanding social and economic phenomena.[44] According to Easterbrook and Fischel, the philosophy of methodological individualism asserts that individuals are the sole bearers of responsibility, and that corporate action or corporate responsibility is merely the aggregate of individual actions.[45] In this regard, the aggregation of various individual actions is the only source of the corporate activity motivation, while the corporation

[41] Bottomley (n 1) 33.

[42] Kukathas and Pettit (n 23) 32–33.

[43] Bottomley (n 1) 15.

[44] Ibid., 30.

[45] Brent Fisse and John Braithwaite, *Corporations, Crime and Accountability* (Cambridge University Press 1993) 18.

itself has no independent value in conducting businesses. And subsequently, the purpose of the corporation can be equivalent to the purpose of maximising individuals' advantages resulting from private bargains through various agreements. However, the philosophy of methodological individualism does not mean that each person's interests will be properly considered. On the contrary, if the transaction improves the overall welfare, if it realises the substantive justice or result justice, it then can be regarded as being efficient even if someone' interests are reduced, according to the economic thoughts of Kaldor-Hicks efficiency.[46]

Putting it simply, in terms of their methodological differences, it is obvious to say that corporate contractualism seeks to achieve the optimal allocation of resources within the capital market; while the corporate constitutional paradigm seeks to ensure corporate participants' interests are substantively guaranteed by means of reliable structures and processes. The political perspective provides a rich analytical foundation for learning and responding to corporate governance issues. The political methodology does not intend to trigger conflicts between the corporate constitutional and corporate contractual paradigms; instead, this broad political analytical basis and the economic approach are essentially complementary in dealing with corporate issues.

4.2.3 Internal Corporate Operation

From the above, the logical roots of each of the corporate contractual and corporate constitutional paradigms determine their different ways of understanding and analysing corporate conducts—one is economic-originated, the other is politics-founded. Oriented to separate directions, the methodology of each paradigm then creates distinct routeways to specific arrangements of corporate governance. The following two sections try to investigate what the real world of corporate governance might look like under the actions of these distinct mechanisms. This investigation will be evaluated from two main sides—the internal corporate arrangements and the corporation's external relationships with public powers.

4.2.3.1 Corporate Constitutions

The current general idea views the corporate constitution as the basic rule and regulation in conducting the internal governance of the corporation. Chapter 2 has given

---

[46] In economic terms, there are two main standards on assessing the efficiency—one is Pareto efficiency, the other one is Kaldor-Hicks efficiency. Pareto efficiency advocates that if one transaction can improve someone's welfare without make other worse off, this transaction is efficiency. But, in reality, Pareto efficiency appears to be very rare. Instead, Kaldor-Hicks efficiency can be wider applied in economic practices. For a survey, see Peter Lloyd, 'Pareto Efficiency', *Famous Figures and Diagrams in Economics* (Edward Elgar Publishing 2010). Joseph Heath, 'Is the "Point" of the Market Pareto or Kaldor-Hicks Efficiency?' (2019) 7 *Business Ethics Journal Review* 21.

a deep analysis of the role of the corporate constitution within a corporate contractual discourse context. Drawing from the analysis of that chapter, we learnt that in the legislative statutes, Section 33 of the UK Companies Act 2006 directly points out the peculiar contractual status of the corporate constitution. Although it shows some distinctions with the contract in the context of contract law, in traditional legal thought, the corporate constitution which expressly draws on the economic criteria in tackling with corporate affairs, establishes a multi-party contractual connection between the corporation and its members just like many other contracts set in a private commercial world that are enforceable by the parties on legal grounds. In a simple word, the corporate constitution seems to be regarded as a contract within the corporation.

Corporate constitutionalism also acknowledges the importance of the constitution, but in a different way. It seeks to provide a counterpoint to traditional legal or Law and Economics notions of 'contract' as the conceptual basis of corporate governance.[47] In the corporate constitutional framework, the constitution both defines the distribution of power within a corporation and establishes the corporation as an economic, social, and political entity.[48] It stays at the centre of corporate governance which defines and creates the main structures and processes of the corporation. Derived from a political understanding of the constitution, it is based on a set of principles and values which may be not explicitly expressed in written content, but still conditional when exercising corporate power and authority.[49] Unwritten conventions, identifications and practices which stay outside the corporate constitution, but commonly exert great impacts on the behaviours of corporate directors, managers and members, must also be taken into account. Therefore, both the written elements (including internal rules of the corporation and relevant sections of the legislation) and unwritten elements (including common law doctrines) could be regarded as the corporate constitution.

The consequence of developing a corporate constitutional framework is that the constitution, which embodies an accumulation of powers and responsibilities between the state and the corporation, as well as within the corporation, among the corporators,[50] instead of the contract, establishes the foundation of corporate governance. In the corporate constitutional context, the constitution arrives at a different conceptual framework that endows different meanings compared to corporate contractual thought. According to Bottomley, the corporate constitution has double meanings—one is the internal aspect which deals with relations inside the corporation; while the other is the external side which concerns the relations between the corporation and the state or society. In other words, the constitution of the corporation recognises the complex interplay between public orderings and private actors. Based on this idea, the corporate constitutional paradigm thus intends to set up

[47] Bottomley (n 1) 14.

[48] Ibid., 59.

[49] Ibid., 49.

[50] Ibid., 64.

a framework within which we can realise the interaction between state contributions and corporate inputs to the "governance of, and governance within, corporations".[51] The following analysis is going to focus on the internal corporate conduct-related corporate governance; while the corporate constitution's external aspect will be illustrated in the last part of Sect. 4.2.

4.2.3.2 Internal Relationships Among Corporate Participants

Both contractual and constitutional approaches identify the same constituents and individuals—the shareholders, directors, internal auditors, and others as relevant insiders, but the relationships among these different groups are viewed differently. As discussed in Chapter 2, although there are different conceptions of "contracts", the contract-based models—no matter the traditional legal model or the law and economics model—reach a consensus of reducing complicated relations among corporate constituents to agreements between pairs of private legal or economic participants.[52] Especially, the law and economics model tends to simplify the internal relationships among various corporate actors as bilateral or multilateral contracts, and the corporation correspondingly is reduced to a "nexus of contracts".

However, the idea of contract appears to over-emphasise the interactions between individual corporate participants which means that it ignores the independent value of the corporation. Unlike the corporate contractual analysis that is based on economic assumptions, corporate constitutionalism appears to present a more realistic view of corporate conducts. A constitutional framework captures the dual-dimensional roles of the corporation—an entity embracing a complex internal organisational operation, and a social actor holding strong relationships with the state and the external regulatory environment. In corporate constitutional terms, the internal relationships among corporate members cannot be purely recognised as contracts; instead they are actually complicated, various and variable interplays between not only individuals, but also between groups and organisations. By categorising the corporation as a body politic, the corporation itself essentially is an independent, rigorous and effective system where collective corporate purposes can be constituted through members' "coordination interactions".[53]

Within the corporation, derived from the political thoughts, the internal corporate operation refers to "matters of institutional design"—mainly including structures and procedures which obviously are also at the centre of the liberal democratic thought that has exerted great impact on the modern constitutional approach.[54] By embedding

---

[51] Ibid., 56.

[52] Ibid., 30.

[53] Russell Hardin, 'Why a Constitution?' in B Grofman and D Wittman (eds), *The Federalist Papers and the New Institutionalism* (1989) 101. Citing from Bottomley (n 1) 13.

[54] Richard Bellamy and Dario Castiglione, 'Constitutionalism and Democracy–Political Theory and the American Constitution' (1997) 27 *British Journal of Political Science* 595, 602. Citing Bottomley (n 1) 47–48.

three principles—accountability, deliberation and contestability—into corporations' daily life, corporate constitutionalism provides an evaluative framework for the structures and processes by which decisions are made to decide whether the institutional design operates properly, and establishes a normative framework to analyse the legitimacy of decision-making in particular corporations, as well. Therefore, rather than reaching substantive outcomes and interests, the internal institutional design under the corporate constitutional paradigm intends to ensure the vindication and authority of corporate decision-making processes.

It can therefore be concluded that the contractual concept in corporate governance establishes a one-dimensional inner relationship between individuals; while the constitutional concept acknowledges the intricate dynamics of power, hierarchies, loyalties, and control systems, which can change over time and differ across decision-making contexts,[55] and sets up a more stereo framework within the corporation. And these three main mechanisms of corporate constitutionalism—accountability, deliberation and contestability—lay the foundation for the decision-making process and structure which can be used to evaluate the internal operation of certain corporation.

4.2.3.3 Shareholders' Status

For Bottomley, from a pragmatic viewpoint, the shareholder primacy model is still a "powerful grip on the mind-set of corporate managers and officers", and shareholding has been an important phenomenon in economic and political terms.[56] Thus, like the corporate contractual models, Bottomley's framework does not aim to promote any radical changes or reforms to the fundamental corporate structures or the legal environment surrounding corporations.[57] He tends still to work with the prevalent shareholder primacy model in which directors should put shareholders' interests ahead, although many corporate law scholars nowadays have advocated lots of weighty critiques of that model and urged greater attention to other stakeholders' interests.[58] The critiques mainly come from two sides—one is from shareholders' incapability of playing a role in corporate control. Chapter 2 of this book also raises the same concern which points out that shareholders, as passive investors, cannot be relied upon solely for legitimating corporate powers. The other side of the critique could be that the shareholder-primacy model impedes other groups' interests in essence. If we place shareholders as the priority in the distribution of corporate interests,

---

[55] Bottomley (n 1) 31.

[56] Ibid., 8.

[57] Ibid.

[58] For example, John E Parkinson, 'The Contractual Theory of the Company and the Protection of Non-Shareholder Interests', in *Corporate and Commercial law: Modern Developments* (Lloyds of London Press 1996). Jeroen Veldman, 'The Separate Legal Entity and the Architecture of the Modern Corporation' in *Shaping the Corporate Landscape Towards Corporate Reform and Enterprise Diversity*, Eds. Boeger and Villiers, (Hart Publishing 2018). Lorraine Talbot, 'Why Shareholders Shouldn't Vote: AM Arxist-progressive Critique of Shareholder Empowerment' (2013) 76 *The Modern Law Review* 791.

other stakeholders are in danger of being relegated to a lower tier that offers little opportunity for their rights to be considered and ensured.

In Bottomley's approach, while he notes shareholders' passivity in corporate matters, he contends that "the observed shareholder passivity and lack of activism should not serve as the basis for normative or policy-driven corporate law reform".[59] There should be a new approach designed to activate shareholders' participation and resuscitate the use of "voice" rather than "exit" as an appropriate response of members. Second, as explained by Bottomley, what resulted in little effect were some radical attempts at stakeholder-oriented reformation which seemed to depart too much from the prevailing understandings of corporations. He thus avoids such dramatic revolution of corporate concepts, instead starting with a small step to make a gradual approach to corporate governance reform.

Bottomley therefore tries to embark on a fine tune of the shareholder-primacy model to avoid certain exclusivity of other groups' interests. He argues for a corporate constitutional framework that could be regarded as a new approach to discuss the shareholders' role in the corporation and the foundation for considering the interests of other stakeholders within the corporation.[60] Corporate constitutionalism is designed as a flexible framework which takes a serious attitude towards the prevalent shareholder-primacy norm—no need to have a fundamental change on existing corporate structures and operations, but to open up a new perception of the role shareholders as members rather than purely as rentiers.[61] The change of shareholders' status is one of the key points of corporate constitutionalism. According to Bottomley, the prevalent recognition of shareholders as investors who purely care about short- or medium-term dividend returns, and who have an economic-efficiency and wealth-maximisation oriented relationship with the corporation, is not the only, or the best arrangement in corporate governance. Instead, corporate constitutionalism regards shareholders as active members who should be involved in deliberative and contestable processes whether in formal or informal occasions. Shareholders in the corporate constitutionalism paradigm can be the conduit of other stakeholder constituents' voice. In other words, consistent with the deliberative principle, which does not mandate the full and direct involvement of all individuals impacted by a decision, even within the shareholder primacy framework, stakeholders may not engage directly in corporate decision-making, although their interests can still be acknowledged and represented through shareholder action.[62]

Therefore, there tends to be no distinct contrast between corporate contractualism and corporate constitutionalism in terms of their attitude on shareholders' status. However, within the corporate constitutional mechanism, shareholders are not passive rentiers that exercise little impact on corporate affairs, rather they are active members who are pivotal in ensuring the operation of corporate decision-making structures and procedures because their collectively passive behaviours would impair

---

[59] Bottomley (n 1) 10.

[60] Ibid.

[61] Ibid., 8.

[62] Bottomley (n 1) 72.

the overall economic and social operations.[63] There is an expectation therefore that shareholders will have different overall goals in constitutionalism—they should be "responsible shareholders" seeking to ensure the company is running well.[64] The conception of "member" that is given to shareholders entails not only the shared features between them, but also a symbol of "participation, identity and identification, responsibility and obligation".[65] Thus, in contrast with the economic idea of viewing shareholders as private investors and owners of corporate property who are marginalised in corporate decision makings, the political perspective thinks of them as members and requires more focus on shareholders' collective participation in decision making. Bottomley's distinctive ideas on shareholders intend to explore more possibilities beyond those we already have in the corporate law and corporate practices. He hopes these more acceptable small attempts could finally lead to fundamental reforms in corporate governance.

4.2.3.4 The Legitimacy of Corporate Managerial Power

As recognised in Chapter 2, it is a general rule that the board is an independent and important decision-making organ with relative autonomy from the general meeting, instead of a pure agent of those shareholders. For example, the case of *Automatic Self-Cleansing Filter Syndicate Co Ltd* v *Cunninghame*,[66] established the principle that the board grants exclusive powers to manage or supervise the management of corporate affairs. It means that the shareholders, no matter as individuals or in general meeting, may not intervene in the exercise of that power. In addition, with the dramatic increase of corporations' size and capital in modern society, the directors are the corporate participants who really manage the daily running of the corporation and amass great power in their hands.

There thus arises a fundamental problem in justifying that accumulated managerial power. This problem is also the "underlying theme" in all kinds of debates of corporate governance, as identified by Bottomley.[67] Two ideas are usually applied to legitimate this arrangement, and they are the basis of the way in which UK company law is outlined. The first one is recognition of majority rule which ensures directors' power can be legitimated by the approval of a majority voting of shareholders. The second one is that freedom-interfering activities, including directors granting great managerial power, can be justified by the "voluntary and informed consent" of shareholders whose freedom is getting influenced or interfered with.[68] Thus, the

---

[63] Jonathan Charkham and Anne Simpson, *Fair Shares: The Future of Shareholder Power and Responsibility* (OUP Oxford 1999) 1.

[64] Stephen Bottomley, *The Responsible Shareholder* (Edward Elgar Publishing Limited 2021).

[65] Bottomley (n 1) 13.

[66] *Automatic Self-Cleansing Filter Syndicate Co Ltd v Cuninghame* [1906] 2 Ch 34.

[67] Bottomley (n 1) 10.

[68] Ibid., 32, 143. According to Bottomley, in some times shareholders' consent may be actual, such as shareholders give actual vote on specific issues; but in most cases, this consent tends to be implicit

contractual models—the traditional legal model and the law and economics model—both engage in giving reasons for delegating the centralised corporate power to the board of directors. The conception of contract embedded in both models constitutes the basic rationale of directors' authority. As noted in Chapter 2, for the legal model, shareholders' empowerment is the ultimate source of managerial power legitimacy; while even going further, for the law and economics model, the notion of freedom of contract asserts that the legitimacy of directors' power is presumed to be naturally included in the agreement between directors and shareholders. Therefore, it can be concluded that the theory of corporate contractualism has the effect of locating the company law within the sphere of the private domain, of legitimatising corporate power as originating from the "entrepreneurial activities of the members" and lessening the justification for public regulatory intervention.[69]

In contrast, derived from a political root, corporate constitutionalism provides a distinct normative framework that helps to assess the legitimacy of corporate managerial power. Taking three principles—accountability, deliberation, and contestability as the evaluative basis, this framework seeks to realise power legitimacy by ensuring the quality of all of the formal or informal processes and structures in corporate power operation or decision making. These three interrelated principles correspond to three key requirements in achieving inclusive and responsive decisions: (1) the possibility for corporate participants to have access to information; (2) the opportunities for those who may be affected by certain decisions to assess, debate and be heard; and (3) the feasibility to review and contest those decisions that are already made.[70] Therein, the principle of accountability which is still the mainstay of the current regulatory framework of the UK company law, helps to ensure corporate constituents, especially shareholders, to be well informed about the status of corporate management. Even if in some cases, for the purpose of sensitive information protection, members may not be permitted to get access to certain information, the accountability mechanism still needs to confirm that information can be used responsibly and efficiently. The principle of deliberation correspondingly sets the standard for evaluating participation and involvement in making corporate decisions; while the third, contestability principle is committed to establishing a review mechanism of corporate governance after decisions have been made.

Bottomley gives a detailed explanation to identify how managerial power could be justified by following three principles. "Accountability" is not an unfamiliar term in corporate governance. As a general rule, the board meeting is a pivotal arena within which the accountability mechanism is exercised. The conducts of those office holders should comply with relevant rules and standards, and their powers should be constrained by the mechanism of accountability. However, despite this, the accountability mechanism in the corporate constitutional context should also provide the availability of diffusing corporate decision-making power, and a plurality of checks

in their activities of buying shares and correspondingly accepting the pre-existing conditions in the corporate constitution.

[69] Janet Dine, *The Governance of Corporate Groups*, vol 1 (Cambridge University Press 2000) 4.

[70] Bottomley (n 1) 68.

and balances, in order to prevent the improper exercise of power.[71] The allocation of decision-making authority extends beyond the formal division between shareholders and directors. It is also necessary to consider the distinct functions performed by various actors who operate outside the formal governance structures, including independent non-executive directors, independent chairpersons, internal and external auditors, institutional investors, as well as other relevant components of the corporate organisation.[72] Notably, as a main part of accountability, auditors within the corporate constitutional approach could be seen as a bridge that connects both the internal and the external dimensions of the corporation. The independence of both internal auditors and external auditors is important in constructing the processes and structures of corporate governance because they are the gatekeepers of the corporation that guard and ensure the information flow accurately and efficiently inside and outside the corporation.

It is also possible to see in Bottomley's analysis that a decision derives the majority of its legitimacy from the deliberative process that precedes it.[73] Another piece of the threefold corporate constitutional principle, "deliberation" which perceives the process of how to reach a decision is as important as the outcome. It is important to note that attention need not be confined solely to the primary forums such as the general meeting and the board. Corporate constitutionalism promotes a "broad and multi-layered" understanding of deliberation, highlighting the diversity of roles, discursive viewpoints, and the range of opinions and arguments involved.[74] It means that all relevant persons' interests, values and views have an equal and real possibility to be taken into account during the debates and discussions which are prior to a decision. It is also expected that within a deliberative system, decision-making participants could move from their individual preferences to a collective corporate interest, because private interests alone are insufficient to justify a final decision which is in the name of a corporation. Thus, the legitimacy of corporate decisions can be confirmed through deliberation not only by acquiring majority votes or reaching desirable results, but also by identifying to what extent the procedures guiding the formal adoption of certain decisions are based on deliberations of the persons concerned.[75]

However, the above mechanisms—checks and balances supplied by the accountability principle and discussions and debates assured by deliberation—seem to be limited in preventing the risks of arbitrary or self-serving behaviours through majority votes. Thus, bringing Philip Pettit's thought on republican political theory into the

---

[71] Ibid., 70.

[72] Ibid., 71.

[73] A Tschentscher, 'Deliberation as a Discursive Feature of Contemporary Theories of Democracy: Comment on John S. Dryzek' in Anne van Aaken and others, *Deliberation and Decision: Economics, Constitutional Theory and Deliberative Democracy* (Taylor & Francis Group 2004) 72, 76.

[74] Bottomley (n 1) 119. Bottomley's idea on threefold categorisation was from William Rehg and James Bohman. See from William Rehg and James Bohman, 'Discourse and Democracy: The Formal and Informal Bases of Legitimacy in Habermas' *Faktizität Und Geltung*' (1996) 4 *Journal of Political Philosophy* 79, 86–88.

[75] Bottomley (n 1) 111.

corporate context, Bottomley seeks to apply the idea of contestability to fill the loophole of his corporate constitutional legitimating mechanism.[76] It is workable as a separate legitimating mechanism insofar as certain decisions are made that disobey the factual possibility that they could be contested and thereby could be subject to a form of review.[77] This shows a permanent chance for relevant persons who are influenced by an already-made decision to contest and give their voices, rather than choosing the option of exit. It gives the minority the prospect of a "fairer and better outcome".[78] As explained by Bottomley, contestability in the corporate area mainly focuses on contestation by members (shareholders), and some directors who may contest the decision made by shareholders and other directors. In general, shareholders therefore are still playing a key role in the legitimating processes. Through the mechanism of contestability, the interests and perspectives of both majority and minority shareholders should be continuously monitored to ensure that all corporate members can take ownership of and identify with the decision-making process, and can see their interests advanced and their views respected.[79]

In summary, the key theme of corporate constitutionalism is to ensure the processes and structures in decision-making relying on accountability-deliberation-contestability principles. Decision-making could be the most apparent and direct manifestation of power implementation. By borrowing ideas from the establishment of a democratic state, power legitimacy in corporate constitutional thoughts is supported by the above three mechanisms that could constrain the dramatic accumulation and expansion of that power.

In terms of whether the economic model or the political model better fits the daily operation of corporations, there are various arguments in academia. Referring to Bottomley's identification of certain scholars in his book, Dallas and Eisenberg are the two distinct scholars who present wholly opposite ideas towards each model—Dallas focuses on the political nature of the firm and perceives managers as strategic players in the corporate power coalitions[80]; while Eisenberg prefers the economic model and depicts it as better reflecting institutional legitimacy.[81] However, corporate constitutionalism, as clarified by Bottomley, does not intend to demonstrate that the political model could substitute for the economic one; rather this paradigmatic model intends to give an alternative option in legitimating corporate powers—both models are not in conflict, but complementary.

---

[76] Bottomley particularly borrows ideas from three main works: Philip Pettit, *Republicanism: A Theory of Freedom and Government* (Oxford University Press 1997); Philip Pettit 'Republican Freedom and Contestatory Democracy' in I. Shapiro and C. Hacker-Cordón (eds), *Democracy's Value* (1999) 163; and Philip Pettit 'Democracy, Electoral and Contestatory' in I. Shapiro and S. Macedo (eds), *Designing Democratic Institutions: Nomos* 42 (2000) 105.

[77] Bottomley (n 1) 74.

[78] Ibid., 146.

[79] Ibid., 145. Bottomley's idea refers to Pettit (n 76) 184–185.

[80] Lynne L Dallas, 'Two Models of Corporate Governance: Beyond Berle and Means' (1988) 22 *U. Mich. JL Reform* 19, 25–26.

[81] Melvin Aron Eisenberg, 'Corporate Legitimacy, Conduct, and Governance-Two Models of the Corporation' (1983) 17 *Creighton L. Rev.* 1, 17.

4.2.3.5 Decision-Making

As acknowledged above, corporate constitutionalism provides a distinct paradigm to assess the legitimacy of corporate decision-making. The ideas of accountability, deliberation, and contestability focus on the processes by which corporate decisions are made. In order to fit into this three-fold normative framework, decision-making as the key part of corporate power operation should correspondingly be understood in an alternative way. In contrast with corporate contractualism pursuing specific outcomes, Bottomley advocates that "*how* decisions are made is as important as the outcomes that they achieve".[82] Corporate decisions are important, not simply because they substantively affect corporate participators' interests, but also because "a corporation's decision to 'downsize', relocate, or expand its operations can have a significant impact on local and national economies and on social policy".[83] The quality of corporate decisions (including both informal decisions made daily by directors and managers and the formal decisions made annually at general meetings) in the corporate constitutional framework thus are asked to be guaranteed through certain processes and structures. Three main principles—accountability, deliberation and contestability—are thus adapted into corporate governance to avoid the general meeting becoming a "procedural hurdle", and to prevent the boardroom being a "rubber stamp" in corporate decision-making processes.[84]

First, the principle of accountability seeks to ensure a plurality of power separations within the corporation. A formal division of corporate decision-making power between the general meeting and the board is a mainstay of corporate life. But in the corporate constitutional context, corporate decision-making is not restricted to this formal dual structure. Bottomley employs the concept of separation of corporate power in a broader and more flexible manner.[85] According to him, the separation of powers (or, more accurately, separations of powers) involves recognising the roles of independent non-executive directors, independent chairpersons, external and internal auditors, institutional shareholders, and other relevant components within corporate organisations.[86]

Second, the board meeting and the general meeting are also the key deliberative platforms of the corporation, but they are not the only ones. Corporate constitutionalism requires to construct a forum that embodies a wider application of the deliberative principle to ensure the quality of decision-making processes. This richer forum may include online chat-sites, the business media, and mechanisms for representing specific groups of interests at general meetings.[87] The concern, then, is to create and sustain structures and processes that prevent unauthorised, excessive, or

---

[82] Bottomley (n 1) 15. My emphasis added.

[83] Ibid., 2.

[84] Ibid., 111.

[85] Ibid., 71.

[86] Ibid.

[87] Ibid., 72.

insufficient exercises of authority and power within a corporate decision-making system.[88]

The third principle of contestability is maintained, to give permanent possibility for members (or directors) who are affected by specific decisions, to contest effectively. Generally, decisions are made by majority rule. This rule entails a double meaning—"a majority of voting shareholders" or "a majority of voting shares".[89] Consequently, a minority of shareholders who have a majority of the voting shares are capable of controlling corporate decisions. But the corporate participants who own a small proportion of voting shares may hardly have a word on specific decisions. The majority rule in contractual context seems to give rise to the problem of minority protection; but according to the democratic assertion, those who are substantially impacted by decisions should be involved into the processes of making such decisions. By relying on the contestability mechanism, those members (or directors) in a minority could get an opportunity for their voices to be heard, rather than simply selling their shares to exit.

In summary, the three principles of accountability-deliberation-contestability establish a distinct evaluative framework to the structures and processes of corporate decision-making. To be clear, the framework in general ensures the inclusivity or responsivity of corporate decision-making with the accountability mechanism to ensure access to information, with the deliberation mechanism to ensure constituents' involvement in decision-making procedures, and with the contestability mechanism to ensure the possibility of challenging and reviewing those decisions. Thus, corporate constituents, from this triple framework to a large extent, can be properly informed; those who are affected by the decisions get the opportunity to assess and debate, the corporate information can be used properly, responsibly and effectively, the corporation as a whole can be assured by a stable review mechanism. However, the accountability-deliberation-contestability mechanism seems still to remain in a theoretical and ideal basis and has not been verified in practice.

4.2.4 External Regulatory Regime and the Corporation

As stated above, the constitution in the corporate constitutional paradigm has two dimensions—the internal part which connects members and directors in a corporation; the external part which locates the corporation in its broader societal, economic and political contexts. Unlike the corporate contractual paradigm which denounces regulatory interference, corporate constitutionalism treats state involvement in corporate issues as being necessary. In this sense, the corporate constitutional framework stresses the importance of the state and regulation in improving the quality and furthering the integrity of corporate decision-makings.

[88] Ibid., 81.

[89] Ibid., 46.

The justification for enabling state inputs into the corporate arena originates from republican political theory.[90] In general, the republican idea entails a claim that, through legal processes and structures, which to a large extent constrain unaccountable and unwarranted activities, the state should and can be beneficial for public values generally. To clarify, the logic behind this republican proposition is that if state actions—the behaviours of the government, the legislators and the agencies that administer laws—can be constrained by certain effective ways, there is no need automatically to view these public actions as a threaten to private freedom.[91] Moreover, what is also important to note is that, in contrast with the corporate contractual paradigm's failure in verifying managerial power legitimacy, the external dimension of corporate constitutionalism focuses on justifying corporate power through government and judicial oversight, which can help limit the power of such organisations while acknowledging their continued importance.[92] These republican views suggest a way to positively approach the creation of political mechanisms within the corporate sector. On one hand, it calls for the law and the state to impose responsibilities that prevent the unchecked concentration and misuse of corporate power. On the other hand, it promotes the public interest and the common good, which includes preventing unfair or oppressive actions, applying objective standards to assess corporate behaviour, and ensuring accountability in the exercise of power within corporations.[93]

However, although the above ideas of corporate constitutionalism perceive that the corporation's status as legal actor is relying on state inputs, the state should not be situated at the core stage of this external regulatory scheme, rather, it is in a "de-centred" position.[94] A balance between the state and corporate actions is an important concern. It is suggested by Bottomley that the state should establish mandatory standards, including the prevention of oppressive or unfair conduct and ensuring financial and decision-making accountability.[95] Moreover, despite binding obligations, "empowering rules, facilitative rules, and guidelines" which enable corporate participants to flexibly alter certain rules in terms of specific situations, should also be included in the external regulatory mechanism. In addition, corporate constitutionalism could not promise "one rule fits all", because the state's role played in corporate governance will rely on different factors and types of the corporation. Thus, rather than detailed prescription on the relationship between the state and corporate issues, a standard-oriented approach is more appropriate to be applied.

What is also worthy of notice here is the issue of public procurement because it was a major aspect of Carillion's relationship with the government or Carillion's

---

[90] Bottomley (n 1) 56.

[91] Pettit (n 76)148–150.

[92] Mark Seidenfeld, 'A Civic Republican Justification for the Bureaucratic State' (1992) *Harvard Law Review* 1511, 1574.

[93] Bottomley (n 1) 57.

[94] Clifford Shearing, 'A Constitutive Conception of Regulation' (1993) *Business Regulation and Australia's Future* 67, 73.

[95] Bottomley (n 1) 65.

external aspects. Bottomley does not specifically discuss this issue, but we could still give some basic speculations here based on the key values of corporate constitutionalism. As stated in Chapter 2, the government, as the contracting party of public procurement contracts with Carillion, more likely regarded itself as a customer rather than keeping its regulatory role. This could have raised a conflict between the government's regulatory role and its role in public procurement contracts. However, corporate constitutionalism, as stated above, realises the complex interplays among different roles that are involved in corporate operations, and also recognises their various identities when dealing with corporate issues. Corporate constitutionalism's core message is that, in political theory, the state plays a unique role in safeguarding and promoting public values, which are ultimately based on individual conceptions of "the public interest" or "the common good".[96] In this sense, when the government seems to be in a paradoxical situation in public procurement contracts, this book perceives that the state should firstly ensure their public functions of protecting and furthering public interests, rather than prioritising their "private" interests as a customer or a party of contracts.

4.3 Some Similarities and Connections Between These Two Paradigms

The similarities and connections of these two paradigms are important in verifying Bottomley's idea that both paradigms are complementary and compatible within the corporate governance mechanism. Corporate constitutionalism aims to remind us of, and rekindle our interest in, key principles already embedded in our corporate law system,[97] rather than urging corporate scholars to embrace a novel concept.[98] It therefore delves deeper into a political paradigm based on the current system of corporate law and corporate governance, for practical and pragmatic reasons. Thus, there may be some overlaps between the contractual and constitutional paradigms in terms of some ideas on corporate conduct.

First, like corporate contractualism, the liberal perception of the constitution also advocates the individual freedom concept. In order to construct his corporate constitutional framework, Bottomley absorbs various versions of constitutional theory, including liberal, deliberative and republican theories among which there seems to be no generally-accepted clear cut.[99] Although Bottomley stresses the latter two theories, it is still safe to say that corporate constitutionalism respects private rights and concerns within the dynamic interactions between individuals and members' coordination. In particular, the liberal democratic idea of constitutional theory clearly

---

[96] Ibid., 56.

[97] Ibid., 179.

[98] The quotation is raised by Pettit Philip. See from Philip (n 76) 105. Quoted from Bottomley (n 1)179.

[99] Bottomley (n 1) 49.

entails an intention of constraining the exercise of public power for the assurance of individual citizens' interests.

Second, within the corporation, both paradigms comply with the shareholder-primacy tradition. As stated above, both paradigms regard shareholders as an important part of the corporation. This is evident not only in concentrating on shareholders' capital interests, but also in the patterns and arrangements of corporate decision-making mechanisms. No matter how they operate, both paradigms treat the general meeting as a necessary decision-making organ. Their evaluative framework is all based on the dual decision-making system.

Third, some important principles of corporate constitutionalism, such as "accountability", "separations of power", "information disclosure" and so forth are also familiar features in corporate contractualism. Both paradigms have shown their clear intention is to create a system of checks and balances on the implementation of corporate power, although each from a different way of thinking.

However, these similarities do not mean both paradigms can be mixed and viewed as the same patterns of corporate governance. Instead, each paradigm expressly shows a different perspective of the corporation, and coincidentally overlaps in certain aspects. Those similarities show the possibility of connecting corporate constitutionalism and corporate contractualism together in constructing an inclusive and multi-angle corporate governance mechanism.

4.4 Conclusion

Looking back to the literatures on corporate contractualism and corporate constitutionalism, this chapter gives a detailed analysis of the differences and similarities between these two paradigms, ranging from their origins and methodologies to their internal and external aspects of corporate operation, and investigates how each paradigm might theoretically impact on companies like Carillion Plc. The contrast part provides evidence that shows why corporate constitutionalism could be a completely distinct evaluative framework from the prevalent corporate contractualism. For Bottomley, corporate constitutionalism gives an alternative way of thinking for dealing with corporate governance issues, especially issues on managerial legitimacy and decision makings. The compare part, Sect. 4.3, has also more or less referred to some similarities and connections between these two paradigms. It also further demonstrates that although there are distinctions in emphasis, the contractual and political paradigms, which represent the two sides of corporate governance are complementary in corporate governance and both are necessary in constructing a complete underlying theoretical basis of corporate governance system.

However, unlike corporate contractualism, which excludes other understandings on corporations, corporate constitutionalism presents a more comprehensive and broad understanding on corporate governance which admits that corporations embrace individual actions and coordinated interactions, private activities and state inputs, power implementation and duty undertaking. The corporation is not, and has never been, a pure and simple economic mechanism. It was born as a privilege granted with monopoly powers from the state. Corporations evolved from that time only to become a device of exercising control over the economy and polity. Currently, a large corporation encompasses various identities: a legal entity, a government-chartered enterprise bound by the rule of law, a joint-stock company generating dividends for shareholders, and an economic, political, and social institution wielding power both within the organisation and in the broader society.[100] The goal of corporate constitutionalism is not to elevate political ideas above the existing ones, but to offer an alternative perspective on corporations and to encourage scholars to reconsider aspects of corporate governance and law that may be overlooked or underemphasised in current legal and economic frameworks.[101]

This chapter, together with the previous two chapters, establishes a theoretical foundation for the following key part of this thesis. These three chapters play separate roles in laying out the fundamental knowledge and basic understandings—Chapter 2 seeks to analyse the prevalent paradigm of corporate contractualism and shows how Carillion's failure was connected to that contractualist approach; Chapter 3 brings political thoughts into corporate governance and describes the constitutionalist theory and how this would have shaped the company law and corporate governance framework; while this chapter puts corporate contractualism and corporate constitutionalism together and looks at their differences and similarities. With this theoretical knowledge as a strong basis, the following chapters start to combine the theoretical paradigms and the Carillion case together, and to delve deeper in answering the question "could an alternative pattern of political thought—corporate constitutionalism—have prevented Carillion's and any other Carillion-style failure?".

[100] Scott Bowman, *Modern Corporation and American Political Thought: Law, Power, and Ideology* (Penn State Press 1996) 2.

[101] Bottomley (n 1) 179.

Part II The Carillion Case: History, Governance, and Collapse

Chapter 5
The Historical Story of Carillion

5.1 Introduction

The whole structure of this book centres upon on the failure of Carillion Plc and provides a hypothetical approach to investigate the extent to which Carillion's bankruptcy could have been avoided by applying the corporate constitutionalism framework. This chapter and the next chapter set out to provide a critical understanding of Carillion and its collapse.

Carillion Plc, UK's former second largest construction company and one of the biggest suppliers of public sector services, suddenly went into liquidation in early 2018, leaving over 2000 people losing jobs; £2.6 billion pension shortfalls; and nearly £2 billion liability to its suppliers, sub-contractors and other short-term creditors. Not since the US corporate scandal of Enron has there been a case that triggered such severe criticism. Carillion's spectacular downfall has stimulated a series of post-mortems into its demise (*eg.* the Second Joint Report from the Business, Energy and Industrial Strategy and Work and Pensions Committees) and given rise to further inquiries and recommendations on the reform of corporate governance practices (*eg.* the Kingman Review).

From the aftermath investigations of the government reports, academics and practitioners, this high-profile corporate failure demonstrates a connection between weak corporate governance and corporate downfall and epitomises the most significant issues traditionally linked with the dominant corporate contractualist thoughts of the UK corporate governance system. Carillion's failure obviously ushers in an urgent need for an enhanced oversight towards a "radically different approach".[1]

[1] House of Commons Business, Energy and Industrial Strategy and Work and Pensions Committees, *Carillion*, Second Joint Report from the Business, Energy and Industrial Strategy and Work and Pensions Committees of Session 2017–19, HC 769, 16 May 2018, at 3, https://publications.parliament.uk/pa/cm201719/cmselect/cmworpen/769/769.pdf, accessed 31 October 2023.

Y. Yang, *Corporate Collapse and Corporate Governance*, CSR, Sustainability, Ethics & Governance, https://doi.org/10.1007/978-981-96-9666-6_5

5.2 A Brief History of Carillion Plc

This section provides a description of Carillion Plc by briefly tracing its development history from its demerger with the company, Tarmac, in 1999 to its self-destruction in January 2018. This heavyweight's rise and fall takes the book to a real corporate world where profit maximisation is the only motive.

5.2.1 Business Scales

Started from 1999, as a result of a spinoff of Tarmac's construction contracting business and professional services Group business, Carillion Plc rapidly grew to be the UK's second biggest construction and outsourcing contractor, a FTSE 250 corporation with annual revenues of £4.4bn.[2] The rapid growth of Carillion was attributed to its fanatical mergers and acquisitions. Between the years 2006 and 2008, Carillion purchased its main competitors—Mowlem and Alfred McAlpine for £350.3 million[3] and £564.9 million[4] respectively. These two acquisitions were marked as Carillion's major forward steps of being the leading construction company in the UK.[5] In 2011, Carillion's integration scheme expanded to Eaga, a heating and renewable energy supplier. This purchase helped Carillion's business to enter the new market of energy efficiency sectors. But it seemed that Carillion had a fixation on being the number one. In 2014, Carillion was ambitious to be the largest construction company in the UK by seeking to purchase Balfour Beatty, the UK's biggest construction company. However, the acquisition at this time ended with a failure, as Balfour Beatty was sceptical of Carillion's takeover claims on achieving cost savings by the combination of two companies.[6] Even though receiving a rejection of this bid, Carillion still held its stable position as the UK's second largest construction company from 2009 to 2017.

Before Carillion's meltdown, its worldwide supply chain had extended to Canada, the Middle East and North Africa. As of the end date of Carillion Plc, this giant multinational company had about 43,000 employees (about 19,000 in the UK) along with its worldwide extensive supply chains. According to Richard Howson, Carillion's Chief Executive (2012–2017), with the ambition to double the size of the company's

[2] 'The Governance Lessons of Carillion's Collapse | ACCA Global', https://www.accaglobal.com/uk/en/member/member/accounting-business/2018/04/corporate/carillions-collapse.html, accessed 10 March 2024.

[3] 'Carillion Plc, Annual Report and Accounts 2006′ 74, https://www.annualreports.co.uk/HostedData/AnnualReportArchive/c/LSE_CLLN_2006.pdf, accessed 23 February 2024.

[4] 'Carillion Plc, Annual Report and Accounts 2008′ 101, https://www.annualreports.co.uk/HostedData/AnnualReportArchive/c/LSE_CLLN_2008.pdf, accessed 23 February 2024.

[5] 'Carillion Plc, Annual Report and Accounts 2006' (n 3) 6.

[6] 'Balfour Beatty: Five Reasons Why the Carillion Merger Won't Work' (*The Telegraph*), https://www.telegraph.co.uk/finance/newsbysector/constructionandproperty/11035863/Balfour-Beatty-five-reasons-why-the-Carillion-merger-wont-work.html, accessed 23 February 2024.

construction business in the Middle East and North Africa from £500million to £1 billion, Carillion had bidden for 13 construction contracts in Qatar market from 2010 to 2014, but only with one success—the Msheireb bid.[7] On the whole, as reported in Carillion's annual report and accounts 2014–2016, Carillion's global revenue had been steadily growing from 2014 to 2016, respectively reaching £575.5million, £717.0million and £786.7million each year.[8]

Carillion's large-scope project portfolio could be divided into three main parts—support services (including facilities management, facilities services, energy services, rail services, road maintenance services, utilities services, remote site accommodation services and consultancy businesses in the UK, Canada and the Middle East);[9] project finance (involving offering funding for Public Private Partnership Projects); and construction services (mainly focused on large-scale and long-time construction contracts in the UK and Canada).[10]

Domestically, the company was a very important strategic supplier to the UK government outsourcing projects which delivered contracts ranging from education, health, military, prison to infrastructure. As revealed from Carillion's annual reports between 2014 and 2016, Carillion's revenue for the UK program accounted for more than 70% of the whole-year global revenue. Therein, the public-sector contracts occupied a large proportion of the company's total revenue (33%) and its domestic revenue (45%).[11] In 2016, Carillion carried out around 450 contracts with the government which accounted for approximately 38% of the reported full-year revenue.[12] Indeed, Carillion was over-burdened with its UK businesses in both the public and private sectors, including:

- participating in many iconic projects, including the construction of Royal Opera House, the redevelopment of Battersea Power station and the expansion of Anfield Stadium.

---

[7] 'Letter from Richard Howson to the Chairs Regarding Carillion' 4, https://www.parliament.uk/globalassets/documents/commons-committees/work-and-pensions/Correspondence/Letter-from-Richard-Howson-to-the-Chairs-regarding-Carillion-21-February-2018.pdf, accessed 24 February 2024.

[8] 'Carillion Plc, Annual Report and Accounts 2016', https://www.annualreports.com/HostedData/AnnualReports/PDF/LSE_CLLN_2016.pdf, accessed 12 March 2024.

See also, 'Carillion Plc, Annual Report and Accounts 2015', https://www.annualreports.com/HostedData/AnnualReportArchive/c/LSE_CLLN_2015.pdf, accessed 13 March 2024.

See also, 'Carillion Plc, Annual Report and Accounts 2014', https://www.annualreports.co.uk/HostedData/AnnualReportArchive/c/LSE_CLLN_2014.pdf, accessed 13 March 2024.

[9] 'Carillion Plc, Annual Report and Accounts 2016' (n 8).

[10] Amir Qamar and Simon Collinson, 'Part A: The Causes of Carillion's Collapse—City REDI Blog' 2, https://blog.bham.ac.uk/cityredi/the-causes-of-carillions-collapse-part-a/, accessed 27 February 2024.

[11] 'Carillion: 12 Months on from a PFI Perspective | Bevan Brittan LLP', https://www.bevanbrittan.com/insights/articles/2019/carillion-12-months-on-from-a-pfi-perspective/, accessed 6 February 2024.

[12] 'Carillion Declares Insolvency: Information for Employees, Creditors and Suppliers' (*GOV.UK*), https://www.gov.uk/government/news/carillion-declares-insolvency-information-for-employees-creditors-and-suppliers, accessed 24 February 2024.

- Repairing, maintaining and building infrastructure on military sites;[13]
- Providing 218 schools with catering, facilities management services;[14]
- Providing 11,500 in-patient hospital beds;
- Providing services to maintain prisons in London and the East of England, and in the South West, South Central, Kent and Sussex;[15]
- Being the second biggest supplier offering maintenance services to Network Rail;[16]
- Signing £335million contract to build Royal Liverpool Hospital
- Signing £350million contract to build Sandwell Midland Metropolitan Hospital;
- Signing £745million contract to complete Aberdeen bypass;
- Signing £1.4bn joint venture contract to deliver certain parts of HS2[17];
- And others.

Carillion's downfall obviously could be a catastrophe for the overall society in the UK—the tax payers, the public private partnership projects, and the UK government itself, and even a disaster beyond the national boundary—the workers, contractors, creditors along the supply chain, all had been caught up in this turmoil.

5.2.2 Hidden Problems

Carillion, the outsourcing and construction giant, seemed to be healthy and prosperous, especially with the safeguard of the Big Four global accountancy firms—KPMG was its external auditor; Deloitte was its internal auditor; EY and PWC were tasked with advising and providing specialist help. However, the appearance of a healthy company masked what was really a fragile bubble. With such a wide range

[13] Djuna Thurley and others, 'The Collapse of Carillion—House of Commons' 32, https://commonslibrary.parliament.uk/research-briefings/cbp-8206/, accessed 13 March 2024.

[14] Amir Qamar and Collinson (n 10).

See also, 'Question for Department for Education—UK Parliament', https://questions-statements.parliament.uk/written-questions/detail/2018-01-16/123190, accessed 13 March 2024.

[15] 'Written Statement Prison Competition and Efficiency, HC Deb 18 Nov 2014 C7WS', https://publications.parliament.uk/pa/cm201415/cmhansrd/cm141118/wmstext/141118m0001.htm, accessed 13 March 2024.

See also 'Written Questions and Answers—Written Questions, Answers and Statements—UK Parliament', https://questions-statements.parliament.uk/written-questions/detail/2018-01-15/122617, accessed 13 March 2024.

[16] 'Where Did It Go Wrong for Carillion?' *BBC News* (15 January 2018), https://www.bbc.com/news/business-42666275, accessed 24 February 2024.

[17] 'Private Sector Rail Investment—Thursday 18 January 2018—Hansard—UK Parliament', https://hansard.parliament.uk/Commons/2018-01-18/debates/DFD3E110-A049-4D50-B467-22685AC5E06E/PrivateSectorRailInvestment, accessed 13 March 2024.

See also, 'Question for Department for Transport—UK Parliament', https://questions-statements.parliament.uk/written-questions/detail/2018-02-20/HL5579, accessed 13 March 2024.

See also, Amir Qamar and Collinson (n 10).

of operating scopes, Carillion was labelled as a "Jack of all trades".[18] Although diversified businesses can spread operating risks to a large extent, such diversification, on the other hand, increases the requirement for governance and risk management. Certainly, the high complexity of Carillion's product offerings intensified its operational and strategic difficulty and made the company start to overstretch itself beyond its capacity to do the work it was setting itself up to do. Carillion's recovery plan, released in January 2018, highlighted that the Group had grown too complex, with a focus on the short-term, weak operational risk management, and excessive distractions away from its core operations. Our strategy is focused on simplification, removing distractions and clear actions to address our risk profile and rebuild Carillion into a strong and viable business."[19]

Carillion faced significant criticism in the Second Joint Report of the House of Commons, which pointed out that the company became increasingly reckless in its pursuit of growth. This approach led to little consideration for long-term sustainability or the negative effects on employees, pensioners, and suppliers.[20] Its ambitious mergers and acquisitions mean Carillion should also have taken over the targets' responsibility for pension scheme deficits which essentially laid hidden dangers for the future. According to the Second Joint Report of House of Commons, after Carillion's failure, it left about £2.6 billion pension obligations owed to around 27,000 members.[21]

Moreover, Carillion's world-wide businesses were largely trapped in difficulties. The investigation for the Second Joint Report revealed that abundant contracts signed by Carillion were not well-managed.[22] In some of the large contracts, Carillion exaggerated goodwill, misrepresented profits and lacked prudence in accounting which contributed to the failure of financial reporting. Especially, the Qatari-Msheireb contract proved to be an abject failure which led to the dispute between Carillion's directors and Msheireb Properties, who each claimed the other one owed £200 million;[23] and which was one of the biggest causes of Carillion's bankruptcy.[24] Carillion's directors, Richard Howson blamed the Msheireb contract as a rogue contract,

---

[18] Amir Qamar and Collinson (n 10).

[19] 'Carillion Plc, Group Business Plan, January 2018′ 6, https://www.parliament.uk/globalassets/documents/commons-committees/work-and-pensions/Carillion-Group-Business-Plan-January-2018.pdf, accessed 18 March 2024.

[20] House of Commons Business, Energy and Industrial Strategy and Work and Pensions Committees, *Carillion*, Second Joint Report (n 1) 16.

[21] Ibid., 8.

[22] Ibid., 15.

[23] 'Letter from Msheireb Properties to the Chairs Regarding Carillion', https://www.parliament.uk/globalassets/documents/commons-committees/work-and-pensions/Correspondence/Letter-from-Msheireb-Properties-to-the-Chairs-regarding-Carillion-27-Febraury-2018.pdf, accessed 26 February 2024.

[24] Jordan Marshall February 2018, 'Being Owed £200 m on Qatar Job Helped Send Carillion under, Former Boss Admits' (*Building*), https://www.building.co.uk/news/being-owed-200m-on-qatar-job-helped-send-carillion-under-former-boss-admits-/5091953.article, accessed 26 February 2024.

and in his words, "working in the Middle East is very different to working anywhere else in the world".[25] However, problems in the Middle East were just one piece of the puzzle. Carillion's contracts were not only in trouble with its overseas business practices, but also in the UK. As stated above, Carillion's work spanned from libraries, Army housing, prisons, to hospitals, and schools. The most notorious domestic problems could be the cost overruns on three public sector construction contracts—the £350million Sandwell Midland Metropolitan Hospital, the £335million Royal Liverpool Hospital, the £745million Aberdeen bypass.[26] After its meltdown, only the Aberdeen bypass project achieved operational completion in February 2019,[27] the other two important public hospitals were still unfinished without an exact due date. It is reported that the Midland Metropolitan Hospital and the new Royal Liverpool Hospital may be expected to open in 2022 with almost double costs than their original plans.[28] Apparently, heavily entrenched in the public sector, Carillion's inevitable collapse resulted in a disastrous dislocation for the whole society.[29]

In addition, without sufficient capital injection into its expansion, Carillion was deeply in debt. In total, as of 2017, Carillion's borrowing was more than 8 times as much as 12 years ago. Its average net debt had increased from just over £100 m in 2005 to nearly £850 million in 2017, even though the profits had remained flat. The three main acquisitions of Mowlem, Alfred McAline and Eaga were all funded through high debt. In the construction industry, it is risky to take high-level debt because a positive cash flow should be ensured to fill the loopholes in case big projects go wrong or cost overruns.[30] However, the huge cash gaps created a snowball effect for Carillion in that as more delayed projects incurred higher costs, the company would take on more debt.

Despite the hidden problems of Carillion's business, the overall environment for the construction industry appears to be cloudy as well. After the worldwide financial crisis in 2008, British construction corporations had to accept long-running and price-fixed contracts to maintain market share.[31] This left construction companies exposed once the projects got into delays or outweighed costs. Moreover, the whole

---

[25] House of Commons Business, Energy and Industrial Strategy and Work and Pensions Committees, *Carillion*, Second Joint Report (n 1) 15.

[26] 'Where Did It Go Wrong for Carillion?' (n 16).

[27] 'Aberdeen Bypass Settlement Reached', https://www.theconstructionindex.co.uk/news/view/aberdeen-bypass-settlement-agreed, accessed 26 February 2024.

[28] 'Carillion Collapse: Midland Metropolitan Hospital Work Resumes' *BBC News* (14 February 2020), https://www.bbc.com/news/uk-england-birmingham-51494374, accessed 26 February 2024. See also 'Costs Double for Stalled Liverpool and Birmingham Hospitals, Report Finds' *BBC News* (17 January 2020), https://www.bbc.com/news/uk-england-51137640, accessed 26 February 2024.

[29] 'Carillion: The Company Entrenched in Public Life' *BBC News* (15 January 2018), https://www.bbc.com/news/uk-england-42689717, accessed 27 February 2024.

[30] Amir Qamar and Collinson (n 10) 5.

[31] 'Carillion Shares Plunge after Third Profit Warning | Reuters', https://www.reuters.com/article/uk-carillion-outlook-idUKKBN1DH0QZ, accessed 31 March 2024.

industry is also suffering delays and reduction in the government's public spending after Brexit.[32]

5.2.3 *Ultimate Collapse*

5.2.3.1 Warning Signs

Carillion's collapse was not sudden; rather, the warning signs had been exposed for a long time. In 2015 or even earlier, hedge fund managers had started to detect the cracks behind Carillion's flawless façade from Carillion's balance sheet. They noticed that the company never seemed to generate cash, and the debt over the year was extremely higher than the debt they presented in the balance sheet.[33] For example, as early as August 2015, one information provider, HIS Markit, reported that Carillion was the most shorted ahead of earnings in Europe of the week with 17.1% of shares outstanding on loan.[34]

From 2015, the institutional investor, Standard Life Aberdeen Investments, started to sell its shares because the investor had no confidence in Carillion's high burden of debt being reduced in the near term.[35] Also in the same year, United Bank of Switzerland (UBS) warned that Carillion's total debt was heavier than the company's public stating.[36] Kuglitsch, an analyst of UBS noted that without many "hard assets", Carillion's ratio of net-debt to EBITDA (Earnings Before Interest, Taxes, Depreciation, and Amortization) was about four times which was far more than the ratio of Carillion's disclosure (less one time).[37]

At the end of 2015, a large proportion of shares in hedge funds were placed on bets that Carillion was going to failing.[38] In June 2017, warning signs had also been concealed ahead in the capital market. Carillion's shares were valued at an extremely

---

[32] Ian Mitchell and others, 'Brexit and the UK's Public Finances' (Institute for Fiscal Studies 2016) 8, https://www.ifs.org.uk/publications/8296, accessed 31 March 2024.

[33] Channel 4 (director), *How to Lose Seven Billion Pounds: Dispatches*, https://www.channel4.com/programmes/how-to-lose-seven-billion-pounds-dispatches, accessed 17 November 2024.

[34] 'Most Shorted Ahead of Earnings', https://cdn.ihs.com/www/blog/commentary/pdf/Most-shorted-ahead-of-earnings-21-August-2015.pdf, accessed 18 November 2024.

[35] 'Letter from Standard Life to the Chairs Regarding Carillion', https://www.parliament.uk/globalassets/documents/commons-committees/work-and-pensions/Carillion/Letter-from-Standard-Life-to-the-Chairs-regarding-Carillion-2-February-2018.pdf, accessed 27 February 2024.

[36] House of Commons Business, Energy and Industrial Strategy and Work and Pensions Committees, *Carillion*, Second Joint Report (n 1) 14.

[37] Chris Bryant, 'Hedge Funds Are the Good Guys In Carillion Debacle' (*Bloomberg Quint*), https://www.bloombergquint.com/opinion/hedge-funds-are-the-good-guys-in-carillion-debacle, accessed 31 March 2024.

[38] Emily Whiteley, 'Richard Adams (Finance Director of Carillion)—An Expert in Deceit.' (*Richard Adams (Finance Director of Carillion)—An expert in deceit.*), http://emilywhiteleyfinance.blogspot.com/2019/11/richard-adams-finance-director-of.html, accessed 16 November 2024.

cheap price.[39] All these signs proved in advance that the embattled Carillion was facing big problems. Indeed, only six months before its collapse, the company had issued three profit warnings in July 2017,[40] September 2017[41] and November 2017[42] respectively. Each earnings signal led to dramatic stock crashes.[43] Since the beginning of 2017, Carillion had witnessed its value slump by up to 90%.[44]

5.2.3.2 No Feasible Actions of the Board

However, facing such obvious warning signs, Carillion's board did not take any feasible actions to prevent the company from crumbling. Even as early as November 2016 the internal review of Carillion's Royal Liverpool Hospital management contract stated the company was making a loss, the company's management presented a rosy picture and persisted as a "healthy profit margin" was assumed in their March 2017 accounts.[45] Only four months later, however, Carillion announced a profit warning pointing to an £845 million reduction of its contracts' values, while two months later the reduction figure turned to £1045 million.

It was stated in the Second Joint Report that the board in June 2017 held a "lessons learned" exercise which hoped to find out the cultural, managerial and operational drawbacks.[46] This construction giant nevertheless took a drastic turn in the same year of the "lesson learned" exercise which eventually resulted in the collapse of the business. On 15 January 2018, the company was finally forced into compulsory liquidation, taking with it £1.5bn debt and only £29 m cash left in its account. Its collapse is obviously "the largest ever liquidation in the UK", according to the

---

[39] Rol and others, 'What Carillion Plc Liquidation Means for Shareholders' (*The Motley Fool UK*, 15 January 2018), https://www.fool.co.uk/investing/2018/01/15/what-carillion-plc-liquidation-means-for-shareholders/, accessed 25 February 2024.

[40] 'Investegate |Carillion PLC Announcements | Carillion PLC: Trading Statement', https://www.investegate.co.uk/carillion-plc/rns/trading-statement/201707100700105229K/, accessed 10 March 2024.

[41] 'Investegate |Carillion PLC Announcements | Carillion PLC: Half-Year Report', https://www.investegate.co.uk/carillion-plc/rns/half-year-report/201709290700092047S/, accessed 10 March 2024.

[42] 'Investegate |Carillion PLC Announcements | Carillion PLC: Update', https://www.investegate.co.uk/carillion-plc/rns/update/201711170702318037W/, accessed 10 March 2024.

[43] Gill Plimmer, 'Carillion Probe Pulls No Punches on Individuals or Institutions' *Financial Times* (15 May 2018), https://www.ft.com/content/aad5cb88-5820-11e8-b8b2-d6ceb45fa9d0, accessed 19 November 2021.

[44] 'Carillion in Fresh Shares Plunge on Latest Profit Warning' (*Sky News*), https://news.sky.com/story/carillion-in-fresh-shares-plunge-on-latest-profit-warning-11129790, accessed 15 March 2024.

[45] Plimmer (n 43).

In Carillion reporting regarding to 2016–2017 financial year, it was £5.2bn in revenue, 14% higher than the preceding year.

[46] House of Commons Business, Energy and Industrial Strategy and Work and Pensions Committees, *Carillion*, Second Joint Report (n 1) 11.

Official Receiver, Dave Chapman.[47] Indeed, Carillion's collapse could be the UK's largest corporate bankruptcy in a decade which had severely put a dent in investors' confidence and dragged down the shares of other peer sectors such as Balfour Beatty Plc and Galliford Try Plc.

In addition to this, there could be a wider societal issue. Stakeholders including employees, suppliers and creditors suffered immediately from Carillion's collapse. There would be repercussions for the taxpayers and society more widely with Carillion's failures of building hospitals, schools and other essential public services as the company was involved in 450 construction contracts with the UK government. When such massive corporations collapse, the whole society suffers not only financially but also with significant losses in welfare. From this corporate catastrophe, there is a need to take a deep look at Carillion's internal corporate governance and its external checks and balances.

5.3 How Carillion Made Decisions in Real Circumstances?

It was reported that in the last stage of Carillion's life, there were four contracts which caused great financial difficulties to the company and behaved as the main contributor to Carillion's demise, including three UK deals—Royal Liverpool University hospital, Midland Metropolitan hospital, and the Aberdeen western peripheral route; and one oversea contract in Qatar for the 2022 Fifa World Cup.[48] This book focuses on the domestic case of Royal Liverpool University hospital, together with Carillion's corporate governance reports, to establish and analyse how decisions were made in Carillion.

With the initial £15 million equity investment plan of Carillion,[49] the public private project (PPP) of Royal Liverpool University hospital started in 2013 and was proposed to be completed in March of 2017.[50] It was estimated that the construction value of this contract was worth £335 million.[51] Through this contract, Carillion expected to get a long-term return along with £300 million of revenue over 30 years.[52] This contract also had a direct impact on the wide range of public lives. According to Carillion's 2013 annual report, the company pledged to fill 60% of the jobs with local workers through this contract. It also committed to creating 100 apprenticeships,

---

[47] 'Carillion Contracts Complete Transfer' (*GOV.UK*), https://www.gov.uk/government/news/carillion-contracts-complete-transfer, accessed 23 February 2024.

[48] Simon Goodley, 'The Four Contracts That Finished Carillion' *The Guardian* (15 January 2018), https://www.theguardian.com/business/2018/jan/15/the-four-contracts-that-finished-carillion-public-private-partnership, accessed 15 November 2023.

[49] 'Carillion Plc, Annual Report and Accounts 2013′ 27, https://www.annualreports.co.uk/HostedData/AnnualReportArchive/c/LSE_CLLN_2013.pdf, accessed 21 March 2024.

[50] 'Carillion Plc, Annual Report and Accounts 2014′ 23, https://www.annualreports.co.uk/HostedData/AnnualReportArchive/c/LSE_CLLN_2014.pdf, accessed 13 March 2024.

[51] 'Carillion Plc, Annual Report and Accounts 2013' (n 49) 29.

[52] 'Carillion Plc, Annual Report and Accounts 2014' (n 50) 23.

providing work placements for young people, offering tailored construction training for the unemployed, and supporting young offenders in gaining skills through the Construction Skills Certificate Scheme (CSCS).[53] From 2013 to 2016, the outlook of Carillion's PPP segment in its annual reports appeared to be positive. However, until 2018, Carillion's new-year business plan started to reveal that there was a huge amount of working capital outflow driven by large legacy contracts, including the Royal Liverpool University hospital contract. Not talking about Carillion's commitment to the public, the completion day of this multimillion-pound PPP project is still unassured to date. More seriously, back in November 2016, the internal peer review had pointed out that Carillion underrated the completion costs of this hospital contract which would cost £53.9 m more than Carillion's estimate.[54] With the contract further delayed and unforeseen flaws detected, by December 2019, in addition to £285 m already spent, the completion would cost £300 m.[55]

Here, this book seeks to track and examine Carillion's corporate governance reports from 2013 to 2016 and 14 written records of board minutes from 2012 to 2017 to evaluate further its decision-making conducts during the terms of this hospital contract.

Carillion's corporate governance reports and the board minutes separately told two different stories. In its detailed corporate governance reports, Carillion presented a fancy picture of its corporate governance in which rigorous management structures and processes, a high standard of ethics and integrity, and accountability had been put in place. However, its short board-minute written records from the board, suggested there were no substantial issues to be discussed. For instance, in reaction to UBS's warning about Carillion's aggressive accounting, the board minutes from 2 April 2015 noted Richard Adam's brief and unconvincing response. He expressed disappointment with the UBS note, which had criticised their target price of 235p. Adam explained that the note had considered average debt, the pension deficit, and reverse factoring, but failed to acknowledge that these issues could affect any organisation. Additionally, when The Times inquired about a potential rights issue similar to Serco's, this was firmly rejected.[56]

In other words, as the Finance Director, Richard Adam simply classified Carillion's financial issues as common problems for any organisation and did not take any actions to prevent subsequent financial catastrophe. Other board minutes also recorded purely simple sentences and did not provide much detail about the company's decisions on the big projects and financial status. Only until 9 May 2017,

---

[53] Ibid., 18.

[54] David Price, 'Carillion Understated Hospital Costs by £70 m' (*Construction News*, 26 March 2018), https://www.constructionnews.co.uk/news/contractors-news/carillion-understated-hospital-costs-by-70m-26-03-2018/, accessed 8 January 2024.

[55] 'Liverpool Hospital Completion Delayed by Two More Years', https://www.theconstructionindex.co.uk/news/view/liverpool-hospital-completion-delayed-by-two-more-years, accessed 9 January 2024.

[56] 'Carillion Plc, Minutes of a Meeting of the Board of Directors, 2 April 2015' 5, https://www.parliament.uk/globalassets/documents/commons-committees/work-and-pensions/Carillion-report/Carillion-Board-minutes-2.4.15.pdf, accessed 9 January 2024.

the board minutes noted that, the last Finance Director Emma Mercer pointed out that she had identified "*some issues with which she was not comfortable*".[57] Emma Mercer could be the first *whistleblower* on Carillion's accounting issues, but everything seemed to be too late.

Additionally, a presentation by EY to Carillion's board in 2017 highlighted five major issues at the final stage of the company's operations. These included: prioritising short-term gains over long-term sustainability, an unnecessary level of complexity, a lack of visibility and transparency in performance despite multiple layers of management, an overload of data made difficult to interpret due to complex reporting systems, and unclear value provided by the Group to the business's performance.[58]

Thus, from these clues, this book seeks to establish how Carillion made decisions in real circumstances. Carillion looks like an empire dressed in the cloak of a modern corporation ruling with top managers and directors. Seemingly, it embraces all the features of a good publicly held corporation, including a scientifically rational managing structure, a positive relationship with shareholders and other stakeholders, sustainable corporate governance, commitment to the public and so on. However, when the research digs deeper, the word to describe such an entity is "monarchy" or, in Elles' words a "despotic corporate government",[59] in which the rulers on the top make decisions without transparent information, sufficient deliberation, constructive challenge and feasible checks and balances mechanism. It is fair to say that structurally, the formal division of power between the general meeting and the board is dysfunctional. The power of the general meeting was overwhelmed by the managerial power and was unable to exercise its power within Carillion.

The collapse of Carillion in 2018 exposed deep failures in corporate governance and financial oversight, yet meaningful accountability has only gradually begun to materialise in the years since. Many of those in senior positions appeared to operate behind a firewall of formal compliance, ostensibly adhering to governance regulations while advancing personal interests—for instance, by raising their own remuneration and awarding performance-linked bonuses. Years later, the UK courts were still grappling with the disqualification of directors. As Tribe notes, this may be partly attributable to the tendency of plc directors to rely on professional advisers, which courts have previously accepted as grounds for exoneration.[60] In October 2023, the former Chief Executive Officer, Richard Howson, was disqualified from serving as

---

[57] 'Carillion Plc, Minutes of a Meeting of the Board of Directors, 15 May 2017' 1, https://www.parliament.uk/globalassets/documents/commons-committees/work-and pensions/carillion/carillion-board-minutes-15-may-2017.pdf, accessed 9 January 2024.

[58] 'Extract-from-EY-Presentation-to-Carillion-Board-22-August-2017.Pdf' 6, https://www.parliament.uk/globalassets/documents/commons-committees/work-and-pensions/Carillion/Extract-from-EY-presentation-to-Carillion-Board-22-August-2017.pdf, accessed 9 January 2024.

[59] Richard Sedric Fox Eells, *The Government of Corporations* (Free Press 1962) 11.

[60] John Tribe, 'Carillion: Move to Disqualify Directors Signals UK Getting Tougher on "corporate Wrongdoing"—Articles—Liverpool Law School—University of Liverpool', https://www.liverpool.ac.uk/law/news/articles/carillion-move-to-disqualify-directors-signals-uk-authorities-getting-tougher-on-corporate-wrongdoing, accessed 7 January 2024.

a director for eight years. According to the Insolvency Service, Howson had caused Carillion to present a false picture of the company's financial health in its 2015 and 2016 accounts, including the concealment of deteriorating contract performance and the wrongful recognition of revenue from complex transactions with Wipro. These misstatements led to substantial overstatements of profit and understatements of net debt—by over £100 million in each year. He also failed to ensure that auditors were informed of these material matters. In effect, the financial statements issued under his leadership did not give a true and fair view, as required by Section 393 of the Companies Act 2006 and applicable international accounting standards.[61]

At the same time, scrutiny of Carillion's external auditor, KPMG, has also proceeded slowly.[62] It was not until July 2023 that the Financial Reporting Council (FRC) concluded two investigations and issued Final Settlement Decision Notices imposing sanctions against KPMG LLP, KPMG Audit Plc, and two former partners.[63] The first decision concerned the audits of Carillion's financial statements for 2014–2016 and additional work conducted in 2017, leading to sanctions against KPMG LLP and former partner Peter Meehan. The second decision related to the audit of transactions in the 2013 accounts, resulting in penalties against KPMG Audit Plc and Darren Turner, the partner responsible. These delayed enforcement outcomes—more than five years after the company's collapse—underscore the systemic inertia in holding both directors and auditors accountable, and suggest a need to reconsider the timeliness and robustness of regulatory responses to corporate failure.

This section tries to get into Carillion's boardroom "black box" to investigate the real processes of this authority's decision making by learning from limited overt sources within this company. However, the restricted information collected for this book is still insufficient to pierce the veil to reveal Carillion's real operational conditions, and this could also be empirical evidence to prove how hard it is for an outsider to gain access to some information that was supposed to be transparent. The Carillion case also shows us how Luke's three-dimensional power had been exercised in a real company.[64] The most straightforward and easily observed corporate managerial power could be found in the traditional decision-making body of Carillion, namely the boardroom and the AGM. Even though at this level, not all corporate participators can get involved in the decision-making processes, but they at least know what decisions would be made through publicly available information so that it is easier for people to identify whether their interests have been affected or not. But power can also be presented in latent and subtle ways—a second level of power through deciding what can be included in discussions and how these discussions may be

[61] 'Former CEO of Carillion Disqualified' (GOV.UK), https://www.gov.uk/government/news/former-ceo-of-carillion-disqualified, accessed 11 April 2024.

[62] Jasper Jolly, 'Carillion Tribunal: Former KPMG Staff Turn on Each Other' *The Guardian* (11 January 2022), https://www.theguardian.com/business/2022/jan/11/carillion-hearing-former-kpmg-staff-turn-on-each-other, accessed 22 January 2024.

[63] Sanctions against KPMG LLP, KPMG Audit Plc and Two Former Partners' (FRC (Financial Reporting Council)), https://www.frc.org.uk/news-and-events/news/2023/10/sanctions-against-kpmg-llp-kpmg-audit-plc-and-two-former-partners/, accessed 11 April 2024.

[64] Steven Lukes, *Power: A Radical View* (Macmillan International Higher Education 2004) 19.

presented and controlled; the third level through modelling how people think. From Carillion's recorded board minutes, we see very few detailed discussions and analysis of important contracts or other public-related sectors. In other words, some big decisions were hidden by those decision makers. Those elements of publicly available information can be regarded as a selected result. Moreover, by constructing big personalities in the boardroom and creating a culture of "fear and confusion" in the company, insiders of Carillion were inhibited from challenging Carillion's strange accounting treatments. Carillion's boardroom structure will be further analysed in the next chapter.

5.4 Conclusion

Before addressing what a corporation should be and do, it is essential to conduct an objective analysis of its current state.[65] To summarise, this chapter has presented a story of "recklessness, hubris and greed" of Carillion Plc. Facing this spectacular corporate downfall and the subsequent social and financial turmoil, a joint report issued by the UK government's Department for Business, Energy and Industrial Strategy and Department for Work and Pensions entitled *Carillion* has dissected the reasons for its collapse and has blamed Carillion's boardroom, auditors, regulators and the government itself, identifying failures in governance and accountability that needed to be addressed by enacting recommendations. Carillion's collapse was marked by unethical leadership, a toxic board culture, ineffective non-executive directors and chair, manipulation of accounts, and failures in both internal and external audits, highlighting a significant lack of stakeholder accountability. This was not merely the failure of a company, but of a corporate accountability system that often allows those at the top, along with the surrounding firms, to emerge unscathed while others bear the consequences.[66]

Indeed, Carillion's collapse was not the result of isolated incidents, but rather the outcome of a systematic failure—both within the company and in the wider regulatory environment. The following chapter will therefore examine Carillion's internal accountability mechanisms, as well as the external checks and balances that were meant to provide oversight.

---

[65] Richard Sedric Fox Eells, *The Meaning of Modern Business: An Introduction to the Philosophy of Large Corporate Enterprise* (Columbia University Press 1960) 94.

[66] Sean Lyons, Corporate Defense and the Value Preservation Imperative: Bulleproof Your Corporate Defense Program (CRC Press 2016) 98.

Chapter 6
Carillion's Collapse and Corporate Governance

6.1 Introduction

This chapter explores both the internal corporate governance arrangements of Carillion and the external systems of checks and balances—such as regulators, auditors, institutional investors, and government oversight mechanisms—that are designed to prevent corporate misconduct and systemic failure. Central to this discussion is the extent to which the company's governance structure, and the broader governance system in which it was embedded, contributed to the chain of decisions and omissions that led to Carillion's downfall.

Carillion's case invites scrutiny not only of the behaviour of individual directors, executives, and auditors, but also of the deeper institutional and systemic weaknesses that allowed governance failures to persist unchecked over time. Was Carillion a victim of a governance system that was, in itself, dysfunctional? Did its collapse signify merely a failure in execution, or did it expose structural flaws in the UK's model of corporate oversight and accountability?

While various proximate causes have been identified—from aggressive revenue recognition and over-reliance on government contracts to poor risk management and short-termism—the chronic disorder in Carillion's internal governance and the systemic inadequacies in external accountability mechanisms must be recognised as critical contributors to its failure. As Solomon observes, Carillion's experience demands that we view corporate governance not only as a matter of structure and compliance, but as a living system whose health determines the survival of major corporate entities.[1]

Indeed, the House of Commons Joint Report on Carillion issues a stark warning: without deep reflection and meaningful reform, "Carillion could happen again, and soon".[2] This chapter therefore aims not only to provide a detailed account of the

[1] Jill Solomon, *Corporate Governance and Accountability* (John Wiley & Sons 2020) 4.

[2] House of Commons Business, Energy and Industrial Strategy and Work and Pensions Committees, *Carillion*, Second Joint Report from the Business, Energy and Industrial Strategy and Work and

Y. Yang, *Corporate Collapse and Corporate Governance*, CSR, Sustainability, Ethics & Governance, https://doi.org/10.1007/978-981-96-9666-6_6

governance breakdowns within Carillion, but also to critically assess what the failure reveals about the broader architecture of corporate governance in the UK.

The chapter is structured as follows. The next section looks into Carillion's internal corporate governance arrangements, followed by a discussion in Sect. 6.3 on the role of external checks and balances. Section 6.4 considers to what extent the broader UK corporate governance system might be held responsible for Carillion's collapse. The chapter concludes with some final reflections in Sect. 6.5.

6.2 Internal Corporate Governance Arrangement

Carillion Plc had been a vast conglomerate, with a complex set of subsidiaries. Carillion's meltdown seemed to set off the domino effect within the Carillion Group. The parent company, Carillion Plc and its subsidiaries had become the subject of a compulsory or provisional liquidation with effect from 15 January 2018.[3] On the same day of Carillion's compulsory liquidation, the five subsidiary companies, Carillion Construction Limited, Carillion Services Limited, Planned Maintenance Engineering Limited, Carillion Integrated Services Limited and Carillion Services 2006 Limited also entered into bankruptcy proceedings.[4] More than that, the number of insolvent subsidiaries of the Carillion Group had ballooned to 94 so far.[5]

Why did these subsidiary companies also get into financial turmoil after the parent company Carillion Plc's collapse, even though they all had the independent corporate personality? That is because within the corporate group, companies may be under common administrative or financial control.[6] Or in other words, companies in the Carillion business group were bonded with the same system of governance relationship. The existence of governance problems in any companies could be easily expanded and exacerbated within the whole group, the problems then could eventually result in exponential collateral damage to the unitary internal governance system. In consequence, if there was a failure to spot the problem in time, the incipient corporate governance disaster of Carillion Plc would sweep through almost the whole Carillion Group.

This section is devoted to investigating the internal governance arrangement of Carillion Plc and examines the problems they had that destroyed this corporate giant.

Pensions Committees of Session 2017–19, HC 769, 16 May 2018, at 5, https://publications.parliament.uk/pa/cm201719/cmselect/cmworpen/769/769.pdf, accessed 31 October 2023.

3 'Court and Tribunals Judiciary—Carillion Group', https://www.judiciary.uk/wp-content/uploads/2015/03/carillion-group-cmo1.pdf, accessed 17 March 2024.

4 'The Ongoing Deconstruction of Carillion' (*Restructuring Global View*, 31 January 2018), https://www.restructuring-globalview.com/2018/01/the-ongoing-deconstruction-of-carillion/, accessed 14 March 2024.

5 PricewaterhouseCoopers, 'Carillion Group' (*PwC*), https://www.pwc.co.uk/services/business-restructuring/administrations/carillion.html, accessed 15 March 2024.

6 Nathaniel Leff, 'Capital Markets in the Less Developed Countries: The Group Principle' (1976) 3 *Money and Finance in Economic Growth and Development* 97.

It will keep eyes on its core decision-making mechanism—the boardroom which took the ultimate responsibility for Carillion's internal control, and the annual general meeting of shareholders; the internal and external auditors; the relationship with employees and other stakeholders.

6.2.1 Core Decision-Making Mechanisms—The Board and AGM

In the tradition of corporate governance, the dual decision-making structure—the boardroom and annual general meeting are the two core decision-making components of corporations. The board of directors is granted the managerial power from shareholders. The board power may then be delegated to more specific strands of power, such as the power of nominating personnel, auditing, deciding remunerations. This section will specifically look at Carillion's core decision-making mechanisms and examine what went wrong in the processes of decision-making.

6.2.1.1 Board and Management

Structure

According to Carillion Plc's 2016 annual report and accounts, the company's boardroom consisted of seven directors: one Independent Chairman—Philip Green, two executives (Group Chief Executive—Richard Howson and Group Finance Director—Zafar Khan) and four independent non-executive directors—Keith Cochrane, Andrew Dougal, Alison Horner and Ceri Powell.[7] Prior to Carillion's first profit warning, in March 2017, there was a slight personnel change that Ceri Powell resigned and had been replaced by Sally Morgan in July 2017. By the time of the collapse of Carillion, Keith Cochrane and Emma Mercer held the positions previously occupied by Richard Howson and Zafar Khan respectively. But in Carillion's final days, Carillion's recovery plan stated that the Carillion Group started to implement structural change to improve the senior management capability. The board was refreshed by appointing new members in the board. The final structure of the boardroom comprised one Independent Chairman—Philip Green; Senior Independent Director—Sally Morgan; Interim Chief Executive—Keith Cochrane; Audit Chair—Andrew Dougal; Audit Chair designate—Justin Read; and two Non-executives—Alan Lovell and Alison Horner.[8] Within the Group Executive team,

[7] 'Carillion Plc, Annual Report and Accounts 2016', at 50–51, https://www.annualreports.com/HostedData/AnnualReports/PDF/LSE_CLLN_2016.pdf, accessed 12 March 2024.

[8] 'Companies House, Carillion Plc Officers', https://beta.companieshouse.gov.uk/company/03782379/officers, accessed 13 November 2023.

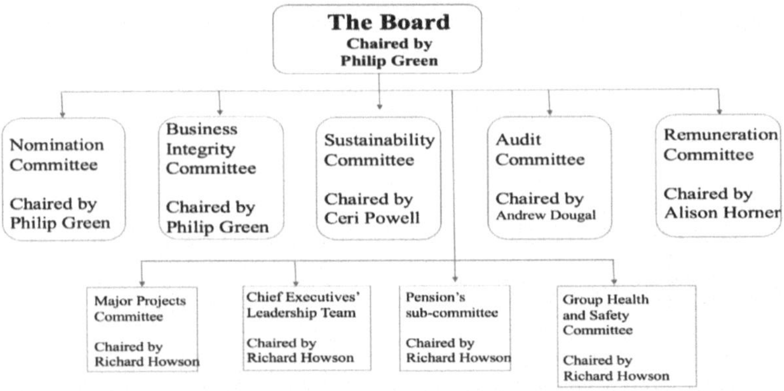

Fig. 6.1 The board structure of Carillion[10]

under the CEO, there were COO—Andy Jones; CFO—Emma Mercer; CHRO—Janet Dawson; Legal and Co Secretary—Richard Tapp; CTO—Lee Watson, and Head of Business Improvement—Donald Muir.

Under the Board's leadership, Carillion Plc had put in place a comprehensive management structure which was comprised of the Nominations Committee, the Business Integrity Committee, the Sustainability Committee, the Audit Committee and the Remuneration Committee (Fig. 6.1).[9]

This is a traditional one-tier board structure which consists of executive and non-executive directors. The non-executive directors have a supervisory role to scrutinise executives' performance, assess the company's risk management and provide constructive challenges to the executive directors. The above pictures and descriptions show a complicated boardroom composition in Carillion. It seems that the board was spread thinly regarding the various specialist functions, but it was still controlled by a few directors with Philip Green chairing three committees and Richard Howson chairing four committees. From this structure, it is hard to see how non-executives would oversee the executives, when instead, non-executives and executives were together building a boardroom "black box" controlled by a few top officials. The following chapters' analysis also proves this speculation here.

Board Activities and Decision Making

Tracing Carillion's fifteen-year Annual Reports and Accounts from 2002 to 2016,[11] this book finds some clues to the decision-making processes of the board. During these fifteen years, the number of board meetings in each year was between 7 to

[9] 'Carillion Plc, Annual Report and Accounts 2016' (n 7) 54.

[10] Ibid.

[11] The Annual Report and Accounts 2002 is the earliest one, and the Annual Report and Accounts 2016 is the latest one that can be found for this book.

10. The Annual Reports and Accounts between 2003 and 2011 revealed the formal schedule of matters reserved to the board meetings for consideration in the same words. These formal matters cover statutory issues, including the approval of final and interim financial statements, as well as dividend recommendations; appointments to and removals from the Board; the terms of reference and composition of Board committees; approval of group strategy and annual budgets; setting authority levels and financial policies; authorisation of acquisitions or disposals; evaluation of internal control and risk management strategies; and review of corporate governance arrangements.[12] However, there was a big change of the board's main activities in the 2012 report which included another 28 issues that the board dealt with in addition to these formal matters.[13]

In terms of the decision making in the boardroom, according to Carillion's Annual Report and Accounts, directors followed a rigorous division-of-responsibility rule to avoid unfettered power of any individuals in the board. The roles of its Chairman, Group Chief Executive and Senior Independent Non-Executive Director were clearly settled in the reports. In order to ensure compliance with management requirements, the Board and its Committees also kept an appropriate balance of expertise, competence, capability and independence.[14] Especially, Carillion's Audit Committee held a significant position to review the company's financial status, internal control, risk

[12] The Annual Reports and Accounts between 2003 and 2011.

[13] These 28 activities were: "Health & Safety; Sustainability policy and practice; Presentations on the business units' performance and strategy; Group strategy; Risk management; Financial and interim management statements; Quarterly forecasts; Regulatory announcements; Dividends; Monthly management results; Work winning; Three year business plan; Board committee reports; Review of policies such as ethics and business integrity; Annual Board evaluation review; Delegation of authorities; Insurance matters; AGM business; Major projects; Acquisitions and disposals; Regulatory issues and briefings; Succession planning; Directors' share dealings; Appeals committee funding; Review of conflicts of interest; Review of third party benefits; Site visits to operations; Meeting local management and employees".

See from 'Carillion Plc, Annual Report and Accounts 2012′ 47, https://www.annualreports.co.uk/HostedData/AnnualReportArchive/c/LSE_CLLN_2012.pdf, accessed 21 March 2024.

[14] The Nomination Committee was responsible for making recommendations on appointments to the Board and its Committees; reviewing the Group's succession arrangements and overall Board composition to ensure the balance of skills and experience remains appropriate.

The Business Integrity Committee was responsible for reviewing and overseeing the development and implementation of the Group's Ethics and Business Integrity Policy; monitoring the Group's compliance with relevant legislation such as the Bribery Act 2010 and the Competition Act; monitoring the Group's communication and training programmes on ethics and business integrity.

The Sustainability Committee was responsible for reviewing and approving policies, targets and performance in relation to key sustainability initiatives; reviewing and approving the annual Sustainability Report prior to publication; monitoring legislation and/or regulations that might affect the Group or its stakeholders and other matters which could impact corporate reputation and the management of any such matters; engaging with internal and external stakeholders on key sustainability themes.

The Audit Committee was responsible for reviewing and reporting to the Board on the Group's financial reporting to investors, internal controls and risk management processes; making recommendations to the Board on the appointment or reappointment of the external auditor and monitors the effectiveness and independence of the external auditor; directing and reviewing the work undertaken by the external and internal audit functions.

management, regulatory compliance and the independence and effectiveness of the external auditor, KPMG LLP. According to the 2016 report, Carillion's goodwill by the end of 2016 was worth £1,571.0 million which was the largest single element in the balance sheet.[15] In the Audit Committee's reports from the past three years, the external auditor confirmed that the audit plans for 2016, 2015, and 2014 were carried out as agreed with the Committee, with no significant issues raised for the Committee's attention.[16] In summary, Carillion's fifteen-year Annual Reports and Accounts, especially the reports for the last three years, presented a prosperous scene for investors. The board and its committees followed their fiduciary duties owed to the shareholders, and no one broke the rules. Through these reports, they were just willing to send one signal—"everything is fine".

The Board Behaviours in the Real World

However, the rosy picture painted in Carillion's Annual Reports and Accounts did not reflect the reality. To a large extent, Carillion's downfall could be attributed to the board's wrongful behaviours.

Three Key Figures in Carillion's Collapse

The Second Joint Report particularly criticised three key figures in the board – Richard Adam, Richard Howson and Philip Green. Richard Adam, Carillion's Finance Director from 2007 to 2016, was the dominant personality in the company's finance department. In the Chair of the audit committee, Andrew Dougal's words, Adam maintained strict control over the entire finance function, exerting significant influence within the Group, and was defensive when faced with challenges during board meetings.[17] Adam was regarded as the "architect of Carillion's aggressive accounting policies"[18]—an accounting practice of overstating company's financial performance based on optimistic forecasts, before the profits have been

The Remuneration Committee was responsible for reviewing and advising the Board on remuneration arrangements for the Chairman, the Executive Directors and their direct reports.

See from 'Carillion Plc, Annual Report and Accounts 2016' (n 7) 57.

[15] 'Carillion Plc, Annual Report and Accounts 2016' (n 7) 64.

[16] 'Carillion Plc, Annual Report and Accounts 2015', https://www.annualreports.com/HostedData/AnnualReportArchive/c/LSE_CLLN_2015.pdf, accessed 13 March 2024.

See also, 'Carillion Plc, Annual Report and Accounts 2014', https://www.annualreports.co.uk/HostedData/AnnualReportArchive/c/LSE_CLLN_2014.pdf, accessed 13 March 2024.

[17] 'Letter from Andrew Dougal to the Chairs, 5 April 2018', https://www.parliament.uk/globalassets/documents/commons-committees/work-and-pensions/Carillion-report/Letter-from-Andrew-Dougal-to-Chairs-5-April-2018.pdf, accessed 25 March 2024.

[18] House of Commons Business, Energy and Industrial Strategy and Work and Pensions Committees, *Carillion*, Second Joint Report (n 2) 46.

really achieved.[19] Without accurate prospect of revenues and profits, the aggressive accounting easily leads to misrepresentation of Carillion's real business. Indeed, Carillion's aggressive accounting approach created difficulty for the company to withstand contracts deteriorating which finally led up to its collapse, according to Emma Mercer, the last finance director of Carillion.[20]

The other boardroom member who has been seriously criticised is Richard Howson, Chief Executive between 2012 and 2017. The Second Joint Report considers Howson as the "figurehead for a business model that was doomed to fail".[21] In other words, although being a crucial member in the board, Howson was unaware of the unsustainability of Carillion's business model and governance problems laying at the root of the company. During the House of Commons' examination of witnesses, he explained that much of his time was spent managing cash calls or travelling to contracts, as the support services and construction markets, particularly in Canada and the Middle East, were facing challenging conditions that required significant time and effort.[22] Even facing challenges in business, he believed Carillion was still in a sustainable position, and he was also optimistic that Carillion could survive with ongoing support from banks.[23] Moreover, as revealed by the Carillion joint inquiry, after Howson's contract was terminated, his share-related bonuses were deposited into a bank account which would not need to be disclosed to shareholders.[24]

Philip Green, a non-executive director since 2011 and the non-executive Chairman since 2014, was also a detached optimist when Carillion was on the road to demise. It seemed to be the company's tradition that the Chairman of Carillion was also the Chairman in the Nominations Committee and Business Integrity Committee. Thus, when Philip Green succeeded Philip Rogerson as the Chairman of the Board in 2014, he also became the Chairman in the two Committees of management. In his position, Green regarded his role as "cheerleader-in-chief" who always presented a false appearance of corporate prosperity in his statements. Just days ahead of Carillion's profit warning, the board minutes indicated that the Chairman emphasised ongoing efforts to prepare an optimistic announcement for the following Monday, highlighting

---

[19] David Pells, 'Ineffective Risk Management and the Collapse of Carillion' (*PM World Journal*) 4, https://pmworldjournal.com/article/ineffective-risk-management-2, accessed 28 March 2024.

[20] Gurpreet Narwan, 'Carillion's Problem Was Aggressive Accounting, Says Finance Chief', https://www.thetimes.co.uk/article/carillions-problem-was-aggressive-accounting-says-finance-chief-5rsskpjcw, accessed 28 March 2024.

[21] House of Commons Business, Energy and Industrial Strategy and Work and Pensions Committees, *Carillion*, Second Joint Report (n 2) 29.

[22] 'Oral Evidence—Carillion—6 Feb 2018' Q534–Q535, http://data.parliament.uk/writtenevidence/committeeevidence.svc/evidencedocument/work-and-pensions-committee/carillion/oral/78103.html, accessed 26 March 2024.

[23] Ibid., Q413 and Q475.

[24] 'Carillion Agreed Secret Bonus Account for Richard Howson' (*Construction News*, 26 March 2018), https://www.constructionnews.co.uk/news/contractors-news/carillion-agreed-secret-bonus-account-for-richard-howson-26-03-2018/, accessed 21 November 2024.

the company's perceived strengths as an appealing business and referencing planned self-help measures and asset disposals.[25]

Those three directors—the architect of Carillion's aggressive accounting scheme, the figurehead CEO, and the cheerleader and optimist of Carillion's false prosperity—failed to manage and run the company in a reliable and sustainable manner, but exploited the corporate interest by annually increasing their remuneration and bonus payments. Although the company followed the requirement of corporate governance codes that divided the functions of CEO and Chairman, they essentially were still bound together in the same interest group. In 2021, three years after Carillion's collapse, the business secretary Kwasi Kwarteng through the Insolvency Service had launched a legal proceeding to ban Carillion's former 8 Carillion directors (including Richard Howson, Richard Adam, Keith Cochrane, Zafar Khan, Philip Green, Alison Horner, Andrew Dougal and Ceri Powell) from holding senior boardroom roles in the UK.[26] This appears to be a really rare action to disqualify directions' position by formal proceedings in the UK, as observed by O'Connell.[27]

According to Financial Conduct Authority's (FCA) announcement, it is evidenced that these directors had "acted recklessly" and issued "misleading positive market statements" before Carillion's collapse.[28] The FCA's Warning Notice Statement to Carillion and several former executives noted that the executive directors did not ensure the announcements under their responsibility accurately and comprehensively represented the situation. Although they were aware of the worsening conditions and escalating risks, they did not inform the Board or the Audit Committee, thereby undermining appropriate oversight.[29] Clearly, the non-executive directors did not live up to their monitoring roles as presented in the corporate governance codes, such as the Higgs Report (2003) and the Walker Review (2009) which specifically highlight non-executives' independent scrutiny function in corporate governance.[30]

---

[25] 'Carillion Plc, Minutes of a Meeting of the Board of Directors, 5 July 2017' 5, https://www.parliament.uk/globalassets/documents/commons-committees/work-and-pensions/Correspondence/Carillion-Board-minutes-5-July-2017.pdf, accessed 26 March 2024.

[26] 'Carillion: Legal Bid Launched to Ban Former Directors' *BBC News* (14 January 2021), https://www.bbc.com/news/business-55659196, accessed 17 March 2024.

[27] Ibid.

[28] 'Carillion Directors to Face FCA Action for Misleading Investors' *Financial Times* (13 November 2020), https://www.ft.com/content/55a5136a-25a2-43a6-a085-3904ee72f60c, accessed 17 March 2024.

[29] Financial Conduct Authority, 'Warning Notice Statement 20/2, https://www.fca.org.uk/publication/warning-notices/warning-notice-statement-20-2.pdf, accessed 17 March 2024.

[30] For a survey, see *Review of the Role and Effectiveness of Non-Executive Directors (Higgs Report)*, Department of Trade and Industry London January 2003; *A Review of Corporate Governance in the UK Banks and other Financial Industry Entities (Walker Review)*, The Walker Review Secretariat, London 26 November 2009.

The Audit Committee Together with the Internal and External Auditors

Carillion's financialisation and accounting practices were guarded by not only the company's own audit committee but also by the Big Four—KPMG as the external auditor, Deloitte as the internal auditor, EY tasked with the six-month strategic review and PWC tasked with advising and specialist help. However, Carillion's audit committee, internal and external auditors all failed to hold the board to account, allowing Carillion's internal governance and the whole accountability mechanism to fall into disarray.[31] The failure of Carillion's audit functions is an especially major cause of the company's downfall. In evidence to the Second Joint Report, Deloitte was appointed as Carillion's internal auditor since 2010, pocketing on average £775 k each year.[32] It, however, was insensitive to Carillion's risks that only one report had pointed out Carillion's inadequate-control issues of the total 61 reports between 2015 and 2016.[33] The external auditor—KPMG also behaved in the same way—charging high service fees but barely once qualifying its audit opinion, rather as directors' "rubber stamp" helping directors sign off the year-on-year fantastical accounting figures.[34]

The rosy revenues stated in Carillion's Annual Reports and Accounts were really a mirage. Although these auditors and management officials viewed Carillion's collapse as a sudden deterioration, according to Bhaskar, Flower and Seller's simulation of Carillion's finance, the company's financial problems were actually "being stored up for some time (years)".[35] Carillion's "aggressive accounting" appeared to be the key reason for not diagnosing Carillion's financial problems earlier.[36] This kind of accounting practice would stretch the reasonable standards of accounting to recognise as much revenue ahead as possible which could result in a danger of overstating the company's performance and creating an illusion of business prosperity. Through aggressive accounting, Carillion's accounts thus were mixed with real transactions and future potential suppositions. Carillion's financial reporting was

---

[31] Solomon (n 1) 35.

[32] 'Letter from Deloitte to the Chairs, 2 February 2018', https://www.parliament.uk/globalassets/documents/commons-committees/work-and-pensions/Correspondence/Letter-from-Deloitte-Chairman-to-the-Chairs-relating-to-Carillion-2-February-2018.pdf, accessed 29 March 2024.

[33] House of Commons Business, Energy and Industrial Strategy and Work and Pensions Committees, *Carillion*, Second Joint Report (n 2) 54.

[34] House of Commons Business, Energy and Industrial Strategy and Work and Pensions Committees, *Carillion*, Second Joint Report (n 2) 4.

[35] Krish Bhaskar, John Flower and Rod Sellers, *Financial Failures and Scandals: From Enron to Carillion* (Routledge 2019) 76.

[36] In terms of "aggressive accounting", further explanation is added here. Carillion used accrual basis accounting which is a preferred bookkeeping method for revealing a company's accurate financial status. The accruals basis of accounting requires a company's revenue to be confirmed when it is earned, rather than when it is really received. A company with aggressive accounting will try to minimise the prediction of the whole project's costs to guarantee the maintaining of margins on contracts and larger amounts of revenues recognised in advance. 'Accounting tricks: How Carillion duped the market', https://www.globalconstructionreview.com/accounting-tricks-how-carillion-duped-market/, accessed 29 March 2024.

therefore seriously compromised. As accounting became increasingly dependent on fluctuating, forward-looking judgments instead of objective figures, the credibility of performance assessments weakened and external observers grew more sceptical of the accounts.[37]

Moreover, Carillion also had a great amount of revenues that was not signed by clients which made payment uncertain. Besides those "traded not certificated" contracts, many of Carillion's contracts suffered from losses. It was noted in the 2017 audit committee papers that over the period of March-June, more than 18 contracts were mired in losses.[38] Additionally, Carillion's balance sheet was upheld by goodwill (such as company brand, patents, trademarks, copyrights and other intangible assets). Unlike tangible assets, the actual value of goodwill is difficult to define and when Carillion succumbed, its goodwill value would be nothing.

Furthermore, according to Moody's analysis, Carillion's Annual Reports and Accounts were also compromised by the accounting for reverse factoring.[39] Reverse factoring is a supply chain finance instrument by which corporations and the suppliers work together with the banks to optimise the cash flows in the trade.[40] However, the agreements between corporations and their suppliers and the banks are always undisclosed, unless checking the reported amounts as "trade payables" and "other creditors". In Carillion, the company's liability to banks was not clear in its balance sheet, and the main source for the company generating cash was also not evident in its cash flow statement.[41] As analysed by Moody's statistics, Carillion's balance sheet showed the company had bank loans and overdrafts totalling £148 m, but under reverse factoring arrangements that began in 2013, an additional amount owed to banks could be as high as £498 m. This additional figure seemed to be hidden in the amount reported as "other creditors" of Carillion and was therefore not included as borrowings. In a word, Carillion's cash flow and balance sheet were fatally weakened by long-lasting and risky construction contracts; and were also puffed up with exaggerated goodwill. As a result, although the company's last report of accounts showed a prosperous vision of its business, Carillion was merely a "hollow" company which was emptied out by high payouts to shareholders and heavy liabilities to creditors when it went to liquidation. It is unconvincing to say these auditors were unaware of Carillion's real financial problems.

[37] Michel Aglietta and Antoine Rebérioux, *Corporate Governance Adrift: A Critique of Shareholder Value* (Edward Elgar Publishing 2005) 126.

[38] Ibid., 42.

[39] 'Moody's: Carillion's Collapse Exposes Flaws in the Accounting for Supply-Chain Finance Arrangements' (*Moodys.com*, 13 March 2018), http://www.moodys.com:18000/research/Moodys-Carillions-collapse-exposes-flaws-in-the-accounting-for-supply--PR_380769, accessed 31 March 2024.

[40] John Liebl, Evi Hartmann and Edda Feisel, 'Reverse Factoring in the Supply Chain: Objectives, Antecedents and Implementation Barriers' (2016) 46 *International Journal of Physical Distribution & Logistics Management* 1.

[41] 'Moody's: Carillion's Collapse Exposes Flaws in the Accounting for Supply-Chain Finance Arrangements' (n 39).

It is thus remarked here that auditors of Carillion failed to act as effective gatekeepers of transparent and trustworthy financial information. And what is also remarkable here is that failures of Carillion's auditors seem to repeat the same US story of Enron. Responding to the Enron scandal, Coffee raises a "general deterrence" hypobook to explain auditors' incompetence.[42] It is revealed that there is a positive correlation between auditors' benefits with auditors' actions of acquiescing to their clients' aggressive accounting behaviours.[43] Coffee perceives that auditors' client-pleasing behaviours will compromise their independence and mislead investors. Following Coffee's theory, Kershaw proposes an "incentive equilibrium" between acquiesce and independence of auditors. He argues that when the balance shifts towards acquiescence, the risk of audit failure rises.[44] According to Kershaw, changes in audit firms' revenue structures in the UK have heightened their financial reliance on specific clients. More critically, these changes have empowered management to credibly pressure audit firms into compliance.[45] He further contends that litigation, reputational damage, and disciplinary action impose minimal costs on auditors who acquiesce.[46] The regulatory reforms, however, increased the complexity, fragmentation and opacity in audit arena.[47] More than 20 years later, Coffee's theory and Kershaw's statement can even offer an explain to the misbehaviours of auditors in Carillion. We can still see auditors give up their independence to cater to Carillion's management because the audit firms highly relied on those clients. And the reforms on regulatory frameworks have not rebalanced the equilibrium in favour of independence or checks and balances of corporate governance. The previous criticisms in the literature on auditor standards and independence have still been well and accurate illustrated in Carillion's case.

High Dividend and High Remuneration

Carillion had a progressive dividend policy since its demerger from Tarmac. Especially its five-year compound annual growth rate from 2006 to 2010 was as high as 14%. Its dividend payments, nevertheless, had little relevance to business performance. As a construction company with no steady profits and insufficient cash outflow, Carillion was generous to its shareholders that kept the growth in the dividend payment in the years preceding to corporate failure. Even facing difficulties in volatile cash flows and falling construction volumes, Carillion continued to pay excessive dividends to shareholders. In Carillion's final year, in 2017, the board

---

[42] John C Coffee Jr, 'What Caused Enron-a Capsule Social and Economic History of the 1990s' (2003) 89 *Cornell L. Rev.* 269, 288–293.

[43] Ibid., 288.

[44] David Kershaw, 'Waiting for Enron: The Unstable Equilibrium of Auditor Independence Regulation' (2006) 33 *Journal of Law and Society* 388, 389.

[45] Ibid.

[46] Ibid.

[47] Ibid.

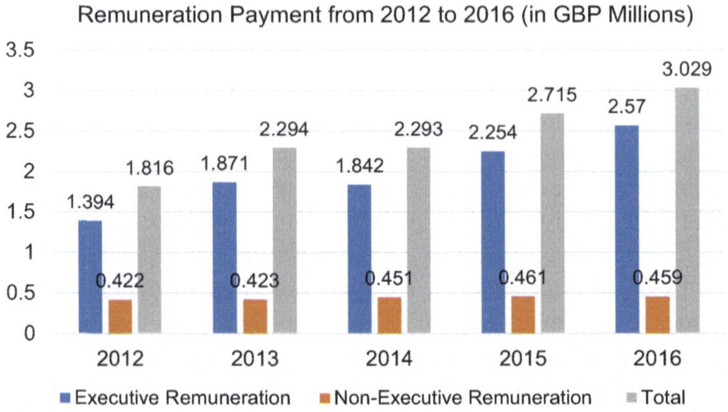

Fig. 6.2 Remuneration Payment from 2012 to 2016 (*Data Source* Carillion Group Annual Reports and Accounts 2012–2016)

had seriously debated stopping dividend payments due to the company's deteriorating financial situation, but Carillion still went ahead and paid out £55 million in dividends.

In terms of the directors' remuneration, as stated above, the boardroom had added an additional 28 activities in 2012. The increasing burdens on the board could be a sign that on the one side the board took more responsibilities of the Carillion Group which put higher demands on directors' competence, and on the other side, the board members held more power in their hands. The most direct manifestation of power increase was the rise in remuneration of Carillion's board members. On Richard Howson's appointment as Group Chief Executive in 2012, his basic salary increased by 45% to £560 k.[48] Despite the increase in the CEO's remuneration, between 2012 and 2016, there had been a year-on-year remuneration rise for all directors (executives and non-executives) from £1.816 million to £3.029 million in total. As of 2016, the total remuneration payment for executive directors— Richard Howson and Richard Adam had jumped 45.8% more than the entire executive payment in 2012. When Adam left Carillion in December 2016, he earned a final pay package up to £1.1 million and offloaded his entire Carillion shares with a total £776 k gain between March and May 2017, just before the dramatic share price drop by mid-July (Fig. 6.2).[49]

A "Rotten" Boardroom Culture

In conclusion, Carillion presented a rotten atmosphere in the boardroom. The whole picture presented above was totally opposite to the rosy one in Carillion's Annual

[48] 'Carillion Plc, Annual Report and Accounts 2011′ 49, https://www.annualreports.co.uk/HostedData/AnnualReportArchive/c/LSE_CLLN_2011.pdf, accessed 21 March 2024.

[49] 'Carillion Plc, Annual Report and Accounts 2016' (n 7) 66.

Reports and Accounts. The true story of Carillion is that: the executives and non-executives together constructed a boardroom "black box"; there were "big" personalities who were especially at fault but with no challenges to the dominant individuals in the board; when facing financial problems, the self-assured boardroom "cheerleaders" were incapable of managing risks; the independent Chairman and non-executives had no capability to monitor and control Carillion's low levels of investment, declining cash flow, rising debt and growing pension deficit; shareholders' interests were always given priority, even employees' pension rights were infringed in consequence of the high dividends; the audit committee together with the internal and external auditors overstated Carillion's profits and lacked prudence in their audit functions; the remuneration committee failed to set appropriate level of remuneration for board members.

6.2.1.2 Annual General Meeting (AGM) and Decision Making

The AGM had a constructive use for the Board to make contact with shareholders and encourage their involvement, according to Carillion's Annual Report and Accounts 2016.[50] Shareholders possessed the voting rights to decide on the main issues about audit, remuneration, appointment or re-election of directors. At the meeting, the Chairmen of the Audit, Business Integrity, Nominations, Remuneration and Sustainability Committees should be involved to answer questions on the work of their Committees.

Regarding shareholder composition, according to the latest three-year (from 2014 to 2016) data, around 80% investors were institutional shareholders, 20% were private shareholders. Most of the board members were shareholders themselves. The share capitals were highly concentrated by top shareholders that approximate half of the shares were held by the top 10, about 90% shares were held by the top 100.[51] In 2016, the institutional shareholders who held substantial amount of interests are BlackRock Inc. (8.81%), Deutsche Bank AG (5.82%), UBS Investment Bank and UBS Group AG (5.08%), Kiltearn Partners LLP (5.01%), Brewin Dolphin Limited (5.00%), Letko, Brosseau & Associates Inc. (4.97%), Standard Life Investments (Holdings) Limited (4.96%).

There was little evidence to demonstrate that the shareholders were well-equipped to exercise their decision-making power or to influence director's decisions. Most institutional shareholders, such as the passive investor BlackRock, the active investors Standard Life Aberdeen and Kiltear Partners, who possessed a large number of shares, were still unable to change Carillion's short-term situation. For them, the unrealistic

[50] 'Carillion Plc, Annual Report and Accounts 2016' (n 7) 57.

[51] In 2016, 77% investors were institutional shareholders, 18% were private shareholders, 5% were other shareholders; the top 10 investors held 43% shares, the top 100 investors held 89% shares. In 2015, 84% investors were institutional shareholders, 16% were private shareholders; the top 10 investors held 50% shares, the top 100 investors held 93% shares. In 2014, 82% investors were institutional shareholders, 18% were private shareholders; the top 10 investors held 45% shares, the top 100 investors held 90% shares.

high dividend was a signal of "not sustainable".[52] Moreover, they also felt they suffered on the battle with Carillion's board and its remuneration committee (RemCo) regarding the high remuneration for directors. According to the voting records from 2013 to 2015, more than 90% shareholders agreed with Carillion's year-on-year rising remuneration. Only months before Carillion's first profit warning announcement, the RemCo intended to continue to increase executives' bonuses, but abandoned after institutional investors protesting this proposal.[53] The AGM then to a large extent was a mere formality to "tick the box". The shareholders hardly participated in real decision-making processes, let alone challenge directors' decisions. The only way for these disappointed shareholders at the end was to sell the shares.

Shareholders' behaviours in Carillion essentially raised questions of the existing Corporate Governance Code and Stewardship Code. Also operating on an apply-or-explain basis, the UK Stewardship Code in particular, presents a framework of principles for institutional investors which is designed to enhance investors' engagement in companies to help improve long-term returns to clients and beneficiaries, and to create sustainable benefits for the economy, environment and society. Shareholders are expected to disclose how they implement the principles of stewardship on an annual basis. However, Carillion's failure casted suspicions on the effectiveness of the Stewardship Code and the efficacy of investors' stewardship role. As highlighted in the Second Joint Report, the existing Stewardship Code lacks the necessary detail to function effectively and, due to its comply-or-explain nature, remains entirely unenforceable. There is a clear need to strengthen it with enforceable provisions.[54] Although Carillion's institutional shareholders had tried to take some measures (always informally, not through voting rights in the AGM) to warn and forbid directors' behaviours, their actions seemed to be too late with not much effect on correcting Carillion's problems. Rather than performing as responsible "owners" caring for the long run of Carillion, their share interests were the real priority considered.

Overall, the above analysis shows a different picture of Carillion's central decision-making mechanism in contrast with its Annual Reports and Accounts. With an absence of trustworthy information about the company and enough influence on the board, the Annual General Meeting merely "rubber-stamped" the decisions of the

---

[52] 'Oral Evidence - Carillion - 7 Mar 2018' Q1116, http://data.parliament.uk/writtenevidence/committeeevidence.svc/evidencedocument/work-and-pensions-committee/carillion/oral/79969.html, accessed 2 April 2024. See also 'Letter from Standard Life to the Chairs, 2 February 2018', https://www.parliament.uk/globalassets/documents/commons-committees/work-and-pensions/Carillion/Letter-from-Standard-Life-to-the-Chairs-regarding-Carillion-2-February-2018.pdf, accessed 2 April 2024.

[53] 'Letter from Carillion to BlackRock, 7 March 2017', https://www.parliament.uk/globalassets/documents/commons-committees/work-and-pensions/Carillion/Carillion-letter-to-BlackRock-7-March-2017.pdf, accessed 2 April 2024.

See also 'Letter from BlackRock to the Chairs, 8 February 2018', https://www.parliament.uk/globalassets/documents/commons-committees/work-and-pensions/Carillion/Letter-from-Blackrock-to-the-Chairs-regarding-Carillion-8-February-2018.pdf, accessed 2 April 2024.

[54] House of Commons Business, Energy and Industrial Strategy and Work and Pensions Committees, *Carillion*, Second Joint Report (n 2) 73.

board. Carillion's Board, senior executives, and both internal and external auditors each demonstrated significant shortcomings in high-level decision-making. Collectively, these deficiencies contributed to a business strategy that aggressively sought growth while paying little attention to long-term viability or the consequences for employees, pensioners, and suppliers.[55]

6.2.2 *Stakeholder Caring?*

6.2.2.1 Employees

Among 43,000 employees who worked in Carillion's extensive worldwide supply chains (including 19,000 in the UK), over 2000 people lost their jobs. Employees who were not at the senior level could be the group who bore the earliest brunt from Carillion's collapse. Although as a high-profile company, Carillion could be an example of workers' exploitation that the company refused to give them adequate rights and enough protections.[56]

Carillion had long failed to make sufficient contributions to its 27,000 members' pension schemes. Carillion's former Finance Director from 2007 to 2016, Richard Adam who recognised the pension schemes as a "waste of money" was the destroyer of Carillion's pension schemes.[57] Over the six years between 2011 and 2016, the company's pension scheme deficit recovery pay was £246 million which was far behind Carillion's £441 million dividend payments. According to the analysis of the Second Joint Report, across Adam's ten-year tenure as finance director, dividends had jumped by 199% compared to 1% increase in deficit recovery payments.[58] The huge disparity between the dividend for shareholders and the pensions for pensioners and employees sent an important message that the company did not balance the interests between shareholders and other stakeholders, rather shareholders' needs were the priority for the board's concern. Moreover, with a rotten culture, Carillion's board and senior management chronically refused to take adequate consideration

---

[55] Amir Qamar and Simon Collinson, 'Part A: The Causes of Carillion's Collapse—City REDI Blog' 2, https://blog.bham.ac.uk/cityredi/the-causes-of-carillions-collapse-part-a/, accessed 27 February 2024.

[56] House of Commons Business, Energy and Industrial Strategy and Work and Pensions Committees, *Carillion*, Second Joint Report (n 2) 70.

[57] 'Sacker and Partners LLP, Carillion Single Trustee—Meeting between Trustee Representatives and the Pensions Regulator Regarding Failure to Agree the 2011 Valuation', https://www.parliament.uk/globalassets/documents/commons-committees/work-and-pensions/Carillion/Carrillion.pdf, accessed 25 March 2024.

[58] House of Commons Business, Energy and Industrial Strategy and Work and Pensions Committees, *Carillion*, Second Joint Report (n 2) 18.

for its workers. Approaching collapse, the company's management team continued to ensure those at the top of the hierarchy would suffer less than the workers and other stakeholders to whom they had accountability by boosting directors' salary and bonus.[59]

6.2.2.2 Suppliers

As estimated by Build UK, a construction trade body, there were around 30,000 companies spanned alongside Carillion's supply chain.[60] Apparently, these suppliers would always be the last paid from any value rescued from the mess when companies collapse.[61] At the point of Carillion's collapse, Carillion owed about £2 billion to its 30,000 suppliers, sub-contractors and other creditors.[62] In evidence to the Second Joint Report, claims were made that Carillion had abused its dominant power in the market by treating another group of stakeholders, the suppliers, with contempt.[63]

First, suppliers suffered from Carillion's payments delay. Under the UK Government's Prompt Payment Code introduced in 2013, businesses are expected to commit to settling supplier invoices within a maximum of 60 days in accordance with late payment regulations, to strive towards making 30-day payment terms standard practice, and to refrain from engaging in conduct that negatively impacts the supply chain.[64] As a signatory of this Code, Carillion should fulfil payments promptly to its suppliers, especially small-scale ones who relied on big companies like Carillion for much of their income. In fact, Carillion had been notorious for late payment and resisted standard payment of 120 days. Especially across Carillion's reporting period, the company subjected suppliers to long delays of paying.

Second, Carillion was trying to squeeze the supply chain to prop itself up. In practice, besides direct payment to suppliers, Carillion had a second payment method which was through the "supply chain factoring" (also known as "reverse factoring" or "supply chain financing") scheme where the company had arrangements with several different banks.[65] Suppliers could get payments from a bank before the standard timescales by selling their invoices to Carillion's bank, but at a discounted rate. Carillion, however, could repay the bank following the standard payment date,

---

[59] House of Commons Business, Energy and Industrial Strategy and Work and Pensions Committees, *Carillion*, Second Joint Report (n 2) 34.

[60] House of Commons Business, Energy and Industrial Strategy and Work and Pensions Committees, *Carillion*, Second Joint Report (n 2) 24.

[61] 'Carillion: The Company Entrenched in Public Life' *BBC News* (15 January 2018), https://www.bbc.com/news/uk-england-42689717, accessed 27 February 2024.

[62] House of Commons Business, Energy and Industrial Strategy and Work and Pensions Committees, *Carillion*, Second Joint Report (n 2) 3.

[63] 'Oral Evidence: Carillion, HC 769' Q356, http://data.parliament.uk/writtenevidence/committeeevidence.svc/evidencedocument/work-and-pensions-committee/carillion/oral/78103.pdf, accessed 7 April 2024.

[64] 'Prompt Payment Code', http://www.promptpaymentcode.org.uk/, accessed 6 April 2024.

[65] 'Oral Evidence: Carillion, HC 769' (n 63) Q352.

acquiring a generous reimbursement period. From this way, Carillion effectively treated payments to suppliers as a form of borrowing, allowing it to mask the fragility of its balance sheet and cash flow position.[66] At the point of its demise, Carillion had got up to £500 million credit for the suppliers who had to cut their privilege in exchange for early payment.[67]

In summary, Sect. 3 has provided a critical evaluation of Carillion's internal governance arrangement by analysing the dual decision-making structure of the board and AGM, the inefficacy of shareholders', especially institutional investors' involvement in making decisions, the ineffectiveness of auditors' functions, the inadequate caring and protections on stakeholders. From the above, Carillion's internal governance mechanism was in an extreme mess, or in Lyons's words – all its "lines of defence" ended in fiasco.[68] According to Lyons, all the way from the boardroom to the front line of operational management established the five internal lines of defence to protect stakeholders and safeguard the company from failure.[69] These five defence lines include the Operational Line Management (the 1st), Tactical Oversight Functions (the 2nd), Internal Audit (the 3rd), Executive Management (the 4th) and the Board (the 5th). From Carillion's case, not only were there very obvious failures throughout its boardroom, executive management, auditors and so forth, there was also a list of weaknesses and deficiencies within each corporate defence component (including the components of corporate governance, risk management, compliance, intelligence to access information, security, resilience, corporate controls, good manner assurance).[70]

When the analysis turns to Carillion's relationship with its stakeholders, the company clearly did not behave ethically and responsibly towards its stakeholders, rather taking a casual disregard for them. Solomon compares Carillion to a "reckless player" in the board game of *Monopoly* who was drawn to expanding with no consideration to its financial situation and obligations to stakeholders.[71] Indeed, the company indulged in crazy expansions and short-term profit motives at a heavy cost to non-senior employees' welfare and the suppliers' privilege. When the company was approaching bankruptcy—of which the directors must have been aware, they continued to squeeze the company by receiving hefty bonuses and massive remunerations. And they tried to disguise the fragility of Carillion's corporate model by using tricks of accounting or loans, such as the "aggressive accounting" and "supply chain financing".

---

[66] 'Letter from S&P Global to the Chairs', https://www.parliament.uk/globalassets/documents/commons-committees/work-and-pensions/Carillion-report/Letter-from-S-and-P-Global-to-the-Chairs-230318.pdf, accessed 7 April 2024.

[67] House of Commons Business, Energy and Industrial Strategy and Work and Pensions Committees, *Carillion*, Second Joint Report (n 2) 25.

[68] 'Carillion: A Case Study of a Corporate Defence Fiasco', https://www.linkedin.com/pulse/carillion-case-study-corporate-defense-fiasco-sean-lyons, accessed 16 March 2024.

[69] Sean Lyons, *Corporate Defense and the Value Preservation Imperative: Bulletproof Your Corporate Defense Program* (CRC Press 2016) 98.

[70] 'Carillion: A Case Study of a Corporate Defense Fiasco' (n 68).

[71] Solomon (n 1) 35.

Carillion's fiasco of internal governance raises serious questions of the existing Company Law and Corporate Governance system—why do we apparently have adequate mandatory and non-binding regulatory corporate arrangement, but these did not work in the Carillion case (not only in this case, but also raising a question mark on other corporate collapses)? This question will be evaluated and answered in next chapter which seeks to find the correlation between Carillion's collapse and the existing corporate governance system.

6.3 External Checks and Balances

Carillion's collapse could also be attributed to the imbalance of the company's external checks and balances. As to the Second Joint Report, the whole system of external checks and balances mainly includes the functions of investors, auditors, advisors, pension trustees, the pension regulator, the Financial Reporting Council, the government and the Corporate Law.[72] The above analysis of this book has referred to the investors' insufficient influence, auditors' incompetence and the advisors' incapability that all led to Carillion's downfall. This section then looks at how the government, regulators and the law played their roles in the approach to Carillion's failure.

6.3.1 The Government

The government was in a paradoxical position—on the one hand, it was the contracting party of public procurement contracts which pursued benefits maximisation of itself; while on the other hand, it had the public functions to protect public welfare and to prevent financial and societal disorders. Unfortunately, the government at the time, Theresa May's government, was unable to keep a trade-off between its private role and public role which resulted in an ultimate failure in both roles.

To clarify, on the one side, as the signatory of 450 outsourcing contracts with Carillion, the government's overriding priority had been spending less while forcing the company to bear tremendous financial risks.[73] The delivery of the UK government's public services largely relies on the outsourcing and contracting with a spend

---

[72] House of Commons Business, Energy and Industrial Strategy and Work and Pensions Committees, *Carillion*, Second Joint Report (n 2) 48–69.

[73] Reuters Staff, 'Carillion Collapse Exposed Flaws in UK Government Policy: Lawmakers' *Reuters* (9 July 2018), https://www.reuters.com/article/us-carillion-collapse-idUSKBN1JZ1H7, accessed 9 April 2024.

up to £251.5 billion each year.[74] The government, however, has long-standing problems in designing, letting and managing these outsourcing and contracts. Carillion's first profit warning was issued in July 2017. Yet as of that point, just one week after the warning, the government awarded Carillion the HS2 contract which was worth £1.4bn and Hestia defence contracts totalling £158 m. Furthermore, in November, two months after Carillion's second profit warning, the government-owned Network Rail signed the London to Corby electrification contract with Carillion totalling £62 m.[75] Additionally, the government sent a direct signal to the outsourcing companies that the spending, rather than the quality, was what the government was preoccupied with.[76] The government's tough attitude on price cutting forced outsourcing companies to sign the overburdened contracts that were beyond their capability. For example, in one of the contracts about prison maintenance, the government assumed Carillion had accurately estimated its own costs; the exact cost revealed, however, was £15 million more. More than that, the government's ineffectiveness had contributed to the Carillion-style problem. The Public Administration Committee's Report highlighted that the government had intentionally encouraged an aggressive approach to transferring risks to the private sector, sometimes attempting to shift risks that it had not fully analysed or understood itself.[77] Thus, the government's pressure on Carillion, no matter in the price and also the risk-transfer aspects, had boosted the company's systematic risks and unsustainable growth.

On the other side, the government also takes a role to ensure the national economy stays on track. Regarding the government's "Strategic Risk Management Policy", the government may designate a company as "High Risk" when various risk signals are uncovered.[78] If a company is "High Risk", a Crown representative should be appointed to monitor the relationships between government and the ailing suppliers. The Cabinet Office is responsible for supervising suppliers' public-available financial information sources to alert potential financial distresses for government.[79] However, even though Carillion announced three profit warnings in 2017, the Crown Representative failed to alert the government during this critical period. And the government's outsourcing contracts were even consequently stepped up by that stage. As Carillion's last resort, the government however rejected the company's financial assistance

[74] 'After Carillion: Public Sector Outsourcing and Contracting - Public Administration and Constitutional Affairs Committee - House of Commons', https://publications.parliament.uk/pa/cm201719/cmselect/cmpubadm/748/74803.htm, accessed 10 April 2024.

[75] 'Carillion Issued 3 Profit Warnings. So Why Was It Still Getting Government Contracts?', https://www.newstatesman.com/politics/staggers/2018/01/carillion-issued-3-profit-warnings-so-why-was-it-still-getting-government, accessed 10 March 2024.

[76] Staff (n 73).

[77] 'After Carillion: Public Sector Outsourcing and Contracting—Public Administration and Constitutional Affairs Committee—House of Commons' (n 74).

[78] 'Carillion Issued 3 Profit Warnings. So Why Was It Still Getting Government Contracts?' (n 75).

[79] House of Commons Business, Energy and Industrial Strategy and Work and Pensions Committees, *Carillion*, Second Joint Report (n 2) 62.

request and bailed it out ultimately. Although the Second Joint Report supported this decision from the taxpayers' perspective, the wound for the economy and the whole society cannot be ignored. The government was a contributor to this fiasco, rather than part of a solution.

6.3.2 The Regulators

The main regulators which were blamed by the Second Joint Report were the Pensions Regulator (TPR) and the Financial Reporting Council (FRC). These two regulators had exposed different problems—the powerful pension regulator was reluctant to use its statutory power; while the weak FRC was passive in scrutiny Carillion's financial reporting arrangements.

The Pensions Regulator is empowered by Section 231 of the Pension Act 2004 to force companies to make a schedule of pension recovery contributions.[80] However, it has never used this power once in nearly 15 years, in terms of the thousands of pension schemes it takes on duty.[81] When the powerless pension trustees sought intervention from the regulator to impose Carillion to fulfil £427 million pension deficit, TPR only led to a recovery of £85 million which was far short of the additional £342 million.[82] For Carillion, it was emboldened to neglect its pension obligations and even insisted on its intransigent approach to resisting adequate pension deficit recovery contributions due to the regulator's empty threat.

The FRC, the regulator of accounts, auditors and actuaries also failed to give enough intervention to deter Carillion in going towards self-destruction, but in a different way, compared to TPR. The FRC takes charges of ensuring high standards of corporate financial reporting and auditing, promoting the integrity of market by issuing the "comply or explain" based Corporate Governance Codes, and maintaining confidence in the external checks and balances system. To exercise its power, the FRC usually operates by agreement with concerned companies to require revisions of accounts or reports, while it can also go to the court to take legal action.[83] But under its existing limited powers, not all directors can be investigated and punished because the FRC can only take action against those who have accounting qualifications.[84] Thus, in respect of Carillion, the weak FRC was timid and passive in challenging Carillion's questionable financial information.

The effectiveness of the FRC has long been debateable. As the main regulator over UK's corporate governance system, its primary function is to oversee financial

[80] Expert Participation, 'Pensions Act 2004' Section 231, https://www.legislation.gov.uk/ukpga/2004/35/section/231, accessed 12 April 2024.

[81] House of Commons Business, Energy and Industrial Strategy and Work and Pensions Committees, *Carillion*, Second Joint Report (n 2).

[82] Ibid., 57.

[83] Ibid., 60.

[84] Ibid., 61.

governance. However, in the Kingman Review, which is a review specifically focused on the FRC, the FRC has been critiqued as "chronically passive", "timid", "useless", and "toothless".[85] For now, the FRC is being replaced by a new independent regulatory agency, ARGA, the Audit, Reporting and Governance Authority. The new statutory regulator for the first time, will gain powers of directly changing corporate accounts, giving more comprehensive and visible reviews to enhance transparency, providing more protections on customers' interests, setting restrict requirements of statutory audit, corporate governance and reporting, overseeing corporate advisors, directly regulating the largest audit firms.[86] By possessing these new powers, the ARGA may impose greater sanctions in response to corporate collapses, including requiring companies to give rapid explanations or, if more serious, to publish a report about the company's running and management conditions.[87]

6.3.3 The Company Law

The law has two effects: the ex-ante effect of affecting business conduct and director's behaviours; and the ex-post effect of remedying managerial misconduct by resorting to court. Under the Companies Act 2006, directors are required to act in "good faith" to promote the success of the company, and to exercise their power with reasonable care, skill and diligence. Breaches of such duties may trigger the proceedings of disqualification as a director under the Disqualification of Directors Act 1986. However, in Carillion's case, it seemed that the effects of law were insufficient to deter directors' misbehaviours in advance or to give liability penalties to those who breached their legal duties. For example, Carillion's mergers and acquisitions highlight the potential for companies to adopt predatory expansion measures that take them beyond their business strengths and expertise into territory where they become vulnerable and they get greedy for profits without having the knowledge for what they have committed themselves to. But the Company Law and the Takeover Code seem to have no effective restrictions on companies' aggressive expansions.

Moreover, Section 172 of Companies Act 2006, in particular, is subjected to great queries. Under Section 172, a director must act "in a way he considers, in good faith, would be most likely to promote the success of the company for the benefit of its members as a whole". In doing so, directors should "have regard to" various considerations, including "the likely consequences of any decision in the long term", "the interests of the company's employees", "the need to foster the company's business relationships with suppliers, customers and others", and "the desirability

---

[85] John Kingman, 'Independent Review of the Financial Reporting Council *(Kingman Review)*', December 2018.

[86] 'Audit regime in the UK to be transformed with new regulator' (*GOV.UK*), https://www.gov.uk/government/news/audit-regime-in-the-uk-to-be-transformed-with-new-regulator, accessed 2 April 2024.

[87] Nina Boeger, Roseanne Russell, and Charlotte Villiers, 'Companies, Shareholders and Sustainability' (2020) 7 *University of Bristol Law Research Series* 17.

of the company maintaining a reputation for high standards of business conduct".[88] This section is often described as an "enlightened shareholder value" approach which sets out a wide range of interests for directors to consider in decision makings.[89] However, the Second Joint Report noted that the deterrent effects of Section 172 of the Companies Act 2006 were inadequate in influencing the directors' behaviour, even when the company had a chance of survival.[90] It means that this section is more like a guidance, rather than a mandatory legal act that has a deterrent effect. When directors breach their duties, Section 172 has hardly ever been used in litigation (*eg. R (on the application of People and Planet) v HM Treasury*[91]) and does not deter directors from wrongful behaviour. Carillion's board failed to adhere to the law by neglecting to consider the long-term consequences of their decisions, the interests of employees, the importance of maintaining business relationships with suppliers and customers, and the need to uphold the company's reputation for high business standards.[92] Even the Board minutes of Carillion on December 2017 showed that Philip Green specifically mentioned the board duties of Section 172 which means that the directors were clearly aware of these duties, but still dared to breach them.[93]

Additionally, since Carillion's compulsory liquidation, there is no impression that the law has played enough of a role in remedying the directors' misconduct. As stated by Gail Cartmail, assistant general secretary of the Unite union, despite the millions of pounds the Carillion collapse cost taxpayers, no individual has been held accountable for any wrongdoing.[94] It was not until three years after the company's collapse, on 12 January 2021, that the Insolvency Service, acting on behalf of the Secretary of State,

---

[88] Companies Act 2006, Section 172 (1).

[89] A large body of literature has identified numerous weaknesses in Sect. 172, see eg: Andrew Keay, 'Section 172 (1) of the Companies Act 2006: An Interpretation and Assessment' (2007) 28 *The Company Lawyer* 106; Deryn Fisher, 'The Enlightened Shareholder: Leaving Stakeholders in the Dark–Will Section 172 (1) of the Companies Act 2006 Make Directors Consider the Impact of Their Decisions on Third Parties?' (2009) 20 *International Company and Commercial Law Review* 10; Kong Shan HO, 'Is Section 172 of the Companies Act 2006 the Guidance for CSR?' (2010) 31 *The Company Lawyer* 207; Andrew Keay, 'Moving towards Stakeholderism-Constituency Statutes, Enlightened Shareholder Value, and More: Much Ado about Little' (2011) 22 *Eur. Bus. L. Rev.* 1; Elaine Lynch, 'Section 172: A Ground-Breaking Reform of Director's Duties, or the Emperor's New Clothes' (2012) 33 *The Company Lawyer* 196.

[90] House of Commons Business, Energy and Industrial Strategy and Work and Pensions Committees, *Carillion*, Second Joint Report (n 2) 67.

[91] *R (on the application of People and Planet) v HM Treasury* [2009] EWHC 3020 (Admin). This case highlights the limitations of the public power (the state, the government and the court) in influencing directors' decisions.

[92] Expert Participation, 'Companies Act 2006' Section 172 (1), https://www.legislation.gov.uk/ukpga/2006/46/section/172, accessed 13 April 2024.

[93] House of Commons Business, Energy and Industrial Strategy and Work and Pensions Committees, *Carillion*, Second Joint Report (n 2) 67.

[94] 'Carillion Collapse Two Years on, Lessons Not Learned, Hospitals Unfinished and Guilty Unpunished', https://www.unitetheunion.org/news-events/news/2020/january/carillion-collapse-two-years-on-lessons-not-learned-hospitals-unfinished-and-guilty-unpunished/, accessed 13 April 2024.

announced that it had initiated director disqualification proceedings in the public interest against eight former directors of Carillion.[95]

However, the recent decision to abandon the case against the five non-executive directors raises further doubts about the effectiveness of legal mechanisms in securing accountability.[96] The collapse, which caused significant public and financial harm, has yet to result in any formal finding of liability or wrongdoing through the courts. This state of affairs has not only undermined public confidence in the regulatory response to corporate failure but also calls into question whether existing legal tools are adequately equipped to ensure timely and meaningful enforcement in high-profile insolvency cases.

We can have a brief conclusion here on the external checks and balances. It is clear to see from the above analysis that the government, the regulators, and the mandatory legal framework all indulged Carillion's wrong doings. They failed to prevent Carillion's problems before they expanded to become a broader societal problem. Even worse, many years after Carillion's failure, there is no clear result on how to deal with the mess made by the company. The slow response and measures of the government, the regulators and the corporate governance regulatory framework, in fact, aggravate the negative impacts on the communities who have suffered from Carillion's collapse and further expose the weaknesses of the whole system.

6.4 To What Extent the UK's Overall Corporate Governance System Could Be Blamed in Carillion's Downfall

The above analysis has placed a question mark on the overall corporate governance structure of Carillion. This section aims particularly to evaluate the extent to which corporate contractualism could be blamed in Carillion's collapse.

As discovered in Carillion's annual reports and accounts from 2010 to 2016, Carillion had a relatively fixed boardroom structure which comprised the Chairman, Group Chief Executive, Group Finance Director, Senior Independent Non-executive and three non-executives. In the final days of Carillion, in response to the significant losses, there was a slight reform of leadership structure which changed to a framework with Independent Chairman, Senior Independent Director, Interim Chief Executive, two Audit Chairs, and two non-executives.[97] From this change, the company was

---

[95] 'Legal Bid Launched to Ban Ex-Carillion Directors from Top Boardroom Roles' (*the Guardian*, 13 January 2021), http://www.theguardian.com/business/2021/jan/13/legal-bid-launched-ban-ex-carillion-directors-top-boardroom-roles, accessed 20 March 2024.

[96] 'Carillion Disqualification Proceedings Dropped—but Where next for NEDs?—Macfarlanes', https://www.macfarlanes.com/what-we-think/2023/carillion-disqualification-proceedings-dropped-but-where-next-for-neds/, accessed 11 April 2024.

[97] 'Carillion Plc, Group Business Plan, January 2018', https://www.parliament.uk/globalassets/documents/commons-committees/work-and-pensions/Carillion-Group-Business-Plan-January-2018.pdf, accessed 18 March 2024.

desperate to regain public confidence in its operational and commercial controls. But obviously, it failed. Under the board, there were four principal committees—the Audit Committee, the Remuneration Committee, the Nominations Committee and the Business Integrity Committee. But since 2014—the year with a new Chairman,[98] Philip Green, taking office, the management team expanded to nine committees. For example, in 2016, the Board Committees involved Nominations Committee, Business Integrity Committee which were all chaired by Philip Green, Sustainability Committee which was chaired by Ceri Powell, Audit Committee which was chaired by Andrew Dougal, and Major Projects Committee, Chief Executive's Leadership Team, Pensions Sub-Committee, Group Health and Safety Committee which were all chaired by Richard Howson.[99] Although these committees were spread thinly, corporate decision-making power was still centralised in a few leaders' hands. Especially Richard Adam, the architect of Carillion's aggressive accounting was to be blamed as the "financial supremo"[100] who was allowed to control all of Carillion's financial aspects without proper interrogation and enough challenges.

Although Carillion's corporate governance mechanism was unresponsive to its crisis, hedge funds had long been sending a clear message that Carillion was in trouble as early as 2015. In March 2015, UBS (Union Bank of Switzerland) analyst, Gregor Kuglitsch, seemed to be the first to give a crucial check on Carillion's aggressive accounting highlighted Carillion's extended supplier payment terms and its "reverse factoring". He also warned that there was a "profit shortfall" and the company was more leveraged than it reported.[101] Then by October 2015, Carillion had become the most popular share to "sell short".[102]

The institutional investors also soon took actions to sell their shares. In the letter from Standard Life Aberdeen to the MPs of Work and Pensions Committee Business and Energy and Industrial Strategy Committee, this institutional investor explained that, on the underneath of Carillion's flawless balance sheet, they had discerned the problems of Carillion on a number of fronts, including Carillion's corporate strategy, its vulnerability to the deterioration of market conditions, financial management and balance sheet.[103] Despite being a major institutional investor, we still felt

---

[98] Before 2014, the principal Board Committees of Carillion only consisted of the Audit Committee, the Remuneration Committee, the Nominations Committee and the Business Integrity Committee.

[99] 'Carillion Plc, Annual Report and Accounts 2016' (n 7) 52.

[100] Channel 4 (director), *How to Lose Seven Billion Pounds: Dispatches*, https://www.channel4.com/programmes/how-to-lose-seven-billion-pounds-dispatches, accessed 17 November 2023. In Channel 4's documentary, one of the insiders said, "when the numbers didn't come to where he wanted them to be, he would simply say to the management go back and do the numbers again."

[101] 'Hedge Funds Are the Good Guys In Carillion Debacle' *Bloomberg.com* (16 May 2018), https://www.bloomberg.com/opinion/articles/2018-05-16/hedge-funds-are-the-good-guys-in-carillion-debacle, accessed 19 November 2023.

[102] Ibid.

[103] 'Letter from Standard Life to the Chairs Regarding Carillion 2-February-2018', https://www.parliament.uk/globalassets/documents/commons-committees/work-and-pensions/Carillion/Letter-from-Standard-Life-to-the-Chairs-regarding-Carillion-2-February-2018.pdf, accessed 18 November 2023.

constrained in our ability to influence the financial decisions made by the management of any company we invest in.[104] Moreover, the responsibility of these institutional investors seemed not to be centred on assisting a company in managing its operations effectively. Instead, their primary duty was to manage investment risk and enhance the value of the assets under their management for the benefit of their clients and customers.[105] In other words, their first duty is to make money for their clients. Thus, if the risks of a particular investment outweigh the expected returns, our final option as active investors is to reduce our exposure or fully divest from those assets and reinvest in other opportunities.

In this sense, Carillion to a large degree was a typical "ownerless" publicly-held company under the economic-oriented corporate contractualism. Shareholders' wealth is always regarded as a good tool for decision making than profit,[106] even if shareholders have little knowledge on the real condition of the company. Carillion's directors and managers clearly knew this rule well. Showing no care about their company's volatile cash flows, they purely prioritised and focused on shareholders' dividend pay-outs which could falsely signal that Carillion seemed to have a steady financial situation, even though Carillion was actually taking on £7billion of liabilities.[107]

It was a sad story for Carillion that if shareholders could get satisfactory returns, then the capital market could stay steady, even though the company was heading towards its demise. Shareholders' satisfaction on their dividends could be a tool that had been used by Carillion's financial director to keep the company's share prices looking healthy. Investors and other relevant stakeholders cannot get the right information from the market. Shareholder primacy nowadays does not only mean shareholders can get priority in interests' distribution, but a good sign is related to companies' operation condition. If they are satisfied, then the share prices would look attractive. That is what we have seen from the Carillion case.

In addition to Carillion itself, the UK government could also be a hidden cause of Carillion's downfall. In recent years, the government outsourced more and more public services to private companies. But with the impacts of the 2008 financial turmoil, the inputs for public services drove down. The Government appears to have prioritised unduly the cheapest bids of private companies, but without consideration for the "things like robustness, commitment and long-term sustainability".[108]

---

[104] Ibid.

[105] Ibid.

[106] Emily Whiteley, 'Richard Adams (Finance Director of Carillion)—An Expert in Deceit.' (*Richard Adams (Finance Director of Carillion)—An expert in deceit.*), http://emilywhiteleyfinance.blogspot.com/2019/11/richard-adams-finance-director-of.html, accessed 22 November 2023.

[107] Ibid.

[108] 'Oral Evidence—Sourcing Public Services: Lessons to Be Learned from the Collapse of Carillion—24 Apr 2018', http://data.parliament.uk/writtenevidence/committeeevidence.svc/evidencedocument/public-administration-and-constitutional-affairs-committee/sourcing-public-services-lessons-to-be-learned-from-the-collapse-of-carillion/oral/82098.html, accessed 7 February 2024.

This is a dangerous sign in the market because it will incentivise private companies to aggressively undercut the prices of bids, even with low interest or a loss. As demonstrated in former chapters, Public Private Partnership projects, which are one of the main parts of Carillion's project portfolio, are supposed to be associated with "fat cat" private corporations ripping off the public strategic sectors, but in reality, the profit margins are often too small for the contracts to be profitable.[109] According to the investigation report of National Audit Office (NAO), whilst Carillion got considerable profit in its local government contracts (with 13 to 15% operating margin), its contracts in facilities management services only had a 1% operating margin, and the construction projects in building the Aberdeen bypass, the Royal Liverpool University Hospital and the Midland Metropolitan Hospital incurred huge losses.[110]

The House of Commons Public Administration and Constitutional Affairs Committee report highlighted serious concerns regarding the Carillion case, noting that the government's focus on minimising costs and maximising risk transfer stemmed from a highly transactional approach to contracting.[111] In other words, the government transferred their risks to the private sector with the lowest price. On the face, it seems that the PPP would be a win–win for both the public and the private sides: the government would be more efficient to complete infrastructure constructions without taking the burden of financial risks; while the companies could get profits from these lucrative contracts.[112] The market would also guarantee the taxpayer's value.[113] However, what Carillion has shown is that this is just a theory. As revealed by Wong, both the government and companies can become trapped in a "deal-making" mindset, failing to address risks beyond the scope of the contract.[114] Given the feature of the PPP construction structure, the bid winner will get a large chunk of payment upfront which can be used to pay the company's other debts. This large amount of upfront cash thus is associated with the ongoing running of the bidder. The truth therefore is "everyone bids each other to death" even "operating

---

See also House of Commons and Public Administration and Constitutional Affairs Committee, 'After Carillion: Public Sector Outsourcing and Contracting, Seventh Report of Session 2017–19' 2, https://publications.parliament.uk/pa/cm201719/cmselect/cmpubadm/748/748.pdf.

[109] 'Carillion: 12 Months on from a PFI Perspective | Bevan Brittan LLP', https://www.bevanbrittan.com/insights/articles/2019/carillion-12-months-on-from-a-pfi-perspective/, accessed 6 February 2024.

[110] National Audit Office, 'Investigation into the Government's Handling of the Collapse of Carillion' 6, https://www.nao.org.uk/wp-content/uploads/2018/06/Investigation-into-the-governments-handling-of-the-collapse-of-Carillion.pdf.

[111] House of Commons and Public Administration and Constitutional Affairs Committee (n 108) 25.

[112] Simon Goodley, 'The Four Contracts That Finished Carillion' *The Guardian* (15 January 2018), https://www.theguardian.com/business/2018/jan/15/the-four-contracts-that-finished-carillion-public-private-partnership, accessed 15 November 2023.

[113] Ibid.

[114] Karen Wong, 'The Collapse of Carillion: Regulatory Failure in the Contract State' (2019) 4 *LSE Law Review* 1.

on wafer-thin margins", as Sam Cullen, an analyst of the investment bank, Jefferies, stated in the Guardian.[115]

The key issues that related to Carillion's breaking down are concluded as following:

- The company was too complex, with too many distractions outside of the core business;
- Frantic mergers and acquisitions. For example, in board minutes for April 2015, Howson stated that growth appeared to hinge on acquisitions and leveraging adjacent opportunities to achieve higher margins and continuous additions.[116]
- Taking on too many risky and unprofitable projects;
- Aggressive accounting;
- Financial department can control the way that how their financial strength presented;[117]
- Increasing average debt position and absence of underlying profit growth;[118]
- A culture of "fear and confusion": that no insiders dare to challenge Richard Adam's accounting treatments;[119]
- All the powers of accounting were accumulated in Richard Adam's hands;
- Not enough challenges from the auditors and independent non-executives;
- Board power was centralised in a few leaders' hands;
- A strong personality in the Board;
- Directors cared more for their own remuneration rather than the company.[120] There was a change in bonus rules that if the company were to collapse, directors' bonus had no need to be paid back.[121]
- Dysfunctionality of all the auditors;
- No care of the employees and their pension funds;
- The Pensions Regulator made a few empty threats to Carillion, rather it tended to be friend with business;
- Limitation of shareholders' ability in corporate governance;
- Shareholders' return being regarded as a good tool for checking on share prices, and also a good sign of the company was running well;

---

115 Goodley (n 112).

116 'Carillion Plc, Minutes of a Meeting of the Board of Directors, 2 April 2015' 4, https://www.parliament.uk/globalassets/documents/commons-committees/work-and-pensions/Carillion-report/Carillion-Board-minutes-2.4.15.pdf, accessed 9 January 2024.

117 Dan McCrum and Gill Plimmer, 'Carillion Draws Short Sellers' Attention' *Financial Times* (12 October 2015), https://www.ft.com/content/d90be254-6e98-11e5-8608-a0853fb4e1fe, accessed 19 November 2023.

118 Ibid.

119 Channel 4 (director) (n 100).

120 'Carillion bosses focused on their own pay rather than the company' (*Construction Enquirer News*), https://www.constructionenquirer.com/2018/03/07/carillion-investors-question-kpmg-auditing/, accessed 21 November 2023.

121 'Carillion Plc, Annual Report and Accounts 2016' (n 7) 78.

- Dysfunctionality of regulators, government and the law. They were blind to the crisis that had long been revealed;
- Government's inability in managing PPP (public–private partnership) projects;
- Overall environment for construction and Brexit.

The whole picture of Carillion being presented was the dysfunctionality prevalent in both internal and external governance. The combination of incompetence and governance failure created a "Legal Ponzi Scheme" within Carillion, involving the manipulation of financial figures, paying large dividends despite inconsistent cash flows, using anticipated revenues to settle debts with lenders or suppliers in a bid to stay afloat, and allowing the board of directors to retain their bonuses while facing no legal consequences.[122] In a nutshell, it seemed that both Carillion's internal governance, (including its boardroom, management, non-executive directors, auditors) and the government, the market for corporate control, could be subjected to varying levels of opprobrium. Moreover, the inefficiency of the external checks and balances was even exacerbated by the utility of principles-based soft law. Without fully external supervisions on Carillion's conducts, Carillion built a firewall for directors wielding powers. Based on the above analysis, it is safe to argue here that corporate contractualism is a determining factor to Carillion's failure.

6.5 Conclusion

Carillion's collapse has exposed the fundamental shortcomings of a contractualism-based corporate governance model. The company's internal accountability mechanisms, ranging from the managerial accountability of senior executives to the board of directors, the responsibility of board sub-committees to the full board, the accountability of independent executives, to the broader notion of stakeholder accountability, were in essence, dysfunctional. This fragmentation and lack of oversight highlight the urgent need to establish more robust accountability frameworks across all levels of corporate governance, particularly in large corporations.

More than six years after Carillion's bankruptcy, however, there has been a disappointing lack of meaningful academic, theoretical, or regulatory advancement toward deeper corporate accountability. Despite the widespread recognition of its failures, Carillion has not led to a comprehensive rethinking of the underlying governance structures that enabled such mismanagement to persist unchecked.

The company's downfall also reflects the inadequacy of relying on market forces, commonly referred to as the "invisible hand", to ensure effective corporate discipline. The assumption that competitive pressures would automatically lead to efficient and responsible corporate behaviour was decisively undermined. In response,

[122] Emily Whiteley, 'Richard Adams (Finance Director of Carillion)—An Expert in Deceit.' (*Richard Adams (Finance Director of Carillion)—An Expert in Deceit.*), http://emilywhiteleyfinance.blogspot.com/2019/11/richard-adams-finance-director-of.html, accessed 16 November 2023.

the Kingman Review, published in December 2018, recommended replacing the Financial Reporting Council (FRC) with a new independent statutory regulator—ARGA (Audit, Reporting and Governance Authority)—accountable to Parliament, and equipped with a clearer mandate, enhanced powers, and improved leadership. Although expectations have been placed on ARGA to initiate change, such reform remains insufficient. As the House of Commons Joint Report on Carillion observed, what is now required is a "radically different approach."[123]

The Carillion case also lays bare the limitations of corporate contractualism in providing effective checks on corporate conduct. Under this model, there was no adequate constraint on Carillion's aggressive expansion, risky acquisitions, unsustainable dividend payments, or its overreliance on suppliers. Equally, the company's disregard for employees' pensions and the absence of a functioning supervisory mechanism over board conduct and project risks further illustrate the failure of a governance system rooted in market logic and private ordering.

This chapter has argued that such a contract-based view of company law and governance is ultimately unhelpful in addressing the realities of modern corporate behaviour. The failures that led to Carillion's collapse were not mere operational mishaps but systemic defects in a governance framework unable to detect or mitigate risk from within the corporate firewall. A more normatively grounded and structurally attentive approach is therefore essential.

The next chapter will turn to Bottomley's theory of corporate constitutionalism, exploring it not only as a theoretical concept but also as a practical alternative. By embedding these ideas in a real corporate case study, it will evaluate the potential of this approach to reshape corporate conduct and prevent failures akin to Carillion's within the UK's governance regime.

---

[123] House of Commons Business, Energy and Industrial Strategy and Work and Pensions Committees, *Carillion*, Second Joint Report (n 2) 84.

Part III Applying Corporate Constitutionalism: Hypothetical Evaluation and Critical Reflection

Chapter 7
Reassessing Carillion's Collapse from Corporate Constitutional Perspective

7.1 Introduction

At the very beginning of his book, *The Constitutional Corporation—Rethinking Corporate Governance*, Bottomley states that his desire to create a conceptual framework for analysing corporate law issues, which could serve as an alternative to the dominant law and economics model, remained steadfast.[1] Inspired by his words, the following two chapters try to utilise his corporate constitutional conception as a distinct evaluative paradigm to elaborate corporate governance issues around the case of Carillion. From this book's standpoint, Bottomley's alternative conceptual framework could provide valuable ideas for responding to corporate scandals and failures and could give a positive-oriented approach to preventing a future Carillion-style collapse.

From the above description and analysis of corporate contractual and corporate constitutional theories, and from the compare and contrast approaches between these two paradigms, this book highlights certain key themes of corporate governance: in terms of the internal governance, "corporate constitution", "decision-making" (including the dual decision-making structure and processes between the general meeting and boardroom), "the inner relationships among corporate participators" "legitimacy of corporate power", "threefold mechanisms of accountability-deliberation-contestability" are prominent to be considered; when talking about the external governance of the corporation, the "roles of regulators, government, and the law in regulating the corporation" are the mainstay to be analysed.

Concomitantly, chapters 7 and 8 will seek to apply the above corporate constitutional thoughts to the Carillion case under each theme and consider the potential impacts for companies like Carillion if such corporate constitutional ideas were embedded within the corporate governance system. These two chapters set out to

---

[1] Stephen Bottomley, *The Constitutional Corporation: Rethinking Corporate Governance* (Ashgate Publishing, Ltd 2007) XIV.

Y. Yang, *Corporate Collapse and Corporate Governance*, CSR, Sustainability, Ethics & Governance, https://doi.org/10.1007/978-981-96-9666-6_7

make some assumptions based on the theoretical foundation that the earlier chapters have built up. Quite legitimately therefore, chapters 7 and 8 are speculative in their nature. This means that whether corporate constitutionalism could have prevented Carillion's failure cannot be proven from the real operation of Carillion itself, but rather may be a logical inference from the theoretical analysis that has been developed. Chapters 5 and 6 figured out what Carillion looked like under the corporate contractual paradigm, identifying the key factors leading to its failure. Correspondingly, the logic here is that, if corporate constitutionalism provides an alternative paradigm that would be able systematically to deter such flaws identified that contributed to Carillion's demise, then it is fair to argue that corporate constitutionalism could have prevented Carillion's failure. This chapter will apply corporate constitutionalism to Carillion's story in a broad and general way to find the points connecting this alternative framework to Carillion's case. Chapter 8 will identify the necessary changes if Carillion were operated in a corporate constitutional way. Finally, a critique will be presented in Chapter 9.

This chapter will apply, through a process of speculation, ideas on how corporate constitutionalism could be embedded within Carillion's corporate governance arrangements. Just as the term implies, corporate constitutionalism is developed from a political understanding of corporate constitutions which sustains the notion of interactions between the public and the private. Internally, the corporate constitution sets out to mediate the interplay between the individual and the collective; while externally, it also recognises the complex relations between the corporation and the external regulatory regime and the state. Thus, the hypothetical processes in section three will be evaluated mainly from two aspects—the "internal" and "external" governance of Carillion within the corporate constitutional paradigm.

The internal part will first present a detailed literature review on the corporate constitutional accountability-deliberation-contestability mechanism which carries the key ideas within Bottomley's internal corporate governance arrangement. Then, the book will consider what Carillion might look like if it accepts such an internal arrangement. The external part investigates what the role of the government, regulators and the entire UK's corporate governance system should be in the case of Carillion's breakup under this alternative way of thinking.

7.2 An Assumption of Applying Corporate Constitutionalism into Carillion

This book sets out to use a corporate constitutional way of thinking to examine Carillion's failure and to evaluate whether corporate constitutionalism could provide a useful framework in breaking Carillion's "firewall".

Chapters 2, 3 and 4 lay out a theoretical foundation on which the whole book is based. Chapter 3 highlights the distinct characteristics of corporate constitutionalism under several themes which are derived from the core values of political constitutional thoughts, including the "corporate constitutions", "internal relations among corporate members", "shareholders' status", "legitimacy of corporate managerial power", "decision-making", and the "external relations with the state and regulation". In light of those specific points of focus, Bottomley's corporate constitutionalism shows us a whole picture of corporate governance in political terms. As acknowledged in Chapters 3 and 4, in the process of the construction of corporate constitutionalism, Bottomley learns from various political theories, mainly including liberal constitutionalism, communitarianism, and republicanism which respectively are concerned with personal rights and interests, private rights and overall interests, and the common good of all members. One of the biggest features in the process of establishing such a constitutional framework in the corporate context is that Bottomley neatly bypasses the debates among different political theories—he intends to learn purely from the key values and concepts of these theories that can be usefully deployed to set up a corporate constitutional paradigm. He never mixes corporations and public constitutional governmental mechanisms, rather he reiterates many times in his works that these values and concepts should be adapted to fit into the unique corporate constitutional systems.

Another feature could be that, instead of pursuing a dramatic reformation of the corporate form, corporate constitutionalism starts with an easy step, and then triggers subsequent gradual changes in corporate governance. Corporate constitutionalism is not totally inscrutable to the basic legal structure. Rather, by rediscovering and re-aggregating some significant ideas in the corporate world that have long been ignored by the current dominant contractual paradigm, it tends to rebuild a different comprehensive evaluative framework. Bottomley's corporate constitutional normative framework is, thus, based on existing corporate governance rules and practices.[2] Some aspects of this political paradigm can be easily connected to the incumbent formal legal arrangements of the corporation. It is this prudent step of conceptual reformation that makes it possible for the book to look back to Carillion's failure, and to explain its collapse from a cautious, understandable and feasible viewpoint.

Based on the above theoretical foundation, this part sets out to suggest a way of connecting corporate constitutional thoughts to the already broken-down company Carillion Plc; and it also tends to present a different path in tackling Carillion's corporate governance issues in a way that contrasts with corporate contractualism. As stated in Chapter 1, the theoretical application of corporate constitutionalism to Carillion case has a double meaning—Bottomley's idea gives a wholly different evaluative approach on Carillion's matters; conversely, using the Carillion case could also be regarded as an examination on his corporate constitutional approach. To be more precise, on the one side, starting from the current system and practices of UK's corporate governance, this book utilises Bottomley's corporate constitutional paradigm as an evaluative framework to analyse the real case of Carillion Plc, and to evaluate Carillion's decision-making structure and processes according to whether

[2] Ibid., 76.

it can "embody and uphold certain values and principles".[3] This corporate constitutional framework does not ask for certain outcomes, but it indeed provides a basis for the insiders and the outsiders to understand and assess what the corporate structure and processes are doing.[4] On the other side, the real case of Carillion can be used to figure out whether this evaluative framework could have legally practical consequence in the corporate world, and what further steps need to be taken to enhance this corporate constitutional approach.

7.2.1 Methodology—Filling the Gap Between the Theoretical Basis and Real Practice

It should be admitted that there is a gap between the theory and the practice. Before the hypothetical application process, this book should at first figure out how can we combine the Carillion case and corporate constitutional theoretical framework together. This refers to the methodological issues. Drawing from Rule and Mitchell's research, there are four dimensions of the theory-case relation: theory *of* the case, theory *for* the case, theory *from* the case and a dialogue *between* the theory and the case.

As explained by Rule and Mitchell, "theory *of* the case" tells how the case is selected and formed. This refers to a process of constructing a case or "imagination of the case and the invention of the study" in Bassey's words.[5] It requires the researcher to define the "bounded system" of the case, identify its components, determine what is included and excluded, and clarify what the case represents.[6] The "theory *for* the case" means using cases to test theories. This connects to a deductive approach which entails "a general theory (a hypobook) and then tests the theory in practice".[7] The "theory *from* the case" means the new theory is generated from the case which contains an inductive approach. The dialogue *between* the theory and the case" concerns the mutual conduct between theory and case. According to Rule and Mitchell, one can utilise theory to define, select, and problematise the case, while also leveraging the case to generate new theoretical insights.[8] By re-conceptualising the "theory", "practice", and "research", these two authors seek to recognise the open-ended interplays among them.

---

[3] Ibid., 16.

[4] Ibid.

[5] Michael Bassey, *Case Study Research in Educational Settings* (McGraw-Hill Education (UK) 1999) 24.

[6] Peter Rule and Vaughn Mitchell John, 'A Necessary Dialogue: Theory in Case Study Research' (2015) 14 *International Journal of Qualitative Methods*, 4.

[7] Ibid., 5.

[8] Peter Rule and Vaughn Mitchell John, 'A Necessary Dialogue: Theory in Case Study Research' (2015) 14 *International Journal of Qualitative Methods*, 4.

The method used in this book could belong to the second dimension—"theory *for* the case". Through a deductive approach which moves from the general to the specific, the research sets out an existing theory or generalisation, and sets out to test the outcomes if applying the theory to the case.[9] In other words, this method requires the research to commence with a general theory and examine whether the specific instance and the theory match or not. Ultimately, this theory-testing approach may lead to confirmation, revision or rejection of the theory.[10]

Following the deductive approach, this book perceives that if Carillion's problems could have been solved, then Carillion could have been saved. So, if corporate constitutionalism can offer a solution for Carillion's issues, then it is safe to argue that the corporate constitutional framework could have prevented Carillion's failure. The standard to test the corporate constitutionalism framework therefore is whether such a framework could fix Carillion's problems which have been listed above. The theory-testing approach will be propelled by inserting corporate constitutionalism into the detailed structures and processes of Carillion's corporate governance, including the themes of "shareholders' involvement", "the board and managers", "stakeholder's status", "auditors", "external checks and balances (including the external auditors, the law, the regulators, and the state)". Quite legitimately, because of Carillion's demise, this can only be a hypothetical testing approach. Additionally, there are limitations in using the logic inference to test the theoretical application against a real case. But it is still a meaningful way of contributing original ideas in the aftermath of Carillion's collapse.

The following theory-testing approach contains two parts—a general idea of bringing corporate constitutionalism into Carillion and a detailed examination of the interaction between the framework and the case under each theme. The later examination will be approached in Chapter 8. The subsequent content of this chapter 7 involves construction of a theory-to-case bridge, to establish a broad corporate constitutional "world" in Carillion and to see how Carillion could have been operated in that "world".

7.2.2 Internal Governance—A Broad Structure

In general, what corporate constitutionalism advocates within the internal governance is a complete mechanism of checks and balances that contains three most basic principles—accountability, deliberation and contestability. Thus, the main task of applying corporate constitutionalism into Carillion's internal governance is to construct a comprehensive accountability-deliberation-contestability mechanism which paves a different way in sustaining a legitimate system of corporate managerial power.

[9] Kenneth F Hyde, 'Recognising Deductive Processes in Qualitative Research' (2000) 3 *Qualitative Market Research: An International Journal* 82, 83.

[10] Rule and John (n 8) 4.

7.2.2.1 The Establishment of a Complete Accountability-Deliberation-Contestability Mechanism

The accountability-deliberation-contestability mechanism sits at the fulcrum of Bottomley's corporate constitutionalism. This section will examine the core values of the accountability-deliberation-contestability mechanism and try to analyse the outcomes of bringing this trinity into Carillion's internal governance.

Accountability

Bottomley reminds us that the processes and structures of accountability should be stressed as important as its content or subject matter. He does not intend to create novel structures and processes, rather applying and stressing those already in existence whose significance in accountability is not always realised.[11] Bottomley's corporate constitutionalism seeks to examine the necessary structures to achieve "structural accountability". Under his corporate constitutional framework, companies, especially the large ones, cannot be insulated from the democratic control of the state, rather their operations should be correspondent with political constitutional values. Borrowing from political constitutional understandings, corporate constitutionalism regards "the division and separation of corporate decision-making power" as the key to an effective accountability structure.[12] That is, by guaranteeing that decision makers are held to account as much as possible, their powers can be controlled and constrained within the corporate political system. Corporate constitutionalism is designed mainly from two angles to ensure decision makers are held accountable—the division of dual decision-making powers, and the separation of multiple levels of powers within the corporation.

The Division of Dual Decision-Making Powers

The dual decision-making powers between shareholders and directors are the only decision-making fora with legal recognition in a corporation. For Bottomley, the formal division of decision-making power between the board of directors and the general meeting of shareholders sits at the core of the accountability mechanism. The general meeting focuses on the basic corporate rules and is entitled to amend a corporation's fundamental structure; the directors' decisions relate to the corporation's daily routine but cannot refer to the alteration of corporate structures.[13] This dual structure means that there are also two kinds of decision-making processes: for the general meeting, mostly held on an annual basis for public companies; it is a "meeting of the corporation" that gathers shareholders and directors together through

---

[11] Bottomley (n 1) 81.

[12] Ibid.

[13] Ibid., 83.

a rigid and formal way.[14] It gives shareholders the right and the authority to require the directors to account and to demand explanations of directors' behaviours. While in directors' meeting, occurring more frequently and with less formality, directors can delegate part of their powers to senior managers. The implementation of the general managerial power is regarded as the "normal politics" of corporate decisions.[15]

This dual decision-making system refers to a distinct concept of accountability—structural accountability. As Bottomley described, structural accountability refers to the dual process, with its inherent constitutional constraints, creating a framework designed to protect specific rights or interests from being easily or hastily interfered with by controlling parties within a corporation.[16] In other words, this vertical power-division structure defines different accountability manifestations of shareholders' and directors' power—directors' "normal political power" holds an ultimate accountability to the general meeting, while the power conduct of the general meeting is scrutinised and deliberated by all shareholders.[17]

The Separation of Multiple Powers

In Carillion, the general meetings and the board meetings all seemed to have minimal effect in corporate governance terms: the former was only an annual event, while the latter were normally held ten times a year. This points to the situation that the formal decision-making processes and structure in corporations do not happen frequently in practice. Decisions occurring in daily corporate life are certainly not limited to the formal fora, instead they should also be presented in a more varied, flexible and frequent way. Thus, to recognise and to ensure the possibility of a separation of corporate powers among different decision makers could be regarded as the second feature of Bottomley's structural accountability.[18]

The idea of separation of powers is deeply rooted in the political constitutional context. In liberal political terms, the exercise of decision-making power should be non-autocratic and should be conducted in an open and accountable manner.[19] To prevent the concentration of public power in the hands of one person, the "holy trinity" of state power (including the legislative power, executive power and judicial power) was raised as a formal doctrine in controlling undue impingement on individual citizens. As noted in the corporate constitutional framework, like political communities, corporations also play a great role in social, economic and political life. Bottomley thus inserts the political ideas of separations of power into the corporate arena, but with a different approach than the classic doctrine of three branches of state power because exercise of power in modern corporate structures is often

[14] Ibid., 84.

[15] Bruce Ackerman, 'Constitutional Politics/Constitutional Law' (1989) 99 *The Yale Law Journal* 453, 461.

[16] Bottomley (n 1) 86.

[17] Ibid.

[18] Ibid., 91.

[19] Ibid.

segmented in uneven and complicated ways that cannot be adequately caught by that traditional classification.

In terms of this separation of multiple corporate powers, there is one important point to be remembered when applying this design to real corporations: there are various types of power separations within a corporation which include not only strict hierarchical monitoring from the top to the bottom, but also overlapping functions between different parts of corporate governance (*eg*. independent and executive directors). Thus, it is to be remembered that there is no one-size-fits-all design of the types of divisions and separations of corporate powers. Although Bottomley has addressed the separations of board power, audit functions, institutional shareholders' power, he does not pursue a dogmatic and predetermined classification of different powers. What corporate constitutionalism really insists on is to ensure a range of separations that is suitable for the specific corporation.[20] Moreover, as an important supplementary mechanism of the separations framework, the role of whistleblowers stands out within corporate constitutionalism. Whistleblowers come from various groups (e.g., employees, corporate officers, advisers, consultants, affiliated companies, and others) who are aware of issues and understand that these problems are unlikely to be identified or addressed through standard channels.[21] Whistleblowing behaviour is of great importance to guarantee the company's openness and transparency. However, what should be notified here is that the corporate constitutional framework encourages whistleblowing, but it is only a complementary mechanism or a safety net of the overall accountability mechanism. Corporate problems should regularly be detected, revealed, and solved through normal internal channels.[22]

In short, the goal of maintaining multiple separations of corporate power is to establish a system of checks and balances that increases the likelihood of identifying, restraining, correcting, and understanding power abuses by one part of the corporate governance system through other parts.[23] To reach such a delicate checks-and-balances system between various corporate powers, corporations are required to reach several standards of their decision-making structures and processes: first, to establish a network of separations of powers in which each decision-making site is connected by this web. Second, on this relational net, each site's power-conducting process is not totally independent or autonomous, instead each separate site of power should be upheld by mutual learning.[24] Third, in the exercise of decision-making power, each

---

[20] Ibid., 93.

[21] Ibid., 107–108.

[22] Marcia P Miceli and Janet P Near, *Blowing the Whistle: The Organizational and Legal Implications for Companies and Employees* (Lexington Books 1992) 282.

[23] Bottomley (n 1) 93. See also from John Braithwaite, 'On Speaking Softly and Carrying Big Sticks: Neglected Dimensions of a Republication Separation of Powers' (1997) 47 *The University of Toronto Law Journal* 305, 341–342.

[24] According to Braithwaite, separation of powers may lead to inefficiency. The way to solve this problem is to emphasise "each separate site of power learning from the know-how of other sites". Quoted from Bottomley (n 1) 110. See also from John Braithwaite, 'On Speaking Softly and Carrying Big Sticks: Neglected Dimensions of a Republication Separation of Powers' (1997) 47 *The University of Toronto Law Journal* 305, 359.

site should allow partial participation and scrutiny of other sites.[25] Fourth, when a site is playing a role as an outside monitor, it should have sufficient independence and autonomy, with the outcome that no site is controlled by another or relinquishes its responsibilities to another.[26]

Deliberation

However, the division and separation of corporate power alone seem to be inefficient and insufficient to contribute to a constitutional corporation, even on the contrary, it may prompt mistrust between each decision-making site and breed a "compliance-oriented, tick-the-box approach" within the corporation.[27] Bottomley, drawing on the work of Braithwaite, perceives that an accountability mechanism thus should be supplemented by a deliberation mechanism where "dialogue" replaces "sanctioning" as the main method of controlling power abuses. The purpose of establishing a deliberative mechanism is to improve the quantity and quality of information that is incorporated into decision making, subsequently improving the quality of decisions themselves.[28]

Bottomley defines deliberative decision-making as the process in which, as much as possible, there should be open and sincere discussions before making decisions, whether in the boardroom or at a general meeting. These processes should culminate in decisions that reflect a collective judgement on the matter being considered.[29] To further understand this term, two conceptual points should be stressed here—"open and genuine" and "collective judgement". With critical assessment of rational argument as the basis, an "open and genuine" deliberation requires fairness and justice of decision-making proceedings, rather than simply concerning the outcomes; it emphasises the use of reasoned arguments during discussion, consultation, and persuasion, rather than the authority of managerial elites and powerful shareholders, or the pre-existing hypotheses about "what is reasonable, feasible, or appropriate";[30] it stresses the equity of participants in deliberations, rather than automatically ignoring the minority who owns a small share of voting power.

In terms of "collective judgement", Bottomley gives clarification on the transformation from "individual interests" to "collective judgement" in the deliberative decision-making structure: deliberation is a process where individual interests are

---

[25] Bottomley (n 1) 93. See also from MJC Vile, *Constitutionalism and the Separation of Powers* (Oxford: Clarendon P 1967) 18–19.

[26] Bottomley (n 1) 93.

[27] Ibid., 110.

[28] Ibid., 120.

[29] Ibid., 112.

[30] Joshua Cohen, 'Deliberation and Democratic Legitimacy' in A Hamlin and P Pettit (eds), *The Good Polity: Normative Analysis of the State* (1989) 22. Citing from Bottomley (n 1) 113.

subjected to competing viewpoints, which are discussed and then shaped into a collective decision that aligns with the corporate interest regarding the issue at hand.[31] To put it another way, a valid deliberation encourages decision makers to shift from their personal preferences to a collective opinion about an undetermined proposal, because only by doing so, can corporate decisions be regarded as being legitimate.[32] This does not mean individuals should abandon their personal interests, but such interests alone are insufficient to reach a legitimate result of decision making within a deliberative mechanism of corporate constitutionalism. Despite corporate interest, deliberative decision making also encourages consideration of the interests of other interests, eg. employees, consumers and the environment. However, a collective judgement is not the same as unanimity of corporate decisions or majority domination of decision making, rather it follows with the existing majority voting rule. That is, on the one hand, to achieve collective judgement does not require unanimity; on the other hand, deliberative decision making only accepts a majority vote in which the minority could have open and genuine chances to participate.

To realise a deliberative decision-making process, Bottomley advocates a series of benchmarks against which real corporate activities may be applied: first, a precondition for the effective operation of the deliberation mechanism is to ensure a sound information disclosure system that shareholders are given access to information about the management, business and performance of the corporation.[33] According to Bottomley's statement, that information disclosure process should be mandatory. He shows little faith in regarding the market or security prices as the only avenue of getting information.[34] On the contrary, shareholders are encouraged to assess information disclosure not just based on what it might indicate about the value of their investments, but also by considering its ability to contribute to informed discussions.[35] Second, the corporation should have suitable mechanisms in place to ensure that different viewpoints can be expressed and heard, interests can be communicated, and various perspectives can be considered.[36]

Third, the voting processes, structure and the conduct of corporate meetings should ensure all participants have equal opportunities to express their views and be heard; although corporate constitutionalism acknowledges the passivity of shareholders in decision-making, it advocates for rules, structures, and processes that enable and encourage shareholders to use their roles as members and actively seek to influence the decision-making process.[37] Fourth, large public companies, like Carillion Plc, have difficulties in maintaining a legitimate system of decision making. As discussed

---

[31] Bottomley (n 1) 114.

[32] Ibid.

[33] Ibid., 125.

[34] Ibid., 126. In Bottomley's words, "leaving it solely to the market to produce information, or insisting that all relevant information about a corporation is represented in the market price of its securities, reduces this capacity."

[35] Ibid.

[36] Ibid., 117.

[37] Ibid., 118.

in above chapters, shareholders with widely dispersed shares, to a large extent, are holding the role as passive investors or residual claimants. The reality for shareholders to be involved in detailed deliberations is indeed difficult to be achieved. In this regard, shareholders' decisions are not likely to be totally consistent with corporate interests, rather only an approximation of the corporate interests. The fourth standard therefore requires corporations to adopt a wide-range and multi-levelled concept of deliberation which embraces a plurality of roles, discursive perspectives, opinions and arguments that may potentially be taken into corporate decision-making processes, rather than restricting the focus to the general meeting or the board room.

Fifth, acknowledging shareholders' limitation in deliberative inputting, the corporate constitutional framework requires a supplementary model to enhance shareholders' deliberations outside the general meeting. In terms of the practical procedure, he argues that before the formal meeting is settled, shareholders' deliberative processes should begin well. Given the dispersed and pluralistic feature of shareholdings, the corporate constitutional framework embraces a wide, multi-layered scheme of shareholder deliberation.[38] Drawing on Habermas's "concentric circles" metaphor for corporate deliberations and decision-making, Bottomley describes a series of concentric spheres of influence. These extend from the central general meeting to the board of directors, then to non-director managers and other employees, and ultimately to the outermost business world, which includes shareholders (both large and small), market analysts, proxy advisory services, shareholder associations, regulatory bodies, stock exchanges, media commentators, and others.[39] When moving from the periphery to the core, the deliberation processes would subsequently be more constrained. To be more specific, the outer business world has the most activate and continuous informal information transactions, while closer to the core, the activities are gradually less frequent and more formalised. The board of directors behave like a filter to obstruct the "biased, subjective, and sometimes impractical" deliberations from the outside.[40] Only the filtered deliberations can be considered in the board and the general meeting and turned to be an ultimate decision. The task of a deliberative decision-making model, therefore, is to improve the connection and information flow between the outer circle and the centre, in both directions. Because it is correct to say that, from the border to the core, if information is to be converted to authoritative binding decisions, it must rely on the narrow avenue of the central area.[41] It is also the case that the information from the periphery is the original source of the final decisions. In addition, the processes of public opinion and will formation at the periphery decide the legitimacy of decision-making.[42]

[38] Ibid., 132.

[39] Ibid., 132–133. Jürgen Habermas, *Between Facts and Norms: Contributions to a Discourse Theory of Law and Democracy* (John Wiley & Sons 1996) 308, 356.

[40] Bottomley (n 1) 133.

[41] Jürgen Habermas, *Between Facts and Norms: Contributions to a Discourse Theory of Law and Democracy* (John Wiley & Sons 1996) 308, 356.

[42] Bernhard Peters, '*Die Integration moderner Gesellschaften*' (Frankfurt, Suhrkamp 1993). Citing from Bottomley (n 1) 133.

However, Bottomley also reminds corporate scholars to be realistic about deliberations which may have practical limitations on the number and range of information inputs that are considered in decision making. For example, for practical conducts, in order to ensure that shareholders gain timely access to corporate-operation information and can engage in discussions about this information in a manner that will draw the attention of the decision-makers in the 'inner spheres', Bottomley considers some methods by which shareholders could be encouraged to deliberate outside the general meeting, mainly including through internet discussion or information intermediaries. However, both ways of constructing peripheral deliberation should not be overestimated, because the former one cannot guarantee the quality and coherence of deliberation occurred on the internet; while the latter may refer to the practice of proxy solicitation which is an expensive and rarely-used process in the UK.[43]

In addition, deliberation alone cannot prevent the problems of "domination, oppression or unfairness" in corporate issues.[44] All the other matters of deliberation, such as the tensions, unevenness and unpleasantness in the deliberative processes also reveal that deliberation is only one piece of corporate constitutionalism, and to complete the whole picture of this framework, in addition to structural accountability and deliberation, there should be an avenue of contestability.

Contestability

The mechanism of contestability is backed up by the idea of enhancing the review system within the corporation. Together with the above accountability and deliberation mechanisms, these three interdependent mechanisms reinforce each other and provide benchmarks against which the real corporate operation and regulatory scheme can be assessed. The purpose of contestability is to encourage shareholders' willingness to give their voices rather than exiting when certain improper decisions are made.

The corporate contractualism approach to corporate governance perceives that the quality of corporate decisions can be naturally assessed and improved by various markets for corporate control, the managers, and the company's products and services. However, within this contractualised framework, the issue could arise where shareholders lack preemptive confidence in directors' decisions, as they would have to wait for the outcomes to unfold. If directors and managers are allowed to make corporate decisions without fear of challenge, it could increase shareholders' mistrust and raise suspicions about managerial behaviour.[45] A contestatory mechanism of corporate constitutionalism nevertheless intends to consolidate shareholders' confidence in the ex-ante managerial actions and to raise the belief that how decisions have been achieved is as important as the substance of these decisions. Contestability itself works as a distinct mechanism to challenge improper exercise of managerial power

---

[43] Bottomley (n 1) 137–141.

[44] Bottomley (n 1) 120.

[45] Ibid., 73.

and to force directors and managers to be liable for their behaviours. It also plays as a legitimating mechanism insofar as the factual possibility of shareholders', especially minority shareholders', contest and review towards each corporate decision can be respected and guaranteed.[46]

As revealed by Bottomley, contestability has already played a part in company law. Although his discussion is based on the Australian regime, certain actions can still be found in the UK's Companies Act 2006—for unfair prejudice (Companies Act 2006, s994 and s996), the derivative claim (Companies Act 2006, chapter 11), the protection of class rights (Companies Act 2006, Chapter 9).[47] In his work, he highlights the strong public enforcement function of the statutory derivative claim which is tied to the constitutional dimension of a corporation, rather than the nexus of contractual connections between personal corporators.[48]

However, relying excessively on court-based forums of contestation might be counterproductive, because that may undermine directors' activity and impede the interpersonal relationships within the corporation.[49] Corporate constitutionalism also respects the value of "in-house" fora for contestation. The core concept of contestability in corporate constitutionalism is to promote the deliberative resolution of issues, while maintaining the possibility of invoking more independent and public methods. In this context, internal forms of contestation can still lead to effective outcomes.[50] To put it another way, deliberation, in-house contestation and judicial contestation are encouraged by corporate constitutionalism to be arranged in priority order—full deliberations are to be considered as a first resort that would otherwise then trigger the more rigorous in-house approaches (eg. questioning in the general meeting) and courtroom-based options in dealing with disputes. In the case of *Isle of Wight Railway Company v Tahourdin*, Lindley LJ also expressed a preference that, "this Court has constantly and consistently refused to interfere on behalf of shareholders, until they have done the best they can to set right the matters of which they complain, by calling general meetings".[51]

In a nutshell, there are a few core principles for inserting the contestability mechanism into a real company. First, the key task of a contestability mechanism is to ensure the possibility of contestation is realistic, rather than having actual contestation in every corporate decision because frivolous or vexatious contestations may bring reverse consequences to a company. To avoid the risk of needless challenges, it is important to cultivate an open and deliberative decision-making culture in the first place. Second, contestability views that the legitimacy of corporate decision-making

---

[46] Ibid., 144.

[47] Citing from Bottomley (n 1) 74, but with an alteration in terms of regulatory region.

[48] Ibid., 168.

[49] Ibid., 149.

[50] Ibid., 150.

[51] *Isle of Wight Railway Company v Tahourdin* [1884] LR 25 Ch D 320.

is attributed to shareholders' confidence in the processes of decision making.[52] In this light, contestation of corporate decisions is essential to create a decision-making process where shareholders can have their interests advanced and their ideas acknowledged.[53] Contestability should be a real available choice for shareholders, and the contest avenues within a corporation should not be overly limiting, excessively complicated, or distant.[54] Third, the corrective role of the contestability mechanism applies in various scenarios. It is not confined to decision-making processes but also addresses issues such as the failure to make decisions or take action, managerial behaviors that overlook or ignore relevant interests, and decisions made arbitrarily or improperly, all of which can be challenged through contestation.[55] Fourth, contestability also concerns the collective dimensions of corporate life. In Bottomley's word, "it should not be thought that contestability is limited to the pursuit of shareholders' individual interests or the protection of their personal rights". In other words, contestation can still be raised when only corporate interests are involved and there is no direct gain for individual shareholders.

In conclusion, this section has elaborated the focal points of accountability-deliberation-contestability mechanism of corporate constitutionalism. This triad image sets the basis of the internal governance system in which the legitimacy of the allocation of corporate power, shareholder's status, and the interaction between the individual and the collective are compiled from a corporate constitutional way of thinking. Corporate constitutionalism views accountability, deliberation and contestability as the key principles around which the corporate governance system ought to be constructed. These three interrelated principles emphasise particularly the issues of the structures and processes in making corporate decisions—the accountability mechanism focuses on the structural accountability whereby a division of the dual powers and the separations of multiple corporate powers are to be taken; the deliberation mechanism seeks to ensure the processes of decision making are open and genuine; while the contestability mechanism works as a review mechanism to ensure the possibility of challenging improper managerial conducts.

---

[52] Bottomley (n 1) 145. This idea is developed from Tom Tyler's work on the importance of perceptions about procedural fairness. Tom Tyler, 'Why People Obey the Law' (1990) *New Haven: Yale University Press.*

[53] Ibid. Bottomley's idea comes from Philip Pettit, *Republicanism: A Theory of Freedom and Government* (Oxford University Press 1997) 184.

[54] Bottomley (n 1) 145.

[55] Ibid., 146.

7.2.2.2 How the Accountability-Deliberation-Contestability Mechanism Leads Us to Approach Carillion's Problem—A General Idea

The above context provides a detailed literature study on Bottomley's work in establishing a corporate constitutional accountability-deliberation-contestability mechanism in a company. His ideas are both descriptive and prescriptive: on the one hand, these three principles are not unfamiliar in the corporate world. But the expressions of those principles have long been overlooked or mixed with some corporate contractual values (eg. efficiency, freedom of the market).[56] What Bottomley has done is to revive and rebuild them in corporate governance. On the other hand, Bottomley's perspective is normative, as he contends that these three principles ought to be regarded as overarching standards—on par with goals like efficiency and profit maximisation. They should be incorporated into judicial reasoning, legislative reform, academic analysis, and corporate practice when addressing governance conflicts, contemplating legal changes, or managing corporate operations.[57] His work is grounded in practical relevance rather than detached theoretical abstraction. He presents corporate constitutionalism as a critical and evaluative framework intended to inform and shape corporate conduct, particularly in responding to corporate scandals. Towards the conclusion of his study, he acknowledges that simply placing greater emphasis on the principles of accountability, deliberation and contestability would not alone have prevented corporate collapses such as HIH Insurance or Enron. Nonetheless, he argues that a legal and corporate environment which places excessive weight on economic imperatives and prioritises shareholder interests has contributed to a culture where such scandals are more likely to arise. Although he does not claim that these principles will automatically improve managerial or shareholder behaviour or ensure responsible decision making, he expresses doubt that any sustained improvements can occur without giving due attention to these values. He therefore regards them as necessary, though not in themselves sufficient, for enhancing corporate governance and ethical conduct.[58]

This section will insert the accountability-deliberation-contestability mechanism into Carillion's decision-making structure and processes and evaluate what its internal governance might look like.

Corporate constitutionalism defines corporations as decision-making organisations in which certain structures and processes must be followed in order for corporate power to be implemented legitimately. The concern of corporate constitutionalism on the whole is to set up and uphold frameworks and procedures designed to prevent improper, excessive, or insufficient uses of authority and power within the corporate decision-making structure.[59] Applying corporate constitutionalism to Carillion

---

[56] Ibid., 171.

[57] Ibid.

[58] Ibid., 172.

[59] Ibid., 81.

therefore focuses on Carillion's structures and processes in which, and by which, the accountability, deliberation and contestability might be realised.

Accountability has a necessary role in underpinning decisional authority. From a law and economics understanding, accountability is characterised as a solution to the agency problem—the tensions between the shareholders who are entitled to the ownership of the company and the professional managers who are the real controller of corporate running. Accountability is therefore presented as a crucial element of the checks and balances system, embedded within the shareholder-manager relationship to promote improved corporate performance, enhanced transparency, increased managerial efficiency, a stronger form of shareholder democracy, and similar outcomes.[60] Accountability is also quite a familiar word for corporate scholars. In the UK, much of the present hard-law and soft-law regulatory regime focuses on constructing and maintaining the mechanisms of accountability in corporations. Especially when a new round of corporate collapse arises, accountability becomes a vital academic and practical discipline in finding solutions to corporate problems. From the first Cadbury Report to the latest Corporate Governance Code 2018, during nearly 30 years, numerous reports and reviews on corporate governance and accountability have been implemented in the UK. The Turnbull Report, the Stewardship Code 2010, Corporate Governance Code 2016 and 2018, and other efforts to enhance directors' conduct of effectiveness, shareholders' involvement, and the transparency and accountability of internal control are imperative in the wake of each wave of corporate crisis. And in the newest version of Stewardship Code (2020), five focal points,—namely, encouraging investors to integrate environmental, social and governance factors (ESG) into the consideration of investment; giving more focus on investors' purpose, values and culture; emphasising the roles of asset owners and service providers in corporate governance; enhancing greater transparency—concern how investors exercise stewardship across asset classes beyond listed equity have been given great considerations in enhancing the accountability mechanism.

However, as many scholars have observed, accountability is today burdened with various meanings and has lost its core value. It is defined through elements such as procedures, outcomes, information disclosure, avenues for redress, and adherence to regulations, and is distinct from notions like evaluation, efficiency, effectiveness, oversight, and responsibility.[61] At its core, accountability often appears too ambiguous to serve as a practical tool for evaluating or regulating corporate conduct.[62] As a result, the accountability system tends to be devalued with too many different contexts, proponents and assumptions.

---

60 Ciarán O'Kelly, 'Corporate Governance and Resentment', *European Group of Public Administration: Annual Conference* (2019) 13. See also Melvin Dubnick, 'Accountability and the Promise of Performance: In Search of the Mechanisms' (2005) 28 *Public Performance & Management Review* 376.

61 Ralph M Kramer, *Voluntary Agencies in the Welfare State* (University of California Press 1981) 290.

62 Bottomley (n 1) 77.

By examining Carillion's ten-year Annual Report and Accounts from 2006 to 2016, this book finds few words that clarify the company's accountability mechanism. Only in the report of 2016—seeming to be the most detailed version about accountability—there is an independent part with two short paragraphs entitled "accountability" claiming that:

> The Board remains committed to ensuring that its communications with shareholders continue to present a fair, balanced and understandable assessment of the Company and its prospects. Both the Audit Committee and the Board received drafts of the Annual Report and Accounts to facilitate review and to provide an opportunity for challenge and discussion.
>
> The Board is responsible for determining the nature and extent of the significant risks it is willing to take in achieving its strategic objectives. Principal risks and uncertainties associated with the Group's business are summarised on pages 32 to 37 of the Strategic report. The Board has an Audit Committee which monitors and reports on the Group's risk management systems. The Audit Committee also considers how the Board should apply corporate reporting and internal control principles and is responsible for maintaining an appropriate relationship with the Company's auditor, KPMG LLP. The 2016 report of the Audit Committee is set out on pages 61 to 64.[63]

From this short description, one could identify the key features of "accountability" from the perspective of Carillion's top management. To them, accountability mainly means dealing with two kinds of relationships: the boardroom with shareholders and the boardroom with auditors (including the Audit Committee and KPMG). The accountability mechanism is designed to ensure the company's operation status and its prospect, to ensure review, challenge and discussion, to evaluate risks, to comply with reporting and internal control rules.

However, even though a central aim of this book has been to follow some clues to establish what is the real meaning of accountability in Carillion, it is still a challenge to identify how the accountability mechanism really works, how it could be a trade-off to corporate official authorities. What Carillion brings us is a vague, indiscriminate and unworkable structure of accountability.

Even more severe, in Carillion's case, the company's accountability system seems to construct a "firewall" or a special zone which insulates directors and senior managers from the consequences of their conducts. In essence, accountability has a necessary role in sustaining and underpinning the decisional authority of corporations.[64] However, accountability in effect allows giant firms, like Carillion Plc, to keep themselves beyond specific political and social norms. Like a "special economic zone",[65] the corporate actors and capital holders of Carillion were insulated from the political democratic control of the state,[66] simply inserting accountability to justify

---

[63] 'Carillion Plc, Annual Report and Accounts 2016' 57, https://www.annualreports.com/HostedData/AnnualReports/PDF/LSE_CLLN_2016.pdf, accessed 12 March 2024.

[64] Marc Moore, 'The Neglected Value of Board Accountability in Corporate Governance' (2015) 9 *Law and Financial Markets Review* 10, 11.

[65] A special economic zone is often light on regulation and highlights the ways that some countries "carve up their own territory so they can better engage and compete in global markets". See from Aihwa Ong, *Neoliberalism as Exception: Mutations in Citizenship and Sovereignty* (Duke University Press 2006) 5. Citing from O'Kelly (n 60) 6.

[66] O'Kelly (n 60) 23.

their authorities. Hiding behind this accountability "firewall", Carillion's directors and senior managers could still receive massive rewards and evade blame when things went wrong.

Thus, it is safe to argue that accountability today appears to be limited in being a legitimating substrate to underpin managerial power. This is why endless business scandals and collapses still happen even though we never seem to tire of re-examining accountability in corporate governance.

Ultimately, we may raise a question—how could the accountability featuring in the corporate constitutional context lead us to a different outcome in Carillion's story? From the above analysis, the conclusion may be that equal attention should be paid to the procedures and frameworks through which accountability operates, not just to the specific duties or content of accountability itself—reflecting what Bottomley referred to as "structural accountability".[67] To elaborate, when addressing the substance of accountability, the key question becomes whether legal focus should remain limited to financial and fiduciary reporting, or be broadened to encompass the "triple bottom line", including financial, environmental, and social responsibilities.[68] However, when focusing on processes and structures, the primary analysis would revolve around issues such as auditor independence, board composition, and the necessity of board oversight.[69] Both the substantial contexts and procedural concerns are important in rebuilding Carillion's accountability mechanism.

The other two principles—deliberation and contestability are specialised in corporate constitutionalism. They seem not to be used as often as the term "accountability". But in parallel with the above statement, we can assume that attention should be given to both the processes and structures of deliberation and contestability, alongside the content or subject matter of the related obligations.

In this sense, learning from Bottomley's analytical structure, we can roughly depict a picture of Carillion's internal governance within corporate constitutionalism. Unlike corporate contractualism, which brings about exchanges between individuals, corporate constitutionalism emphasises co-ordination between corporate participants. Structurally therefore, a new type of network of separation of powers within Carillion should be designed.[70] Holding the shareholders' role at the centre, there is a web linking shareholders, the board of directors, auditors and the whistleblowers together as the prominent actors in constructing an effective corporate accountability structure. As revealed above, in general, this network is required to ensure that when one decision-making site exercises its power, others should have the opportunity to get sufficient transparent information and subject it to scrutiny. And when that site plays its monitoring role over others who exert the power, the independence of the site should be guaranteed. To illustrate, for example, when the board exerts their

[67] Bottomley (n 1) 80.

[68] Ibid.

[69] Ibid., 81.

[70] In this network, shareholders are still the central party of the corporation. But they should also take their responsibilities. In terms of shareholders' responsibility, this will be analysed in next chapter.

powers, their decisions should not be made in a "black box", rather all other groups of corporate participators are able to know what kinds of decisions they are making, and how they are making such decisions. These groups' scrutiny can be enforced by the mechanisms of deliberation and contestability—they can talk about, discuss these decisions and challenge if those decisions affect their personal interests or the general interests, because one of the underlying fundamentals of corporate constitutionalism is that the legitimacy of corporate managerial power is granted from the one whose interests are affected by that power. We have already seen the failures of the traditional supervisory groups of non-executives and auditors in Carillion. In this regard, the scrutiny role therefore is not only adopted by these specific functionalised groups but should be expanded to a broader corporate constitutional concept.

In addition to this corporate-power-separation network, there should also be mechanisms to ensure different voices of shareholders are heard to encourage a wide-range and multi-levelled deliberation within the company. Moreover, there should also be a transfer avenue from the deliberation and contestability. When the company cannot ensure a full deliberation and discussion, corporate participants (mainly shareholders, as Bottomley stressed) should be able to challenge. However, we should note that the key arguments of corporate constitutionalism are concerned with the relationship between shareholders and the board of directors.[71] Although the accountability principle calls for multiple powers, and the deliberation principle welcomes full discussion among different corporate participants, the establishment of a new web is still based on the shareholder primacy norm, rather than expanding to a stakeholder-involved approach.

7.2.3 The External Dimension of Carillion

The above sections show the general ideas on how corporate constitutionalism utilises the principles of accountability, deliberation and contestability legitimate corporate managerial power in the internal side of Carillion. This section looks at its external or public dimension under the discussion of the corporate constitutional paradigm. The external aspects of corporate constitutionalism concerns two issues—how can we understand the public values of the corporate constitution and where should the rules that govern corporate affairs be located—the public or the private side?[72]

7.2.3.1 Carillion's Corporate Constitution

The corporate constitution is a bridge to connect the internal and external dimensions of the corporation. This section is concerned with how corporate constitutionalism understands the externality of the corporate constitution. As Dine acknowledged, a

---

[71] Bottomley (n 1) 5.

[72] Ibid., 3.

company's constitution functions not only as a contract but also as a mediator of the rights and responsibilities of those involved in the ongoing operations of the business.[73] Instead of a contract, the corporate constitution typifies the convergence of power and responsibilities both internally and externally. A corporate constitution from the corporate constitutional perspective has multiple functions—it defines the members' (or shareholders') status and interests and constructs structures and processes to mediate the relations between the corporation as a whole and the state, and the relations between the individual interests and the common good within the corporation.

The corporate constitution consists of corporate legislation and corporate internal rules (normally known as the memorandum and articles of association). They all represent the particular structures and processes that define the rights, duties, powers, and functions assigned to the members and officers of the organisation,[74] which are essential to legitimising their corporate decisions. However, the judicially or statutorily created standards, as the upper law, take precedence over the internal rules of corporations.[75] And these superior rules can be determined and altered without the direct participation of corporate members, which is a necessary feature of corporate constitution. In terms of the internal rule, unlike the case law under the corporate contractual understanding that exempts non-members and non-membership interests of members of a corporate constitution,[76] the corporate constitution accepts a wider meaning. Outside the memorandum and articles of association, there must be other sources, such as the agreements signed between shareholders, that reveal the ground rules on power and authority arrangement.[77]

Additionally, regarding its forms, the corporate constitution is not restricted to the formal statutory document or internal rules but should extend to a broader context that can be partly written and unwritten. The corporate constitution can be partly written in that it should include both the corporate internal rules and relevant statutory legislation. On the other hand, it can be partly unwritten because there could be some conventions regarding corporate life, such as the common-law doctrines. However, like the conventions in the public constitution of a state, well-accepted and strongly-constructed conventions in corporate constitutionalism cannot be judicially applicable, but only assist in the interpretation or application of the formal rules.[78]

The focal point of a political entity could be its constitution, or articles of association which provides the basis for forming and sustaining the structures and processes. Carillion's articles of association from 2010, posted with Companies House, include

[73] Janet Dine, *The Governance of Corporate Groups*, vol 1 (Cambridge University Press 2000) 2.

[74] Bottomley (n 1) 59.

[75] Ibid., 64.

[76] For example, the case of *Eley v Positive Government Security Life Assurance Company* [1876] 1 Ex D 88; *Hickman v Kent or Romney Marsh Sheep-Breeders' Association* [1915] 1 Ch 881.

[77] For example, *Hopkins Professional Services Pty Ltd & Ors v Foyster Holdings Pty Ltd & Ors* [2001] 39 ACSR 519.

[78] There are also conventions in corporate area. For example, AGM usually will accept the board appointment; and the incumbent directors frequently get the ultimate control over the board composition with the powers of making casual appointments and proxy system of voting.

138 key issues—share capital; calls on shares; forfeiture of shares; transfer of shares; transmission of shares; alteration of share capital; general meetings; amendments; voting; proxies; appointment, retirement and removal of directors; fees, remuneration, expenses and pensions; directors' interests; powers and duties of the board; proceedings of the board; dividends and other payments; capitalisation of reserves; record dates; records and summary financial statements; destruction of documents; indemnity; and others.[79] Additionally, according to Carillion's memorandum of association 2006, there was a broad range of 21 objects of this company's business conduct.[80] These objects seem to cover all the activities of a business entity, although Carillion was positioned as a construction company in the market. Moreover, there seemed to be a conflict between Carillion's articles of association and the remuneration policy in that the former do not give a shareholding qualification for directors, while the latter permits executive directors to hold a net of number of shares until their total shareholding value is up to annual salary.

However, in public constitutional theory, the constitution of a country is the origin of public power, based on the primary condition that the power is restricted within certain boundaries. In Gordon's terms, a political organisation is considered "democratic" when there is broad participation by the general public in shaping public policy. It is also "constitutional" in that it includes institutionalised mechanisms to control power, safeguarding the interests and freedoms of the citizenry, including minority groups.[81] In the context of corporate constitutionalism, a corporate constitution consists of both state and corporate contributions, encompassing both written and unwritten elements.[82] Corporate officials' power and relative activities cannot go beyond the boundary of corporate constitution.

When commenting on the possibilities of applying corporate constitutionalism into Carillion, this book observes the important point that if Carillion were to have a constitution and a constitutional approach, it might be more difficult for Carillion to be able perform such a wide range of services. The company may be much more restricted about what they could and could not do. A free-style market cannot stop the companies from doing all these things. That leads to the question on Carillion's far-stretched business activities (such as its mystifying mergers and acquisitions) that—do they have the expertise and the knowledge to be able to do all those things? This book posits that a constitutional approach could force the company to concentrate on what it was good at. If the company really needs to expand the business activities, there should be an institutionalised mechanism to assess the feasibility of such business. And this would trigger an alteration of the corporate constitution which would then require a wide-range and wide-levelled deliberation, participation

[79] 'Articles of Association of Carillion Plc 2010', https://find-and-update.company.information.service.gov.uk/company/03782379/filing-history?page=6, accessed 29 January 2024.

[80] 'Memorandum of Association of Carillion Plc 2006', https://find-and-update.company-information.service.gov.uk/company/03782379/filing-history?page=8, accessed 30 January 2024.

[81] Scott Gordon, *Controlling the State: Constitutionalism from Ancient Athens to Today* (Harvard University Press 2009) 4.

[82] Bottomley (n 1) 75.

and majority shareholders' voting should occur. Moreover, in order to encourage shareholders to be careful and prospective,[83] before shareholders acquire shares, shareholders should thoroughly understand the rights and potential liabilities they might face, as well as how these may be influenced by the corporation's governance structures.[84] In this regard, when an outsider becomes a shareholder of Carillion, that member should be given a written corporate constitution which clarifies what kind of rights they have, what duties they are expected to fulfil, the procedures of participating in corporate decision making, and the deliberation and contestability approaches that they can go through when their interests are affected.

7.2.3.2 State Regulation and Private Governance

As revealed in Chapter 2, corporate contractualism views corporations as private arrangements that are subject to a "flexible and private-ordering paradigm of law".[85] In responding, the default mandatory rules apply and contractarian logic views these rules as the "endogenous outcomes" in the processes of private bargains that attempts to mimic the market, namely the so called "market mimicking rationale".[86] In contrast, the public-oriented concession theory seems to move towards another extreme point which perceives that corporations are granted their legal status through state approval. The rules that regulate corporate behaviours therefore are rooted in a public ground.

However, in the corporate constitutional context, this is not an either/or question. Rather, this framework recognises and respects the complex interrelation between the public interventions and private ordering in the corporate area where the special state-like actors exert powers that are both both privately established and state-approved.[87] As revealed in Chapters 3 and 5, the purpose of political constitutionalism is to reconcile "the public" and "the private". When applying political thoughts in the corporate arena, the corporate constitutional framework thus emphasises the equal importance of "the private" and "the public" in corporate activities and corporate participants. More importantly, corporate constitutionalism also realises the complexity and variability between "the public" and "the private" and reveals the transformation between these dual features of the corporation. Like political constitutionalism, the aim of corporate constitutionalism consequently is to mediate "the public" and "the private" from both internal and external aspects of the corporation. Internally, corporate constitutionalism acts to balance the private and individual interests of members

---

83 *Bratton Seymour Service Co Ltd v Oxborough* [1992] BCLC 693, 699 per Sir Christopher Slade.

84 Bottomley (n 1) 64.

85 Marc Moore, 'Private Ordering and Public Policy: The Paradoxical Foundations of Corporate Contractarianism' (2014) 34 *Oxford Journal of Legal Studies* 693, 693.

86 Ibid., 708.

87 Bottomley (n 1) 55–56.

with the collective interests of the entire group.[88] Corporate decision-making structures and processes should be ensured by following three key interdependent principles of accountability, deliberation, and contestability. Through the deliberation avenue, by offering great opportunities for corporate participants to exercise their voice, the individuals could be more likely to accept and share a common interest within a company. Meanwhile, externally, corporate constitutionalism is concerned to reconcile the public regulation and internal ordering of corporate issues.[89] A corporate constitution breaks down the barriers between the public side and the private side of a corporation, so that the social concept of supervision and governance can be integrated into the corporate arena.

In a nutshell, the rules that regulate corporate conduct contain both state regulation and private governance, namely that the sources of a corporate regulatory framework are supplied by both the state and the company itself. Both of the values from the public and the private are equal in constructing a regulatory framework in that, on the one hand, the state has an important role in protecting the common good or the public interest from potential threats when great powers are being allocated and exercised by corporations; on the other hand, as an independent system of polities, corporations should get some space to set their own constitutional orderings.

In Carillion's case, Carillion's activities are not purely commercial, although the company's activities are tagged with "private orientation". Publicly traded companies, such as Carillion, entail extensive collaboration between state and corporate entities, have considerable social effects, and are maintained within or necessitate significant infrastructural innovation.[90] It is also the reality that Carillion's demise has resulted in financial turmoil in the UK, leaving workers, contractors, the PPP projects, and the whole society in an uncertain and difficult position. In this sense, Carillion's case offers strong empirical evidence that a companies' actions may have a public consequence—their power cannot be limited in a private spectrum, rather a wider societal sector could be implicated in their decision making. Such power possession and exercise in corporations form the basic justification for public power in prescribing certain terms in governing corporate behaviours. If we apply corporate constitutionalism to Carillion, the company cannot only be seen as a commercial entity for this book, it is rather a "system of government with corporate features" with the underlying theme of "power legitimacy". Facing Carillion's failure, the regulatory framework reform thus should be oriented to facilitate the balance between the public value and the private ordering. Following Bottomley's framework, not at the expense of private interests, a system of corporate law should focus on enhancing the public values, including constraining oppressive or unfair behaviours, utilising objective, rather than only subjective metrics in evaluating corporate conducts, highlighting accountability in the processes of exercising corporate power.[91] Following

[88] Ibid., 16.

[89] Ibid.

[90] O'Kelly (n 60) 12.

[91] Bottomley (n 1) 57.

this direction, the next chapter will examine the reform of law in detail under the hypothetical processes.

7.3 Conclusion

With the theme of "corporate power legitimacy", this chapter presents an initial and general approach and starting point for applying corporate constitutionalism into Carillion's case. For a better understanding of Carillion's corporate governance, this chapter gives a brief review of Carillion's decision-making processes by accessing its board minutes' records. The main body of this chapter attempts to embed corporate constitutionalism into Carillion, both internally and externally. Internally, corporate constitutionalism uses the idea of establishing an accountability-deliberation-contestability mechanism to legitimate corporate power. When it applies to Carillion, under the accountability principle, there should be a variety of power separations. Corporate constitutionalism draws a picture of a power-related web, including the shareholders, directors, auditors and whistleblowers. In this network, the role, composition and responsibility of these corporate actors are expected to present not only individually, but also collectively in group or in a whole. Additionally, the deliberation calls for setting an avenue for individuals within the company to fully discuss the issues that may concern them. The contestability principle ensures the possibility and feasibility for shareholders to challenge. Externally, this chapter analyses the public dimension of Carillion from two aspects—the importance of its constitution and Carillion's relationship with the public external checks and balances.

In a word, all these above arguments essentially are based on one core value of applying corporate constitutionalism into Carillion—corporate governance should be strengthened in its functions of checks and balances, both internally and externally. Compared to corporate contractualism that has established an economics-disciplined, pragmatic, free and relatively non-interventionist corporate governance system in the UK, corporate constitutionalism concentrates on legitimating and separating corporate officials' managerial power, procedural justification of decision making, collective interplays of corporate actors, the common good, de-centralised intervention from state. This book asserts that it is only such a fundamental theoretical reform or a basic value change that can prevent continuous Carillion-style collapses.

Following these general ideas, Chapter 8 continues with an examination of how Carillion would appear if it were to adopt a corporate constitutional approach to corporate governance. Internally, the following chapter will focus on the physical form of Carillion based on accountability, deliberation and contestability principles. It will specifically look at how the main corporate actors, namely shareholders, directors, auditors, whistleblowers behave differently under corporate constitutionalism, instead of the long-standing corporate contractual framework. Externally, some suggestions on the law and UK's corporate governance system will also be evaluated.

Chapter 8
Hypothetical Application of Corporate Constitutionalism to Carillion

8.1 Introduction

Chapter 7 examined the general ideas that underpin the application of corporate constitutional framework to Carillion. As shown above, Carillion, in its role as a political entity, carries two key connotations—it is both a major participant in societal power structures and a forum where power, authority, rights, responsibilities, expectations, advantages, and disadvantages are allocated and exercised. These dynamics occur either actively or passively, individually or collectively, and are shaped by interactions characterised by conflict, control, competition, or collaboration.[1] In other words, within the corporate constitutional context, Carillion therefore is a participant in the wide nation-level constitutional setting; and in the meantime, the company itself is also a constitutional arrangement. Carillion's constitution sits in the middle to mediate the interplays between these two sides. Thus, under the politics-based corporate constitutional framework, Carillion's corporate governance has been examined from an alternative perspective than the contractual approach—within the company, its internal constitutional structure is assumed to be upheld by the accountability-deliberation-contestability mechanism; while the external aspect of corporate constitutionalism considers Carillion as a whole, interrelating with the external regulatory sectors.

Viewing Carillion as a political entity essentially leads to a change in the relationships between corporate participants. Under a corporate contractual framework, the agency relationship between shareholders and managers, protecting the company and shareholders from dishonest or neglectful managers, and monitoring of managers by the shareholders are the key items of concern for corporate governance. However, corporate constitutionalism holds a different standpoint towards relationships within a corporation—it emphasises the connections among corporate actors by viewing

[1] This sentence draws on Bottomley's words in analysing corporate power. See Stephen Bottomley, *The Constitutional Corporation: Rethinking Corporate Governance* (Ashgate Publishing, Ltd 2007) 37.

Y. Yang, *Corporate Collapse and Corporate Governance*, CSR, Sustainability, Ethics & Governance, https://doi.org/10.1007/978-981-96-9666-6_8

them as power alliances. As Dallas argued, in the power model of corporations, managers are "strategic players" in the power alliances, rather than purely agents of shareholders.[2] Similar but broader ideas were presented in Chapter 7 that, within Carillion, shareholders, directors and managers, auditors and whistleblowers are connected by a power-related network. This chapter therefore claims that under corporate constitutionalism, we rather regard their roles as strategic players in the power coalitions within Carillion than reserving their contractual-like status. The most significant genetic difference between a constitutional relationship and a contractual relationship is that the former concerns the checks and balances among various sets of power strength, both in individual or in co-participation relations, while the latter facilitates private exchanges among individual parties by simplifying the internal and external relationships as purely contractual connections. It is this fundamental distinction that decides the two different approaches in dealing with corporate failures.

The delayed and ineffective measures taken to avert Carillion's collapse, along with the resulting economic and social instability, seem to serve as a warning that demands an extensive and ambitious reform agenda aimed at reestablishing corporate accountability systems for the long-term benefit of the public.[3] In this book's view, Carillion's collapse is essentially the epitome of a systematic failure of the checks and balances of UK's corporate governance system—a failure of the internal control of shareholders, directors, internal auditors; and a failure of the external regulatory scheme of the external auditors, the law, the regulators and the government. The corporate contractual approach has proved in Carillion's downfall that it cannot provide efficient approach to detect, deter and correct company's substandard activities before it was too late, rather to some extent, the contractual framework has contributed to the problems in corporate collapses. This book thus argues for a fundamental paradigmatic reform that is oriented to a corporate constitutional approach.

Following these ideas, the key theme of this chapter is to continue the application process and crystallise the general analysis of Chapter 7. The following context will investigate how these ideas could be reflected in Carillion's internal corporate arrangements, with the role of the different corporate actors (shareholders, directors and managers, auditors, stakeholders), and practices and in the external regulatory arrangements. What should be repeated here is that the nature of this chapter is also hypothetical. But the arguments made in this chapter are still logical because they draw on the concrete descriptions and discussions of the corporate constitutionalism framework which have been delivered by Bottomley and analysed in the earlier chapters of the book.

---

[2] Lynne L Dallas, 'Two Models of Corporate Governance: Beyond Berle and Means' (1988) 22 *U. Mich. JL Reform* 19.

[3] House of Commons Business, Energy and Industrial Strategy and Work and Pensions Committees, *Carillion*, Second Joint Report from the Business, Energy and Industrial Strategy and Work and Pensions Committees of Session 2017–19, HC 769, 16 May 2018, at 3, https://publications.parliament.uk/pa/cm201719/cmselect/cmworpen/769/769.pdf, accessed 31 October 2023.

The structure of this chapter is as follows. From Sects. 8.2 to 8.5, the chapter sets out to examine the key roles of shareholders, directors, auditors (internal and external), and whistleblowers in corporate constitutionalism respectively and clarify their characteristic transitions from corporate contractualism to corporate constitutionalism in tackling with corporate failures. These roles are specifically highlighted in Bottomley's work and are also the focal points of Carillion's failure. Based on a corporate power network, Sect. 8.6 then examines their aggregated roles, in different groups or as a whole. In the meantime, Sect. 8.7 will evaluate how the external checks and balances, especially the company law and the corporate governance system, could undergo a radical reform under the corporate constitutional framework. The concluding section then brings the internal control and external regulatory framework together in an attempt to establish a framework that could detect, deter and correct Carillion's problems at an early stage by applying corporate constitutionalist thoughts to the company.

8.2 Shareholder Involvement[4]

Over the past thirty years of corporate scandals and failures, company directors, managers, auditors, legal advisers, financial intermediaries, corporate regulators, and the companies themselves have all faced scrutiny and criticism for their involvement in mishandling corporate governance.[5] However, shareholders, tagged with the label of self-interested "rentiers" of modern corporations, seem to be excluded in the discussion of how to ensure the wellbeing of the company. Despite the existence of the Stewardship Code, they are accustomed to being silent in corporate governance, and only exist as the contextual background of corporate failures or the contributor to directors' and managers' misconduct. There are various factors that feed into shareholders' passivity: the legal norm of shareholder non-intervention in

[4] Stephen Bottomley, *The Responsible Shareholder* (Edward Elgar Publishing Limited 2021) 34. Regarding shareholders' role in corporate constitutional context, Bottomley's recent book, *The Responsible Shareholder,* gives a clear response. In this book, he clarifies the definition of "shareholder" which refers to "a person (natural or corporate) who has a direct legal—as opposed to indirect or beneficial—ownership interest in one or more shares issued by a company". Moreover, the high-frequency trading (HFT) is not in the discussion of responsible shareholders. The definition of HFT is "a form of algorithmic trading performed by computers, to rapidly move into and out of trading positions in microseconds in order to capture fractions of a cent profit on every trade, which when magnified by millions of trades quickly yields a substantial return". See Thomas Clarke, 'High-Frequency Trading and Dark Pools: Sharks Never Sleep' (2014) 8 *Law and Financial Markets Review* 342, 342–351.

And shareholders' involvement and responsibility do not necessarily relate to their duration of ownership. In other words, long-term shareholders are not necessarily expected to incur more responsibilities. Conversely, short-term shareholders' are not necessarily exempt from responsibilities.

[5] Bottomley (n 4) 22.

corporate management limits shareholders' role in impacting corporate daily decisions;[6] the doctrine of limited liability lets shareholders feel free to stand outside of a corporation's irresponsible behaviours; it is the directors who possess managerial and discretion power that are the mainstay of the Company Law's considerations.

The idea of a corporate constitutional framework seeks to challenge the orthodox standpoint which views shareholders as outsiders of corporate management and changes the "ownerless" approaches of corporations under corporate contractualism. Within a corporate constitutional context, the term "shareholder" is replaced by "member" which entails more requirements of "participation, identity and identification, responsibility and obligation" of these corporate insiders.[7] It does not mean shareholders take the management role (although many companies' directors and managers are also the shareholders), but it is the shareholders' task to "watch, monitor, question, seek explanations and make suggestions about how the company is being run".[8] By bringing the shareholders' role into discussion, it is expected to establish a disciplinary mechanism for managerial misconduct and complacency, to set a "moral climate" of corporate governance.[9] Thus, in Carillion's case, the shareholders' role is an important element in providing some impact on the good operation of Carillion.

8.2.1 Difficulties of Shareholder Involvement

In the UK, shareholders' involvement is an important topic that has long been under great consideration in academic discussions and the corporate governance regulatory regime. In academia, many scholars have identified shareholders' significant role in corporate governance. For example, Chiu considers "enhanced shareholder engagement" which offers oversight and governance within the corporate sector, as a key component of effective corporate governance across various companies.[10] And according to Boeger, Russell and Villiers's recent research, there is evidence of increasing numbers of investors contributing to environmental, societal and governance (ESG) issues and regarding sustainability as a strategic measure to avoid business risks and secure economic benefits in the long run.[11]

---

[6] *Automatic Self-Cleansing Filter Syndicate Co Ltd v Cunninghame* [1906] 2 Ch 34.

[7] Bottomley (n 1) 13–14.

[8] Bottomley (n 4) 26.

[9] Richard J Klonoski, 'The Moral Responsibilities of Stockholders' (1986) 5 *Journal of Business Ethics* 385, 388. Citing from ibid.

[10] Iris HY Chiu, 'Reviving Shareholder Stewardship: Critically Examining the Impact of Corporate Transparency Reforms in the UK' (2013) 38 *Delaware Journal of Corporate Law* 983, 1023.

[11] Nina Boeger, Roseanne Russell, and Charlotte Villiers, 'Companies, Shareholders and Sustainability' (2020) 7 *University of Bristol Law Research Paper Series*. In their research, they find that the membership of the UN principles for responsible investment (PRI) had more than 2250 signatories in 2019. In this book' research, this membership had grown to 4800 signatories as of March 2022.

Moreover, with the aim to encourage "sustainable benefits for the economy, the environment and society",[12] the UK's codes of practice set out a list of principles to encourage institutional shareholders to escalate stewardship in corporate governance. Under principles 9 to 11 of the Stewardship Code 2020, investors are expected to have collaborative engagement in certain thematic issues of corporations. In addition, in the BEIS Committee's report published in 2017, the committee attempted to investigate the potential for the UK Investor Forum to set the foundation for shareholders taking concerted actions in corporate issues.[13] The government's 2018 consultation on Insolvency and Corporate Governance highlighted the need to reconsider shareholders' responsibilities, questioning whether institutional investors should play a more active role as stewards and whether more efforts should be made to encourage constructive engagement between company directors and their investors, given recent corporate failures.[14] The Second Joint Report, drawing lessons from Carillion's collapse, also underscores the critical importance of shareholder engagement in holding the board accountable.[15]

However, Carillion's case epitomises the difficulties of relying on shareholders' proper engagement in corporate governance. Carillion's shareholders, who were able to have a say in company's management, mainly consist of two sets of corporate actors—the board members[16] and the institutional investors.[17] In Carillion's Annual Report and Accounts 2016, Carillion's shareholders consisted of institutional shareholders (77%), private shareholders (18%), and others (5%).[18] As revealed in the Second Joint Report, Carillion's six institutional investors to some extent had participated in Carillion's governance mechanism, but with different engagement strategies and preferences. For example, for BlackRock, most of its investments relied

See from 'About the PRI' (PRI), https://www.unpri.org/about-us/about-the-pri, accessed 30 May 2023.

[12] 'Financial Reporting Council, *The UK Stewardship Code* (2020)' 4, https://www.frc.org.uk/getattachment/5aae591d-d9d3-4cf4-814a-d14e156a1d87/Stewardship Code_Dec-19-Final-Corrected.pdf, accessed 25 January 2024.

[13] 'Business, Energy and Industrial Strategy Committee, Third Report of Session 2016–17, Corporate Governance, HC 702, April 2017' 44–52, https://publications.parliament.uk/pa/cm201617/cmselect/cmbeis/702/702.pdf, accessed 3 March 2024.

[14] 'Department for Business, Energy and Industrial Strategy, Insolvency and Corporate Governance, March 2018' 26, https://assets.publishing.service.gov.uk/government/uploads/system/uploads/attachment_data/file/691857/Condoc_-_Insolvency_and_Corporate_Governance_FINAL_.pdf, accessed 3 March 2024.

[15] House of Commons Business, Energy and Industrial Strategy and Work and Pensions Committees, *Carillion*, Second Joint Report (n 3) 48.

[16] Ibid., 71. According to the Second Report, Philip Green, Richard Howson, Zafar Khan, Richard Adam, Andrew Dougal and Alison Horner were Carillion's shareholders. Keith Cochrane and Ceri Powell were not.

[17] Carillion's institutional shareholders included the BlackRock, Brewin Dolphin Ltd, Deutsche Bank AG, Kiltearn Partners LLP, Letko, Brosseau & Associates Inc., and Standard Life Aberdeen.

[18] These shareholders came from UK (69%), Europe (8%), and North America (23%).

'Carillion Plc, Annual Report and Accounts 2016' 57, https://www.annualreports.com/HostedData/AnnualReports/PDF/LSE_CLLN_2016.pdf, accessed 12 March 2024.

on passively managed funds.[19] For this passive institutional investor, the suspension of dividends will trigger an automatic obligation to remove Carillion from tracking indices and to sell this company's shares. And this financial vulture, which had noticed the extreme delays of Carillion's payments to its contractors, at an early age betted on the company's collapse and cashed out £80 million from this bet. Another hedge fund, Naya Capital Management UK got £7.6 million from its demise.[20] While for Standard Life Aberdeen, direct investment was a significant aspect of investment strategy. As early as 2014, in the bi-annual meeting with Carillion's Board, it expressed worries about Carillion's growing pension deficit, excessive debt, poor cash flow, and the board's reluctance to alter its strategic direction.[21] Kiltearn Partners LLP also discovered Carillion's problems in debt and working capital levels, and the unreliability of published financial information.[22] In addition, the Letko, Brosseau & Associates even considered further capital injection after Carillion's first profit warnings. In a word, these investors were clear about Carillion's problems but took different actions on its crisis—hedge funds were like "vultures" extracting the last values of Carillion, but there were still many institutional investors who more or less got involved in the monitoring activities of Carillion's corporate governance. However, those actively involved shareholders never acted "in a co-ordinated manner" to give effectual influence on the board of Carillion.[23] It could be a collective failure of these majority shareholders' stewardship responsibilities.

Carillion's results represented the reality that even institutional investors who had capital and professional advantages, could only exert limited exception to the prevailing view that shareholders should not be responsible for corporate behaviour.[24] Just as Talbot advocated, liquidity, short-term focus, and minimal involvement in corporate governance are key components of shareholders' value maximisation strategies.[25] Shareholders in Carillion who behaved with little interest in monitoring and participating to some extent fit Talbot's description. Shareholders' involvement is essentially situated in a paradoxical position which contains multiple conflicts of interests—first, shareholders are expected to actively monitor directors' and

---

[19] House of Commons Business, Energy and Industrial Strategy and Work and Pensions Committees, *Carillion*, Second Joint Report (n 3) 18.

[20] *KPMG Sued For Billions Over Carillion*, https://www.youtube.com/watch?v=rJI2dBqB3KE, accessed 25 March 2024.

[21] House of Commons Business, Energy and Industrial Strategy and Work and Pensions Committees, *Carillion*, Second Joint Report (n 3) 49.

[22] 'Letter from Kiltearn Partners LLP to the Chairs Regarding Carillion 2 February 2018', https://www.parliament.uk/globalassets/documents/commons-committees/work-and-pensions/Carillion/Letter-from-Kiltearn-Partners-LLP-to-the-Chairs-regarding-Carillion-2-February-2018.pdf, accessed 25 January 2024.

[23] House of Commons Business, Energy and Industrial Strategy and Work and Pensions Committees, *Carillion*, Second Joint Report (n 3) 50.

[24] Bottomley (n 4) 6.

[25] Lorraine Talbot, 'Why Shareholders Shouldn't Vote: A Marxist-progressive Critique of Shareholder Empowerment' (2013) 76 *The Modern Law Review* 791, 791.

managers' behaviours, but their high-quality engagement relies heavily upon transparent and accurate information disclosure which requires those management actors' honest and constructive engagement; second, shareholders seem to be not willing to take any action that will attract public attentions, because this may have an adverse effect on the share values or their financial interests; third, effective shareholder engagement is a resource-intensive activity which normally demands a coalition among shareholders. But given the highly dispersed shareholdings or even some "ownerless companies",[26] shareholders are always consigned to a passive role, and their collaboration is confronted with practical difficulties; fourth, there is a blank in the law or corporate governance codes of requiring shareholders to take some responsibilities other than focusing on their interests.[27] In a nutshell, the above analysis talks about one question—that of shareholder engagement—but it is not easy for shareholders to engage in the operation of corporate activities.

However, corporate constitutionalism is a framework that is based on the "shareholder primacy" model. The framework seeks to encourage and enhance shareholders' participation in corporate governance and promote shareholders' interests in the long run. Moreover, Bottomley's more recent work, *The Responsible Shareholder*, seems to hold an optimistic attitude towards shareholders' involvement. Although this new book is not a sequel to his works on corporate constitutionalism, he clearly identifies that the fresh arguments on the shareholders' role are still building on ideas in the three corporate constitutional principles—accountability, deliberation and contestability.[28] His updated arguments seek seriously to challenge the orthodox norm that views shareholders as corporate outsides. It explores the privileged status of shareholders and the specific rights and responsibilities awarded to them in the corporation, not only "morally", but also "legally". Shareholders should be encouraged (or compelled if necessary) to participate in the structures and processes of corporate decision-making beyond pure considerations on their dividend or share prices. In this sense, shareholders should not remain detached from corporate management; instead, they should be evaluated based on how well they fulfil their responsibilities, and in some cases, held accountable if they fail to meet these duties.[29] That means, shareholders are required to remain informed about the conditions of their companies, rather than only focusing on the daily change of shares prices. Bottomley also gives a series of indicative but not exhaustive description about the ideal type of responsible shareholders.[30]

Bottomley describes the ideal shareholder as someone who stays well-informed about the companies they invest in. This goes beyond tracking share price fluctuations, involving reading company documents, reports, and news, and staying updated through business and financial media. The responsible shareholder understands the

[26] House of Commons Business, Energy and Industrial Strategy and Work and Pensions Committees, *Carillion*, Second Joint Report (n 3) 72.

[27] ibid.

[28] Bottomley (n 4) 25.

[29] Ibid., 8.

[30] Ibid., 25–26.

company's activities, the leadership, and board composition. They are aware of the company's operations, including its supply chains and whether there are concerns regarding human rights, environmental issues, or forced labour. They know the company's policies on workforce diversity, climate change, carbon emissions, and executive compensation, if such policies exist. Responsible shareholders exercise their voting rights thoughtfully, ensuring the election of competent and ethical directors. They also voice concerns, ask questions, and seek clarification, both within and outside the company, through meetings, websites, or even legal means. Importantly, a responsible shareholder can explain why they own shares in a particular company, not only in terms of financial gain but also recognising their role as a member of the company, not just an investor.[31]

From the above, Bottomley gives an indicative, but non-exhaustive description on what features we should see from a "responsible shareholder". This long description sheds light on a few key words of shareholders' responsibility—"information", "voting", "voice", "member", and "sustainability"—which progressively put higher expectations on shareholders. It is required that shareholders should firstly be clear about the company they invest in; at least, they should read companies' public-available documents, and be aware of companies' business scopes and management teams and running conditions. Based on sufficient knowledge and information, shareholders' voting then is the most direct and significant way for shareholders to engage in decision-making processes and decide on many critical circumstances.[32] The second layer therefore asks shareholders to exercise their voting rights/powers in an informed and manageable manner. A responsible shareholder does not only act formally through exercising voting power, but also performs and gives their voice beyond the boundary of general meeting and even outside of the company. Shareholders' informal and formal activities towards corporate conducts signal to directors and managers that "we care about our companies and we are watching your behaviours". In this sense, shareholders are the members or insiders of their companies, instead of pure bystanders who are largely ignoring the benefits and needs of the company. This description also takes "sustainability" issues, such as human rights, environmental or forced labour problems of corporate supply chains, climate change and carbon emission, into consideration. The long-lasting pandemic, the devastating bushfire in Australia and the recent Tonga volcano eruption all raise questions on the future of humanity. Corporations, as a central element of economic, social, and political life both locally and globally, play a significant role in shaping a predictable future.[33] A responsible shareholder, a rational corporate member, ought to take the duty to lead and force the company to a sustainable orientation.

These new standards on being responsible shareholders can also be assimilated into the following discussion about shareholders' participation in Carillion under corporate constitutionalism. Being a responsible shareholder in Carillion in general

---

[31] Ibid.

[32] Borut Bratina and Dusan Jovanovic, 'Shareholders Positive Voting Duty', (2014) *International OFEL Conference on Governance, Management and Entrepreneurship* 1.

[33] Bottomley (n 4) vi.

demands them to know Carillion's running problems, to vote on big decisions (eg. mergers and acquisitions, directors' remuneration pay etc.) deliberately, to give their voices and challenge corporate officials formally and informally, to give enough consideration on the workers, employees, contractors alongside Carillion's supply chains, to care about the long-term running of Carillion, and so forth.

8.2.2 Enhancing Shareholders' Involvement in Carillion Under Corporate Constitutional Framework

This part continues to the hypothetical application of the corporate constitutional framework to Carillion. Given the above analysis on the difficulties of shareholders' involvement, this book can give a simple but strongly defended statement to the questions on shareholders' role—to break up the empire that had been constructed by Carillion's management team, we should use a democratic approach—encouraging different corporate constituents' (not only shareholders) participation to realise separations of power is an inevitable course. The following imaginative arguments seek to look specifically at how shareholders' engagement would be enhanced in this company. It is important to be notified here that these hypothetical suggestions only accord with and are restricted within the practical issues in Carillion. They may provide some concrete inspirations to solve wide-range corporate governance problems, but they cannot be regarded as a generally applicable approach to other corporate collapses.

8.2.2.1 A Written Constitution

Chapter 7 provided a broad idea that the form of Carillion's corporate constitution can be partly written and partly unwritten. The unwritten aspect entails the conventions of corporate life and common-law doctrines, while the corporate constitution is partly written in that it includes both the corporate internal rules and relevant statutory legislation. The internal rules actually are the core to Carillion's corporate arrangement, because they directly refer to Carillion's featured, specified structure and process in decision making. Such rules have the advantage of hardening up and strengthening shareholders' involvement by defining what rights they possess and what responsibilities they should take.

Learning from the written constitution in political terms, this book argues that there should also be a written constitution for shareholders. One may observe that nowadays corporations are equipped with a memorandum and articles of association. However, these memorandum and articles of association are more vested with contractual status. As clarified in Chapter 7, the shareholders' written constitution in this book entails different meanings compared to these private contract-like documents. Under corporate constitutionalism, a corporate constitution should be understood from a political dimension. Like a state's constitution, one of the important functions of a written constitution is that it clarifies the specific rights and responsibilities for the citizens. Many countries, such as Spain, France and Germany even establish constitutional courts to ensure and maintain democratic systems of the state. Thus, under the corporate constitutional way of thinking, a written constitution with clear rights and obligations should be directly supplied to each member on the day they become a shareholder to clarify their constitutional positions or the "citizenship" in the company.[34] Compared to a contract-like memorandum and articles of association, the constitution-positioned internal documents would motivate these members with a sense of responsibility to guard the polity of corporation.

8.2.2.2 Different Expectations on Different Varieties of Shareholders

Different numbers of shareholdings directly relate to the overall capacity of shareholders control in the company. As revealed above, Carillion's shareholdings were categorised with three types—institutional, private and others. In addition to institutional and individual shareholders, the third type of shareholdings were possessed by some directors. Regarding the diversity of shareholdings within Carillion, there should also be different responsibility expectations on those various types of shareholders—the institutional shareholders, the shareholders who also held position in the board, and pure individual rentiers.

The second type of shareholders who also possess management power should be expected to take more responsibilities. Although they only occupied a small proportion of shares (compared to institutional investors' total of 77%), their decision-making powers were still unbalanced and unchallenged. As directors or senior managers, those dual-identity shareholders are asked to take on fiduciary duties to the company. But as shareholders, they are rarely required to explain their actions. Moreover, they can easily impact and dictate other shareholders' vote to fit their decisions. When each shareholder's vote is directed to their preferred decision, the aggregation of individuals' decisions would become an action of the overall company. For example, the continuous rising up of dividends told the reality that even when Carillion had no sufficient cash flow to cover their dividend payments, these dual-identity

[34] In terms of the definition of "citizenship", Lee gives a clear explanation that "the concept of citizenship is closely connected with the concept of a political community, a type of community in which potentially legitimate decisions can be made by some on behalf of all. Citizenship signifies membership in such a community, and for some theorists it also stands for conditions contributing to the stability or legitimacy of the community." See Ian B Lee, 'Citizenship and the Corporation' (2009) 34 *Law & Social Inquiry* 129, 138.

shareholders could still easily exploit the company to fulfil their own wish.[35] In this sense, such shareholders ought to accept more responsibilities.

From this book's standpoint, their powers should be checked by other groups of constituents, such as the auditors, whistleblowers, which will be discussed later, and be separated by institutional shareholders as well. Bottomley establishes a benchmark for "responsible shareholders" to assess their behavior. Shareholders' responsibility is to ensure that, as much as possible, the decisions made by the company's directors and managers align with the shareholders' interests and concerns. They must ensure that corporate decisions are not dominated by the interests of particular directors or shareholders, and that shareholder rights, particularly those related to general meetings, are exercised in a fair and proper manner.[36] If this parameter were applied in Carillion, it could be understood from three dimensions. First, as shareholders, and as directors also, when they exercise dual decision-making powers, they should take other shareholders' interests into account; interests should not be limited to dividends, but expand to a wider ESG-labelled range of issues.[37] The second dimension connects to the idea of separation of corporate powers which prevents corporate decisions from being determined by one group of corporate actors. The third dimension sets the standards of "propriety, fairness and absence of oppression" to make shareholders consider their behaviours as members of Carillion.[38]

To be able to meet these prospective requirements, this book perceives that those dual-identity shareholders' decision-making power should be balanced or reduced in certain ways. First, the formal voting rights of those shareholders who also hold positions in the board should be restricted. We may bring the ideas of dual-class-shareholding structure into these different types of shareholders, namely same shares but different rights. These double-identity shareholders can have dividend payments corresponding to their share proportions, but their voting rights cannot be set equally with other single-identity shareholders.

Second, institutional shareholders broadly act as a strong check-and-balance group to dual-identity shareholders' power. On the basis of institutional shareholders' existing power, this book argues that they should also be equipped with veto power on certain corporate decisions, such as Carillion's problematic mergers and acquisition projects, risky dividend payments, and aggressive accounting issues. As far as we know, shareholders do have voting and veto rights around mergers and acquisitions if they are the target company shareholders, but as in Carillion, the purchasing company shareholders are seemingly denied such a right. This book thus calls for a reform that shareholders in purchasing companies have a say on takeover projects. And in this book's standpoint, this veto power should be exerted in a collective manner and

[35] 'Oral Evidence—Carillion—6 Feb 2018', http://data.parliament.uk/writtenevidence/committeeevidence.svc/evidencedocument/work-and-pensions-committee/carillion/oral/78103.pdf, accessed 9 March 2024.

[36] Bottomley (n 4) 97.

[37] Ibid.

[38] Ibid., 99.

the total share proportion should reach to a supermajority vote. Moreover, institutional shareholders' checks and balances are not only manifested by votes in formal annual general meetings, but also presented informally. In Carillion, institutional shareholders had tried to negotiate with and persuade the management team to take actions on their financial problems, but always acted solely. This book argues that if institutional shareholders could detect severe problems at an early stage, for example, the UBS's analyst gave a warning on Carillion's profit shortfalls and problems of aggressive accounting in 2015, they should have a responsibility to take a collective action to contest or challenge the wrongfulness of management.

Third, as Carillion's annual report and accounts 2016 noted, private shareholders accounted for 18% which generally belonged to a minority group of shareholders. Their small proportion of shareholdings and their limited individual abilities shaped their restricted capacity to influence corporate behaviours. Even in the Second Joint Report, we hardly see specific consideration or discussion of these individuals. That may be because they always behaved like pure rentiers in the market who hardly gave constructive efforts to the operation of Carillion. Yet, in accordance with the principle of deliberation, the voice of this small group of shareholders should not be discounted simply due to their small size of potential voting.[39] If we accept the corporate constitutional framework in Carillion, the avenue for shareholders, especially those individual shareholders to deliberate, and the access of such deliberations to be received by the management should be open, unobstructed and genuine.

Moreover, the protection of these small groups of shareholders is a great consideration for corporate constitutionalism. Bottomley asserts that any interference with another member's interests must be genuinely linked to the interests of the members as a whole, rather than driven by sectional interests (the proper purpose requirement).[40] Additionally, it must align with the interests and concerns of the individual affected by the interference (the avoidance of oppression requirement).[41] This assertion accords with the feature of corporate constitutionalism that entails the consideration of the complex interplays between individual/private interests and collective/public interests of a company—the realisation of one-group interests cannot be at expense of others' interests. This constitutional way of thinking essentially can be and has been a criterion for the court to take into account in real cases. For example, the courts occasionally may impose restrictions on majority shareholders' voting power in the general meeting. If the voting power is exercised beyond the implicit scope of purposes granted by the corporate constitution, the court may hold that the decision made by the majority constitutes an abuse of power. In the case of *Daniels v Daniels*, Templeman J. stated that "a minority shareholder who has no other remedy

[39] Bottomley (n 1) 113.

[40] Philip Pettit, *Republicanism: A Theory of Freedom and Government* (Oxford University Press 1997) 55.

[41] Bottomley (n 1) 125.

may sue where directors use their powers, intentionally or unintentionally, fraudulently or negligently, in a manner which benefits themselves at the expense of the company".[42]

In summary, the corporate constitutional framework provides a new interpretation of "shareholder primacy"—if shareholders' interests are the priority consideration, they should also take on corresponding responsibilities. This book lays out different responsibility expectations of Carillion's three main types of shareholders. For the directors who also possessed shareholdings, although they were not in a majority group, their dual powers that could be exerted both in the board and the general meeting effectively formed a threat to Carillion's sustainable operation. They ought to take more responsibilities and their powers should be balanced by other sites of corporate actors if corporate constitutionalism could be applied to Carillion's corporate governance structure. Moreover, this book also investigates that the private shareholders, who may only be rentiers of Carillion were always situated beyond the boundaries of the reflection. However, from this book' standpoint, they are also an important element in the discussion of corporate constitutional framework because their protections and opportunities of giving voice would directly reveal the extent to which a company embeds constitutional values into its corporate governance. This section has discussed how institutional shareholders as the majority should collectively accept and fulfil their check-and-balance responsibility. The following sections will continue to look at how auditors and whistle-blowers hold their restriction role in the web of power.

8.2.2.3 Three Soft Changes to General Meetings

Drawing from Bottomley's ideas on promoting shareholders' responsibility, three soft reforms on shareholders' meeting could also be applied into Carillion's internal governance without radically challenging the existing UK's corporate governance system. First, the usage of online-meeting technology should be clarified and regulated both in the corporate constitution and the company law because it could potentially enhance shareholders' attendance and engagement in decision-making.[43] Even though Carillion's failure happened before the Covid-19 pandemic where there was a capability to hold an in-person AGM, Carillion's constitution should ensure the legitimate status and relative processes of using virtual online meetings. Carillion's Annual Report and Accounts had confirmed the use of "conference calls" which could be regarded as a type of online-meeting technology. It was recorded that, in 2016, Carillion's Board "met or held conference calls with over 130 institutions, around 50 per cent of which were attended by at least one Executive Director".[44] However, the virtual meetings may also have reverse effects. It is of concern that

[42] *Daniels v Daniels* [1978] Ch 406, 414.

[43] Bottomley (n 4) 143.

[44] 'Carillion Plc, Annual Report and Accounts 2016' (n 18) 57.

directors may more easily control or edit shareholders' questions through online-meeting technology; and shareholders might be more distanced from directors and the operation of companies which may indulge directors to allow them to "ignore difficult issues".[45] Aligning with the trend of technological development, Carillion's constitution and corporate legislation should make clear the processes and legitimate status of utilizing online formats for encouraging shareholders' voice.

Second, in permitting shareholders' "non-binding advisory resolutions" to be put to and voted on in general meetings, the purpose of clarifying the rule on advisory resolutions is also to enhance the extent of shareholders' participation in company management. As discussed in Chapter 2, although directors' power is delegated from shareholders' permission, the law has established tight restrictions around shareholders' involvement in the operation of management power.[46] The principle of shareholders' non-interference deepens the practical impression that directors are the ones to take responsibility, rather than shareholders. This leads to the result in Carillion that, as revealed above, shareholders' involvement was reduced to only deciding on resolutions preferred and presented by the directors (most of them were also shareholders). In terms of this problem, without violations of the existing rules constructed by the body of case law, reinforcing shareholders' express right through advisory resolutions could be a feasible approach.[47] In this way, it is not intended to bind or force the directors to follow shareholders' instructions, rather to give shareholders more opportunities to use soft ways (advice, remind and alert) to be involved in corporate governance. However, proposing advisory resolution should also follow certain rules. As Bottomley suggested, an advisory resolution can be exerted only after other mechanisms, such as questions and comments on the board have been exhausted; it should also be subject to certain thresholds of supporting members.[48]

Third, creating different special classes of shares—the "time-weighted" shares, and "participatory" shares could be a means of "reward" for shareholders who would take their responsibilities.[49] Similar to the above ideas on restricting dual-identity shareholders' voting power, using various classes of shares also departs from the default rule of "one share, one vote". As explained by Bottomley, "time-weighted share" means shareholders' voting power grows in accordance with the length of time of possessing shares; while a "participatory share" refers to a reward for shareholders actively taking responsibilities—if shareholders can fulfil certain governance criteria, they will be given participatory shares which carry superior voting power and dividend rewards.[50] Both classes of shares are only permissive methods to encourage

---

[45] Lisa M Fairfax, 'Mandating Board-Shareholder Engagement' (2013) *U. Ill. L. Rev.* 821, 847.

[46] *Automatic Self-Cleansing Filter Syndicate Co Ltd v Cuninghame* [1906] 2 Ch 34.

[47] Bottomley (n 4) 147.

[48] Bottomley suggests that shareholders who want to propose advisory resolutions should get the support of members "with at least 5 per cent of the votes that may be cast, or at least 100 members who are entitled to vote". See from ibid., 157.

[49] Ibid.

[50] Tamara C Belinfanti, 'Shareholder Cultivation and New Governance' (2013) 38 *Del. J. Corp. L.* 789, 846–850. Citing from ibid., 160.

shareholders to be involved. But from this book' position, Carillion's dual-identity shareholders should be excluded from the scope of both share rewarding.

In conclusion, this book assures for shareholders' a leading role in figuring out, preventing and solving Carillion's problems within a corporate constitutional framework. Based on the principles of accountability, deliberation and contestability, this section provides several imaginative speculations of encouraging shareholders' involvement. However, shareholders' participation is only part of the element on the web of power. Although it is important, to maintain a sustainable corporate ecosystem of Carillion, other corporate actors' roles should also be taken fully into consideration.

8.3 Directors and the Checks and Balances

The above ideas on shareholders' participation of corporate governance do not mean that this book seeks to challenge the idea of separation of ownership and control between shareholders and managers, nor does it mean that shareholders' responsibilities can substitute for directors' and managers' duties. On the contrary, the boardroom problem is the origin of Carillion's downfall. As the above theoretical analysis suggests, it is a legitimacy problem of directors' corporate managerial power—the existing corporate governance system cannot provide a checked and balanced mechanism to that power. Even worse, that power had grown with the connivance of the existing corporate contractual based paradigm. The unchecked and unbalanced power thus led to a systematic issue from both inside and outside of Carillion. In this regard, this book seeks to find a feasible approach that could give sufficient checks and balances to this core power. Internally, based on the principles of accountability, deliberation and contestability, the strength of shareholders, auditors, whistleblowers and other corporate participators individually or collectively could be a trade-off to that power; externally, this book argues for a de-centralised regulatory intervention to that power.

These are all the outside combining or separate forces to monitor or balance corporate managerial power; while inside the boardroom, the non-executives and executives should also be balanced. The non-executives' scrutiny function could be viewed as a crucial strength to executives' power. Just as Solomon stated, an effective board strikes the right balance between the two.[51]

The role of directors and managers, their legal duties, the restrictions on these corporate officials' excessive remuneration payment have always been central legal, judicial, academic and market focuses.[52]Especially in the wave of corporate scandals, the boardroom has always been pushed to the forefront to be blamed and critiqued.

---

[51] Jill Solomon, *Corporate Governance and Accountability* (John Wiley & Sons 2020) 72.

[52] Bottomley (n 4) 1. For a survey of the extensive literature, see Charlotte Villiers, 'Controlling Executive Pay: Institutional Investors or Distributive Justice?' (2010) 10 *Journal of Corporate Law* 309–342; Charlotte Villiers 'Executive pay: a Socially-oriented Distributive Justice Framework' (2016) 37(5) *The Company Lawyer* 139–154; Marc Moore, 'Corporate Governance, Pay Equity, and

In the reflection of corporate crises, the UK's corporate governance system has gradually evolved regarding the board functions. The Cadbury Report laid a basis for the board of directors to be effective by emphasising the structures and responsibilities of the board. In order to strengthen the unitary board structure and improve its effectiveness, the report recommended that the chairman should be separated from the CEO to ensure the division of responsibilities and a balance of power and authority.[53] Stimulated by the notorious scandals of Enron and WorldCom, the Higgs Report (2003) re-stressed the significance of splitting the roles of these two top officials and specifically highlighted non-executives' independent monitoring role in the board.[54] The related Tyson Report issued in the same year also focused on the non-executive function by highlighting non-executives' recruitment and development.[55] Moreover, in the wake of the global financial crisis, the later Walker Review (2009) spotlighted non-executives' performance and behaviours in the banking sector with 39 recommendations.[56] Regarding non-executives' functions, the Review provided insights into their career development, the time commitment to the board, their competences to challenge executives.

However, the continuous reforms of corporate governance codes and the accompanying regulatory documents, and the substantial body of academic research on boardroom checks and balances,[57] seemed not to work in keeping an effective board function in the UK's corporate governance system. Instead, what we have seen from Carillion's analysis is that the executives and non-executives in the board together still created a "black box" lacking sufficient checks and balances. Solomon's research seems to give a response to this unstopped "collapse-reform" circulation. In corporate governance reforms, the government has consistently aimed to maintain a voluntary approach regarding non-executive directors, steering clear of regulation or legislation.[58] That was why when the Higgs Report gave some radical recommendations

---

the Limitations of Agency Theory' (2015) 68 *Current Legal Problems* 431; John Parkinson, 'Evolution and Policy in Company Law: The Non-Executive Director' (2000) The Political Economy of the Company (Oxford: Hart Publishing); Wolf-Georg Ringe, "Independent Directors: After the Crisis." (2013) 14 (3) *European Business Organization Law Review* 401–424.

[53] *Report of the Committee on the Financial Aspects of Corporate Governance—Cadbury Report* (Gee and Co. Ltd., London, 1992) paragraph 4.9.

[54] *Review of the Role and Effectiveness of Non-Executive Directors (Higgs Report)*, Department of Trade and Industry London January 2003.

[55] *The Tyson Report on the Recruitment and Development of Non-Executive Directors (Tyson Report)*, London Business School June 2003.

[56] *A Review of Corporate Governance in the UK Banks and other Financial Industry Entities (Walker Review)*, The Walker Review Secretariat, London 26 November 2009.

[57] For example, Anup Agrawal and Charles R Knoeber, 'Firm Performance and Mechanisms to Control Agency Problems between Managers and Shareholders' (1996) 31 *Journal of Financial and Quantitative Analysis* 377; Eugene F Fama, 'Agency Problems and the Theory of the Firm' (1980) 88 *Journal of Political Economy* 288; Eugene F Fama and Michael C Jensen, 'Separation of Ownership and Control' (1983) 26 *Journal of Law and Economics* 301; Randall Morck, Andrei Shleifer and Robert W Vishny, 'Management Ownership and Market Valuation: An Empirical Analysis' (1988) 20 *Journal of Financial Economics* 293.

[58] Solomon (n 51) 66.

of reform on linking the non-executives and the institutional shareholders which aimed to create a stronger and influencer monitoring instrument,[59] the report received drastic opposite reactions from the business community and companies' directors in the top 39 listed companies with the reason that the greater accountability would be adverse to corporate operations.[60] As Solomon commented on these responses, the Higgs report proposed changes that went beyond the existing, implicit framework of UK corporate governance. Typically, policy recommendations that challenge the status quo face resistance, as they aim to alter people's established attitudes.[61] In other words, the Higgs Report sought to leap away from the voluntary nature of the corporate environment and focused more on monitoring roles of the non-executives and the combing strength of both non-executives and institutional shareholders in checks and balances. These policy changes could be regarded as an underlying reform of the existing corporate contractual based corporate governance system, but this radical reform seemed to touch the interests of someone. The Higgs Report and the later reforms of codes of practice themselves indeed gave valuable suggestions on preventing future collapses regarding certain boardroom problems that had been revealed in corporate running. However, these previous soft corporate governance codes reforms were inadequate in terms of enforcement, and essentially they all failed to change the status quo of the voluntary or "comply or explain" environment of corporate governance.

This book argues that the reforms of corporate governance from Cadbury Report in 1992 to the latest corporate governance code in 2018 to a large extent had provided quick, direct and pragmatic recommendations in terms of the corporate or financial problems, but these codes lacked power and have struggled to change the fundamental logic of the corporate contractual based corporate operations. Under a corporate contractual paradigm, some radical recommendations to enhance non-executives' monitoring competence in soft and non-binding codes are essentially unlikely to be achieved. Instead, the whole corporate governance system will only sustain a loose environment for non-executives' functions, avoiding hard law and regulations. These arguments are not only applicable to the boardroom issues, but can also be applied in the context of other separate functions (auditing, shareholder) and the overall corporate governance system of a company in realising checks and balances.

The continuous corporate scandals of the companies, British Home Stores and Carillion, provide strong empirical evidence to illustrate the previous reforms' failure to establish a balanced board. In this sense, it justifies the necessity of finding a different approach that could trigger underlying reforms of the corporate governance system and could tolerate and encourage radical recommendations or even challenges to the problematic corporate operations. The approach advocated by this book is a corporate constitutional path which takes accountability, deliberation, contestability as the key values of corporate governance. Compared to the existing

---

[59] Higgs Report (n 54) Para. 15.5.

[60] Solomon (n 51) 69. For a survey, see also Alistair Alcock, 'Higgs—the Wrong Answer?' (2003) 24 *The Company Lawyer* 161.

[61] Solomon (n 51) 68.

economics-oriented, efficiency- and profit- pursued corporate contractual paradigm of UK's corporate governance system, corporate constitutionalism emphasises more the checks and balances, full discussions and challenges in this system. Thus, this book perceives that if corporate constitutionalism had been applied to Carillion, first, this constitutional paradigm has a high tolerance for the radical suggestions on enhancing non-executives' and institutional shareholders' monitoring role from Higgs report and other codes. These fundamental and holistic recommendations could be given further consideration. Second, within the existing hard law tracks of corporate governance, directors' duties, for both the executives and the non-executives, are generally formulated in Sections 171 and 177 in Companies Act 2006. As a result, the duties and responsibilities owed by executives and non-executives are presented as the same in the company law with no differences. However, these two kinds of directors are, in practice, significantly different in their knowledge, information, experiences, positions, and functions within the company. This book thus calls for a hard-law level reform to separate these two kinds of directors' duties, specifically ensuring non-executives' monitoring, check-and-balance, and corporate safety-control roles in the boardroom.

In a nutshell, this section looks at the previous corporate governance reforms on non-executive directors. It finds that there were many valuable recommendations in realising checks and balances inside of the boardroom. However, some radical changes for reinforcing accountability and challenges in the boardroom were viewed as being divisive and destructive to corporate operations and were rejected by the business communities and top listed companies' officials who advocated an economic-based corporate contractual framework in corporate governance. The wave of corporate collapses nevertheless revealed the flaws of the existing framework and justifies the corporate constitutional-based underlying reform of the corporate governance system which calls for hard-law level changes to the non-executives' monitoring function.

8.4 Auditors and the Checks and Balances

Audit is a bridge that connects the internal and external dimensions of a company's corporate governance. In Carillion, the internal audit function, including the audit committee and the internal auditors, focused on monitoring the effectiveness of the company's internal processes and controls; while the external auditors of KPMG were responsible for giving independent examination of the accuracy of Carillion's business accounts. They are also the gatekeeper of the company to ensure the independent non-executives and shareholders get transparent and accurate information.

In Chapter 6, this book has illustrated the incompetence of Carillion's auditing functions that contribute to the company's deficiencies of checks and balances. It is acknowledged that Carillion's audit committee, as part of the element of internal control, seemed hardly to challenge the management. "Employed, appointed and remunerated" by the management team itself,[62] an audit committee's primary duty is to sustain the existence of the company, rather than challenging. In Carillion, if the audit committee found financial problems, they would prefer to cover them up to avoid a negative impact on the stock market. Another important component for internal control, Deloitte as Carillion's internal auditor and advisor,[63] was either failed to adequately alert the board to the risks tied to their business activities, chose not to raise those concerns, or was overly dismissive of them.[64] In a word, the checks and balances of all these internal audit mechanisms which should have worked, failed completely. Even worse, when Carillion's directors used various techniques to dupe the market, it is unconvincing to say that these internal auditors did not acquiesce with or collude with the directors' accounting tricks. Moreover, Carillion's collapse also drew acute attention to the dysfunctionality of the external auditor, KPMG. The Second Joint Report observed that during its nineteen-year incumbency, KPMG failed to "exercise—and voice—professional scepticism towards Carillion's aggressive accounting judgements"—it was complicit in Carillion's irresponsible management.[65] Without sufficient scrutiny and challenges to directors' financial decisions, even as Carillion's debts piled up, the directors still took risks to acquire companies and bid for works in uncertain markets.

In KPMG's 19-year-long position in Carillion, the external auditor had already been a part of the benefits community or "pet rubber-stampers" to borrow the government's words,[66] which means that KPMG lost its most important feature as auditor—independence. According to the report of the FRC, published in 2018, not only KPMG, but across the "big four", their audit quality resulted in decline, including a failure to challenge and give appropriate scepticism to management. KPMG especially, had "an unacceptable deterioration in quality".[67] After Carillion's downfall, KPMG has found it hard to extricate himself from the shadow of Carillion's demise. In 2020, the case of *Carillion Plc v KPMG LLP & Anor* referred to Carillion's application for pre-action disclosure regarding the context of Carillion's and its subsidiaries' financial reporting in relation to which Carillion attempted to allege

---

[62] Krish Bhaskar, John Flower and Rod Sellers, *Financial Failures and Scandals: From Enron to Carillion* (Routledge 2019) 84.

[63] Deloitte was the advisor to the project of Eaga in 2011 which was a high-risk and high-debt takeover programme. See from 'Letter-from-Deloitte-Chairman-to-the-Chairs-Relating-to-Carillion-2-February-2018.Pdf', https://www.parliament.uk/globalassets/documents/commons-committees/work-and-pensions/Correspondence/Letter-from-Deloitte-Chairman-to-the-Chairs-relating-to-Carillion-2-February-2018.pdf, accessed 25 March 2024.

[64] House of Commons Business, Energy and Industrial Strategy and Work and Pensions Committees, *Carillion*, Second Joint Report (n 3) 34.

[65] Ibid., 53.

[66] 'Carillion Board Minutes Reveal Last CFO Blew Whistle on Accounting Irregularities—Committees—UK Parliament', https://committees.parliament.uk/committee/164/work-and-pensions-committee/news/97763/carillion-board-minutes-reveal-last-cfo-blew-whistle-on-accounting-irregularities/, accessed 19 March 2024.

[67] Financial Reporting Council, Big Four Audit Quality Review Results Decline, https://www.frc.org.uk/news/june-2018/big-four-audit-quality-review-results-decline, accessed 17 March 2024.

KPMG's auditing negligence.[68] The court however dismissed Carillion's application. At the end of 2021, KPMG has also been involved in a tribunal hearing which was commenced to determine the FRC's allegations against KPMG and its six former auditors. In this tribunal, Jon Holt, UK KPMG's CEO, admitted that misconduct over the audit had occurred.[69] On 12th May 2022, the tribunal ended with a settlement which confirmed a £14.4 m fine to KPMG—"one of the largest fines in UK audit history".[70]

The auditing deterioration in Carillion seemed to tell the same story as the earlier corporate scandals of Enron and it auditor, Arthur Andersen, in 2001.[71] In both stories, we can see the same kind of failures of the auditors—these gatekeepers lacked independence. As Coffee concluded: the "watchdogs" turned out to be "pets" of the management. A notable feature of today's gatekeeping markets is that those responsible for oversight—such as lawyers, investment bankers, and consultants—are usually appointed and paid by the very corporate executives they are meant to oversee, rather than by the investors whose interests they ostensibly protect. This structural arrangement inherently risks compromising their independence, as the advice and judgments they provide may lean toward favouring management. When overseers are chosen and compensated by those they must scrutinise, they are more likely to become compliant allies than effective monitors.[72]

In this book's understanding, Coffee's analysis revealed a truth that all the auditors, no matter the internal or external ones, are in contractual relationships with the corporate managers. In other words, rather than viewing themselves as purely independent "watchdogs", auditors actually are in close contractual "client-ship" with the management team—the people who hire them and pay for them. Under a contractual relationship, it is more about getting in line with the directors and managers to make profits and let the corporate accounts look healthy in appearance.

With regard to the systematic failure of the audit market, the government issued a White Paper in 2021 which provided a list of concrete reform proposals aiming to rebuild public confidence in audit and corporate governance.[73] In this comprehensive report, the Secretary of State for Business, Energy and Industrial Strategy highlights the cornerstone of reform as the establishment of an independent audit

[68] *Carillion Plc v KPMG LLP & Anor* [2020] EWHC 1416 (Comm).

[69] Jasper Jolly, 'KPMG Says Accounting Regulator "Was Misled" over Carillion Audits' *The Guardian* (10 January 2022), https://www.theguardian.com/business/2022/jan/10/kpmg-says-accounting-regulator-was-misled-over-carillion-audits, accessed 25 March 2024.

[70] Kalyeena Makortoff and Kalyeena Makortoff Banking correspondent, 'KPMG to Be Fined £14 m for Forging Documents over Carillion Audit' *The Guardian* (12 May 2022), https://www.theguardian.com/business/2022/may/12/kpmg-fined-frc-audit-carillion, accessed 18 May 2024.

[71] 'The Collapse of Enron and the Dark Side of Business' *BBC News* (3 August 2021), https://www.bbc.com/news/business-58026162, accessed 28 May 2024.

[72] John Coffee, *Gatekeepers: The Professions and Corporate Governance* (Oxford University Press, Incorporated 2006) 335.

[73] Great Britain and Energy & Industrial Strategy Department for Business, (2021) *Restoring Trust in Audit and Corporate Governance: Consultation on the Government's Proposals* (*White Paper*), March 2021.

profession. This new profession would be guided by shared principles and a defined commitment to serving the public interest, extending its oversight beyond traditional financial statements to encompass broader aspects of corporate reporting. Additionally, the Government outlines new regulatory initiatives aimed at boosting competition and mitigating conflicts of interest. These include expanding opportunities for smaller audit firms and introducing mandatory separation between audit and non-audit functions within audit firms.[74] The government reform emphasises the auditors' public-oriented approach, aims to realise a power separation of the big four's audit functions, focuses on sustainability of large companies, and encourages competition or challenges to the dominant audit firms.[75] This recent reform indicates that the government is trying to make radical changes in audit and corporate governance system.

However, this book questions to what extent this reform could realise real checks and balances in auditing functions if it is still based on a corporate contractual fundamentalism. The corporate failures from the US Enron to the UK Carillion, and the auditing scandals from Arthur Andersen to KPMG actually warn us that the problem of lack of independence of auditors has been a long-term matter in corporate governance. The correspondent corporate governance reforms in auditing, from the Cadbury Report which suggested the creation of audit committees to the Smith Report which concerned the relationships between the external auditors, the companies and the audit committee,[76] to the White Paper issued in 2021 seemed never to prevent the problems of auditors. Why? From this book' standpoint, the contractual approach appears to lead to a client relationship in which the auditors, working with the directors and managers, see them and the company as clients and this encourages them to get too close. That is why there have over time been numerous suggestions for devices such as "Chinese Walls" to ensure separation of services within audit firms but this still has not worked.[77] Possibly, the contractual approach leads to a limited way of working and shapes the relationship building in particular ways.

However, if we think about the auditors' role in the corporate constitutional paradigm, they are important in legitimating corporate power and setting the basis for challenging and further investigation.[78] In Carillion, auditors are intermediaries

---

[74] Ibid., 17.

[75] 'Business Secretary Launches Major Overhaul of UK's Audit Regime in Wake of Big-Name Company Collapses' (*GOV.UK*), https://www.gov.uk/government/news/business-secretary-launches-major-overhaul-of-uks-audit-regime-in-wake-of-big-name-company-collapses, accessed 10 May 2024.

[76] *Report of the Committee on the Financial Aspects of Corporate Governance—Cadbury Report* (Gee and Co. Ltd., London, 1992).

See also *Audit Committees: A Report and Proposed Guidance (Smith Report)*, Financial Reporting Council, London UK January 2003. See also White Paper (n 73).

[77] For a survey of "Chinese Walls" in auditing, see 'UK Audit Giants Told to Build "Chinese Wall" after Collapses' (*independent*), https://www.independent.ie/business/world/uk-audit-giants-told-to-build-chinese-wall-after-collapses-39346427.html, accessed 30 May 2024. See also, Harry McVea, *Financial Conglomerates and the Chinese wall: Regulating Conflicts of Interest* (Clarendon Press, 1993).

[78] Bottomley (n 1) 100.

between the managers and the shareholders to ensure that the information passed to the shareholders is accurate and their proposed independence is supposed to help them to remain objective about their judgements of the information presented. They are also a support for the shareholders to be able to exercise their votes in an informed way. Thinking from the perspective of accountability, deliberation, and accountability, the auditors' role is to ease the path for the shareholders who seek to hold directors to account, to participate into the discussions around corporate operation, or to give challenge if shareholders feel they themselves or the common good are being affected.

Thus, this book argues for a corporate constitutional approach in Carillion's audit functions. This is a fundamental and an overall environmental change. A corporate constitutional relationship is about holding the directors to account which is distinct from the voluntary contractual approach in the existing corporate governance system. If we apply this checks-and-balances focused corporate constitutional framework to Carillion's case, the auditors would be required to adopt a monitoring role rather than help their clients simply to have big profits. The difference therefore is changing from a client type relationship to more of a checking relationship to make sure the directors follow processes correctly and honestly—less friendly to clients, more checking and scrutiny of the supervisee. In this regard, we can ensure more objectivity and independence in each of the auditors' services provided. Auditors should be clear about their assistant functions to shareholders to help them get information, so that they need to challenge and deliberate, thus corresponding to the accountability-deliberation-contestability approach. In accordance with the principle of accountability, auditors can ask questions of the managers when examining the reports and, if not satisfied with the answers, they alert the shareholders with a qualified report; by deliberation, they can present the report and explain to the shareholders in AGM what the reports are telling them and they can suggest questions for the shareholders to ask; while for contestability, they could assist the shareholders if not satisfied and help them form challenges. It is thus hoped to see in a Carillion-like context that the constitutional approach would more easily enable the auditors to fulfil the harder gatekeeping and watchdog role.

8.5 Whistleblowers and the Checks and Balances

Whistleblowers are a special group of people being specifically highlighted by Bottomley. They are important in the corporate constitutional framework because whistleblowers have the potential to discover and reveal some instances or patterns of "illegal, improper or illegitimate behaviour" to be brought to light and coped with.[79] In other words, they are part of a crucial element of the checks and balances

[79] Ibid., 107.

mechanism to guard the company's openness and transparency. Thus, under corporate constitutional way of thinking, "we should encourage whistleblowing".[80]

Carillion's unravelling also sparked critical reviews of whistleblowers. Emma Mercer, Carillion's last finance director, identified as a "senior whistleblower" by the government, struggled to call for attention to Carillion's financial irregularities.[81] She took only six weeks after taking up her position to uncover the company's fatal financial problems and immediately to trigger contract reviews. But her alarm did not attract serious concerns from the board—the board refused to accept an independent accounting review, and the contract reviews were proceeded on the basis of the "internal review, the KPMG review and the sub-committee of the Board chaired by Andrew Dougal".[82] In the words of Frank Field, the chairman of the Work and Pensions Select Committee, Carillion's board could only "get KPMG, their pet rubber-stampers, to mark their own homework".[83] In this instance, even Emma Mercer was situated at a top position of the company, but she was still hardly able to trigger sufficient actions of the board. In Carillion, the board, together with the internal and external auditors, were bounded tightly within a beneficial community. Through this shared-interest community, their powers were accumulated together which led to the result that in appearance they were functioning separately and running legally, but in reality, they easily exploited the corporate interests to protect their own interests. They had built a firewall that kept out different voices, even the voice of the person who found a problem and was situated at the top. That could also explain why a whistleblowing action was taken only at the very last stage, even though some employees had already identified Carillion's financial problems as discussed in the former chapters.

From this book' viewpoint, although the whistleblowing procedure is limited in solving Carillion's problem, it remains a valuable complementary mechanism designed to motivate individuals with knowledge of issues—particularly those aware that such problems are unlikely to be identified or addressed through standard procedures—to come forward and raise their concerns.[84] It is a "safety net" which can be raised when other forms of accountability fail. Regarding who can be whistleblowers, corporate constitutionalism accepts a wide definition—they can be both insiders (*eg*. employees, corporate officials) or outsiders (*eg*. professional advisers, consultants, related companies) of the company.[85] Individuals may initiate whistleblowing procedures at any point—whether the issue occurred in the past, is currently taking place, or is anticipated to happen in the near future, according to the UK

---

[80] Ibid.

[81] Simon Goodley, 'Whistleblower Warned Carillion Bosses about Irregularities, MPs Told' *The Guardian* (27 February 2018), https://www.theguardian.com/business/2018/feb/27/carillion-whistleblower-emma-mercer-warned-bosses-about-irregularities-mps-told, accessed 18 March 2024.

[82] 'Carillion Last Finance Chief Blew Whistle on Sloppy Accounting' (*Construction Enquirer*), https://www.constructionenquirer.com/2018/02/27/carillion-last-finance-chief-blew-whistle-on-sloppy-accounting/, accessed 18 March 2024.

[83] Ibid.

[84] Bottomley (n 1) 107.

[85] Ibid., 108.

government's online guidance.[86] In addition to the lax standards on who can raise whistleblowing and on what grounds they can trigger such action, Carillion itself should have established a whistleblowing system to deal with corporate constituents' complaints, questions or challenges on issues of internal corporate control, especially matters about accounting and auditing.

8.6 Summary and the Establishment of a Power Web of Internal Control

This section has provided imaginative assumptions on applying corporate constitutionalism to the shareholders, directors, auditors and whistleblowers of Carillion according to the principles of accountability, deliberation and contestation. Separately considering these various roles is not intended to fragment or compartmentalise expertise and authority. Rather, it serves to highlight the character and function of the interactions among these distinct spheres, or to articulate a networked framework of power separation.[87] We are usually accustomed to discussing their roles as independent and divided parties, but in constitutional language, all those corporate actors should also interact and interplay collectively and they have the strength to keep a power balance or to restrict one group from possessing too much power in a corporation. In the corporate constitutional framework, realising a power balance cannot place too much reliance on just one group of constituents. The above analysis has revealed the same point that only one site will lack capacity to prevent Carillion's problems. For example, while the preceding discussion has critically examined the significance of shareholder—particularly institutional shareholder—engagement, it is important not to idealise them as purely altruistic financial actors.[88] Thus, this book argues that to detect, deter and correct Carillion's problems before it is too late would need all corporate actors to play their part.

But how could this power web be created in Carillion? In Chapter 7, this book depicted a general image of this network of separations of powers—each site's power-conducting process is not totally independent or autonomous, but allows partial participation and scrutiny of other sites. When a particular institutional actor exercises its authority, other actors should be granted access to transparent information and afforded opportunities for adequate oversight; conversely, when an actor assumes an external supervisory role, it must possess adequate independence and autonomy to ensure that no single site exerts undue influence over others or shirks its own responsibilities.[89] This power web should also avoid two or more sites from being

[86] 'Whistleblowing for Employees' (*GOV.UK*), https://www.gov.uk/whistleblowing, accessed 20 March 2024.

[87] Bottomley (n 1) 94.

[88] John Coffee, 'Liquidity versus Control: The Institutional Investor as Corporate Monitor' (1991) 91 *Colum. L. Rev.* 1277, 1334.

[89] Bottomley (n 1) 93.

connected tightly, like the directors and the auditors in Carillion. If these ideas could be embedded into Carillion's internal corporate control, there would be a holistic corporate constitutional approach to drive meaningful and lasting reforms.

For this book, real communication and connection among these different roles are the preconditions of establishing a power web, although they may have conflicting interests. But thinking from another perspective, it is the conflicts among various parties that contribute to a checks-and-balances network. Every party pursues their own interests, and corporate constitutionalism seeks to find a balanced point among these distinct directions of strength. Thus, there should be a mechanism (online and offline) established by representatives of shareholders (excluding the dual-identity shareholders), directors, auditors, and workers. This mechanism is a stage for different interest groups to communicate, deliberate and contest. Especially, directors and auditors should honestly respond to other sites' questions, unless the content refers to business confidential information. Through sufficient interplays, no matter whether arguing critically or mutually supporting, the monopoly of one group would in a way be broken up.

But we should also be clear that there is a great disparity of strength among these distinct groups, such as the directors and workers. Amid the wave of corporate scandals, workers or corporate employees are always presented as the ultimate victims; while the directors or corporate officials who led to the problems of companies could still escape from punishment and even get decent yields. To keep balance in the power web of internal control, numerous corporate failures have told us that we need to bring external regulatory power into corporate internal governance. On the one side, public power should give more protections to workers, small contractors and others who are always at a significant disadvantage and oppressed by elite corporate officials; on the other side, managerial power should be limited and restricted within the regulatory boundary.

8.7 The Reform of the External Regulatory Framework

In the corporate constitutional framework, the external regulatory framework is not insulated from the internal corporate control, rather, it is an important element of strength to keep managerial power legitimized and balanced.

Carillion's failure, however, reveals the implicit connections between the government, conservative politicians and Carillion's directors—they were "clients" or "customers" to each other. It is reported that Theresa May and her Conservative Party accepted a £50,000 donation from the hedge fund Naya Capital Management UK which betted on Carillion's downfall.[90] When the leader of the Labour Party Jeremy Corbyn asked Theresa May why the government did not take control over Carillion's

[90] 'Conservatives Took £50,000 from Firm That Bet against Carillion' (*inews.co.uk*, 18 January 2018), https://inews.co.uk/news/politics/conservatives-took-50000-donation-firm-bet-carillion-118377, accessed 27 March 2024.

disorder sooner, the response was that the government was a "customer" of Carillion, not the "manager" of Carillion.[91] The result was that the government behaved more like a bystander rather than a regulator or saver of Carillion's failure. The government, the elite politicians and Carillion's top managers together siphoned off value for their own private interests without consideration for the public good. Equally, Carillion was also one of the top 100 party donors of the conservative party.[92] It is reported that in 2015, one of Carillion's board members, Philip Green, was one of the business leaders who signed an open letter that urged voters to support the Conservatives. It means that to some extent Carillion could be regarded as a customer to the government because the Conservative Party relied on its donations and its business impact. In this regard, the government would not be harsh to them, instead delivering a light-touch regulatory framework which ensured the company had nothing to fear from the regulations.

Following a free market fundamentalism, the law, the regulations and other external interventions on companies are not the preferred choices of corporate contractualism.[93] The UK company law and corporate governance system, thus, to a large extent, has established a "flexible and pragmatic, and relatively non-interventionist" framework serving businesses' and the shareholders' interests.[94] Nevertheless, in the wake of numerous corporate scandals in the UK, including but not limited to BHS,[95] Tesco,[96] and Carillion, it is time for reflection or critical thinking around the privatisation process of public services and contractualism-founded corporate arrangement. Following a corporate constitutional approach, there should exist a balance between public values and private ordering—individuals' private interests should be respected but this should not incur the sacrifice of the common good. Moreover, the state or the external regulatory framework should and could protect the common good. As Horn contends, the state is deeply involved in shaping the legal and political foundations necessary for the emergence and evolution of corporate governance. Instead of simply acting as an external force that intervenes

---

[91] Heather Stewart and Anushka Asthana, 'Corbyn on Carillion: We'll End Outsourcing "racket" in Rule Change' *The Guardian* (18 January 2018), https://www.theguardian.com/politics/2018/jan/18/corbyn-on-carillion-well-end-outsourcing-racket-in-rule-change, accessed 27 March 2024.

[92] 'The Tory 100: Captains of Industry, Party Donors (and a Few Tax Avoiders)' (*the Guardian*), http://www.theguardian.com/politics/ng-interactive/2015/apr/01/tory-100-industry-captains-party-donors-tax-avoiders, accessed 16 May 2024.

[93] Marc Moore, 'The De-Privatisation of Anglo–American Corporate Law?', *Routledge Handbook of Corporate Law* (Routledge 2016) 47.

[94] Boeger, Russell, and Villiers (n 11) 20.

[95] House of Commons Work and Pensions and Business, Innovation and Skills Committees, *BHS*, First Report of the Work and Pensions Committee and Fourth Report of the Business, Innovation and Skills Committee of Session 2016–2017, https://publications.parliament.uk/pa/cm201617/cmselect/cmworpen/54/54.pdf, accessed 27 May 2024.

[96] In September 2014, the Tesco's profits were discovered to be overstated by approximately £250 million, later revised to £326 million. See from Sean Farrell, 'Tesco Suspends Senior Staff and Starts Investigation into Overstated Profits' *The Guardian* (22 September 2014), https://www.theguardian.com/business/2014/sep/22/tesco-investigators-overstating-profit-250m, accessed 29 May 2024.

in corporate affairs, legal rules and regulatory frameworks are fundamentally constitutive elements in the formation and functioning of modern corporations.[97] In this sense, the external regulatory framework in corporate constitutional understandings is not employed to enhance company efficiency, but rather serves as a fundamentally political manifestation of underlying capitalist principles.[98] In other words, like corporations, corporate governance regulations are also essentially political in nature.

As such, the direction of the fundamental change of the external regulatory framework that is recommended by this book is simple—"let the managerial power be legitimated", or let the law guide the companies to explain, control, and democratise managerial power. This book advocates a regulatory initiative approach to enhance supervision on corporate officials' behaviours and protections for workers and other disadvantaged stakeholders. The current corporate contractualised system of company law and corporate governance system, from this book' viewpoint, has failed in legitimizing and balancing corporate power, thus we need to bring a new corporate constitutional system that hardens up the regulatory boundary, making clear the sanctions and facilitating enforcement measures and infrastructures.

8.8 Conclusion

Drawing on the key ideas of corporate constitutionalism, this chapter has made some radical hypothetical assumptions on the changes to be made to Carillion's holistic corporate governance system, including the internal corporate control and the external regulatory framework. Internally, the accountability-deliberation-contestability mechanism sets the underlying rules of internal structure. Based on this trinity mechanism, it is required that corporate managerial power needs to be checked by shareholders' power and scrutinised by various corporate participants at different levels—individually, in groups or as a whole. In the existing scholarly literature in corporate governance, we seem always to focus on the onefold and separate roles of directors, shareholders, auditors and others, but we rarely look at them as a whole and investigate their interplays. This chapter, however, attempts to evaluate both the separated and aggregated roles of shareholders, directors, auditors, and whistleblowers in Carillion. If we see them as various separate groups, in terms of shareholders, this book argues for a responsible shareholder engagement approach. This is also a shareholder-primacy model, but unlike shareholders in corporate contractualism who gradually have lost their "owners" identity in the corporation, shareholders within corporate constitutional framework are regarded as "members" who ought to take their membership responsibilities seriously in running Carillion. They are thus expected to give warnings and collective pressures to directors when they identify

[97] Laura Horn, 'Corporate Governance in Crisis? The Politics of EU Corporate Governance Regulation' (2012) 18 *European Law Journal* 83, 84.

[98] Ibid.

Carillion's financial problems. Moreover, in the boardroom, an accountability mechanism requires a separation of corporate power in both the hierarchical monitoring, for example between the directors and the sub-committees, and the overlapping functions, for example between the chairman of the board and the CEO and between the executives and non-executives. In Carillion's case, the non-executives could not escape blame in Carillion's ineffective monitoring. Non-executives seem to be in a paradoxical situation—on the one side they should scrutinise executives' behaviours, on the other side they rely on the information provided by executives. However, under a corporate constitutional arrangement, the possession of corporate running information is not a monopolistic privilege of executives, rather with a deliberation mechanism encouraging fully open and genuine deliberations of different corporate actors, that information could be more transparent, reliable and flowing. Auditors, in their separate watchdog role, are also responsible for ensuring an unobstructed and trusted information transition. In opposition to regarding the corporation as their clients within a corporate contractual paradigm, auditors in a corporate constitutional model should adopt a more checks and balances role to monitor the boardroom. Additionally, corporate constitutionalism also holds a place for whistleblowers. Whistleblowing activities may trigger the conflicts between different values—loyalty *vs* openness. Loyalty is more important in corporate contractualism; but constitutionalism is different. Carillion's case tells us, if someone could have triggered the alarm early, Carillion might have been saved from imminent danger. What this book is willing to create in Carillion is an open and transparent environment that gives more space for those people who want to tell the truth.

These different corporate actors also have an aggregated role. The thread that connects those different characters are the power relations—more or less, people in Carillion are affected by the three dimensions of power, directly, indirectly and culturally. This book perceives shareholders, auditors, whistleblowers and the workers as together having collective strength to provide checks and balances against the strong corporate managerial power possessed by Carillion's top officials. In Carillion, their interests are not limited to personal benefits, and they also involve the common good. In this book' view, such common good from an internal corporate governance dimension means the sustainability of Carillion—only in a long-term, healthy running of Carillion, can those corporate constituents' overall interests be safeguarded. These corporate actors interact in a web of power and they all accept scrutiny functions of internal control.

For the external dimension of corporate governance, the regulatory scheme of the company law, the soft codes, state and government regulations are also an important element of checks and balances. The justification for state interference in corporate affairs could be one of the most obvious changes brought by corporate constitutionalism compared to corporate contractualism. Under the latter framework, government and Carillion were more like contractual parties—government was the customer of Carillion in PPP projects; vice versa, Carillion was also a client to the government after donating a large amount of money to the Conservative Party. With such contractual relationships, the external regulatory framework would only deliver light-touch rules to Carillion, even though the government was clear about the company being in crisis. However, in the corporate constitutional framework, this book argues for a decentralised status for the state in the corporate governance system which means that the public power is entitled to intervene in Carillion's running if they detect there is something going wrong, and in the meantime, the public power should respect private orderings of the company, rather than being dominant in business conducts.

In short, this study of Carillion has revealed that the central issue centres on checks and balances, either internally or externally, separately or collectively, in power relations that can be characterised by interplays, conflicts, monitors, control, or regulation. The corporate constitutionalist framework offers a solution by highlighting the collective and collaborative roles of different interest groups within the corporation. However, this book finds that corporate constitutionalism, whilst pursuing a collective checks and balances system to protect the common good, is limited in its focus on a selected set of interest groups or stakeholders. A major drawback is that workers seem to be missing from the interest groups recognised by corporate constitutionalism. This paradigm seems to give less consideration to workers compared to other corporate actors. On the other hand, if a company can follow the principles of accountability, deliberation and contestability, workers may therefore be sufficiently considered, albeit indirectly, through that triple mechanism—workers that constitute an important element of a company may still merit attention, both independently and within the web of corporate power. The following Chapter 9 will provide a more detailed critique on the application of corporate constitutionalism to Carillion and will try to answer the main question of the book: whether corporate constitutionalism presents a viable framework for addressing governance failures?

Chapter 9
Critique and Conclusion

9.1 Introduction

This book has examined the relationship between corporate collapse and corporate governance, using Carillion's demise as a case study. It proposes a thought experiment that explores the possibilities and results of applying the under-researched corporate constitutionalism theory to a publicly held company, Carillion which collapsed in 2018. The central contention is that corporate contractualism and corporate constitutionalism are grounded in fundamentally different theoretical premises, which lead to divergent normative choices in regulating corporate affairs. When applied to real-world companies, these frameworks result in markedly different corporate operations and conceptualisations of the corporation's role in society.

The argument advanced is that within the economically oriented paradigm of corporate contractualism, it is inherently difficult to establish a system of corporate governance that ensures checks and balances and legitimises the exercise of corporate power. The persistent failure of this model to prevent corporate misconduct and collapse lends support to the search for an alternative evaluative framework—one that this book contends may be found in corporate constitutionalism.

To address the core research question—"whether corporate constitutionalism presents a viable framework for addressing governance failures"—the book is structured around a series of subsidiary questions, each addressed in a separate chapter to develop a coherent analytical thread. Following the introduction of the research background and structure in Chapter 1, Chapters 2 to 4 trace the theoretical transition from corporate contractualism to corporate constitutionalism. These chapters respond to key sub-questions: "What is the prevailing theoretical foundation underpinning public companies such as Carillion? What is corporate constitutionalism? What are the differences and similarities between corporate contractualism and corporate constitutionalism?"

Y. Yang, *Corporate Collapse and Corporate Governance*, CSR, Sustainability, Ethics & Governance, https://doi.org/10.1007/978-981-96-9666-6_9

Chapter 2 situates corporate governance within a public value-oriented context, emphasising power, legitimacy, and checks and balances as core evaluative parameters. It argues that the contractarian model fails to legitimise corporate power and ultimately contributes to the dysfunction and collapse of firms like Carillion. Chapter 3, drawing on values embedded in public law and political theory, examines how corporate constitutionalism might support a governance ecosystem rooted in balance, accountability, and legitimacy. It also explores the potential structural features of UK company law and corporate governance under this alternative paradigm. Chapter 4 offers a comparative analysis of the two frameworks, identifying their distinctive logics: whereas corporate contractualism promotes an economically rational, efficiency-driven, and relatively non-interventionist approach, corporate constitutionalism foregrounds accountability, legitimacy, discursive engagement, and a decentralised regulatory role for the state.

Part III, comprising Chapters 5 and 6, presents a detailed empirical investigation into the causes of Carillion's failure, analysing both its internal governance deficiencies and the weaknesses of its external oversight structures.

In Part IV, Chapters 7 and 8 explore the hypothetical application of corporate constitutionalism to the Carillion case. These chapters seek to answer two related questions: "Would a corporate constitutionalist approach to governance have avoided the mistakes that led to Carillion's collapse? And how might corporate governance be reformed in light of the constitutionalist framework?" Chapter 7 integrates empirical findings with constitutionalist theory to evaluate Carillion's governance. Chapter 8 develops a normative hypothetical model of internal and external governance, assessing the respective roles of key corporate actors shareholders, directors (particularly non-executives), auditors, and whistleblowers—in maintaining a system of checks and balances. On the whole, the assessment of a constitutionalist approach is cautiously optimistic.

Nevertheless, corporate constitutionalism is not without its limitations. As foreshadowed in Chapter 1, Carillion also serves as a lens through which to critically examine whether the corporate constitutionalist framework can yield legally practical and enforceable outcomes in the real corporate world. This concluding chapter thus presents a critique of corporate constitutionalism, identifying unresolved tensions and areas of insufficient development. In particular, the application of the model reveals a notable shortcoming: despite Bottomley's emphasis on corporate constituents, the role of stakeholders—especially workers—receives limited attention within his shareholder-primacy-influenced formulation of corporate constitutionalism.

Accordingly, this chapter proceeds in two parts. The first offers a critical evaluation of corporate constitutionalism, focusing on the position and treatment of workers within the framework. The second synthesises the key arguments and findings of the book to offer a final answer to the overarching research question: "whether corporate constitutionalism presents a viable framework for addressing governance failures" This section also reflects on the limitations of the present research and outlines potential directions for future inquiry aimed at strengthening the corporate constitutionalist approach.

9.2 Critique of Corporate Constitutionalism—How Should the Workers Fit in?

Corporate constitutionalism, by its nature, still upholds the principles of shareholder primacy. Shareholders remain at the core of corporate governance, and their interests continue to be a central consideration. However, this framework offers a more expansive conception of the shareholder's role, recognising that with significant power comes corresponding responsibility. Under this model, shareholders are seen not merely as investors fixated on economic returns but as members of a corporate community with an obligation to engage in governance.

As Bottomley explains, by focusing more on shareholders' roles as members of a corporation, rather than merely as investors, and by encouraging and valuing their input through deliberative processes, it becomes possible to use shareholders of all types as a means to incorporate the concerns and interests of corporate employees, tort victims, consumers, and other stakeholders into corporate decision-making.[1] Accordingly, corporate constitutionalism does not imply that other stakeholders are excluded from corporate governance merely because shareholders retain a central role. On the contrary, shareholders can function as conduits, introducing diverse interests and perspectives into corporate deliberation.[2] The model also advocates for substantive legal reforms to encourage shareholders to become actively involved as members, prompting them to engage with the options provided by deliberation and contestation, rather than relying on passivity and exit.[3] Thus, the shareholder primacy model within a corporate constitutionalist framework allows for the participation of a wider range of interests in corporate governance.

However, Bottomley's theory leaves a blank with respect to fitting workers in corporate constitutionalism. In other words, there seem to be no sufficient arguments in Bottomley's work to support strengthening or protecting workers' status. From this book' viewpoint, this group of corporate constituents also merit specific forms of concern and protection of their interests. After Carillion's downfall, with nearly 2000 workers losing jobs, the workers seemed to be the greatest casualties of this corporate scandal. Workers actually had long been neglected by Carillion's managers and the protections from the relevant union was also insufficient. In 2015, it was reported that large construction companies, including Carillion and Balfour Beatty were listed in the government report on blacklisting in employment.[4] Carillion's significant size and scope enabled the company to exert considerable power, allowing it to take

---

[1] Stephen Bottomley, *The Constitutional Corporation: Rethinking Corporate Governance* (Ashgate Publishing, Ltd 2007) 175.

[2] Ibid.

[3] Ibid.

[4] House of Commons Scottish Affairs Committee, Blacklisting in Employment: Final Report (Oral and Written Evidence, HC 272, 2015), https://publications.parliament.uk/pa/cm201415/cmselect/cmscotaf/272/272.pdf, accessed 12 December 2023.

aggressive actions against union memberships.[5] In the existing corporate governance system, the workers thus are essentially marginalised and excluded from the internal corporate control. Within the corporate contractual framework, they are regarded as pure contractual parties who sign their contracts with the company, then do their jobs and get salaries, and are excluded from the real governance of the company. They rarely get rights to express their voice within contractual-based corporate governance mechanisms.

But we can still see that there are already ways in which the UK's company law, corporate governance system, and academia make some efforts to enhance stakeholders' protection. For example, in Chapter 2, this book discussed Section 172 of the Companies Act 2006 which seeks an approach of "enlightened shareholder value". It is also acknowledged that the newest Corporate Governance Code (2018) stressed the importance of stakeholders in promoting a sustainable increase of the UK's economy that could be a sign for the recent development direction of the UK's corporate governance system. Academics have long advocated for the inclusion of non-shareholder constituencies in governance.[6] As Parkinson notes, employees and shareholders both have a vested interest in profitability, as profits are key to job security and income growth.[7] Boeger, Russell, and Villiers have proposed a sustainable governance paradigm that actively mobilises shareholders to pursue sustainability while reconsidering their relationships with directors, employees, and other stakeholders.[8]

Yet these efforts, while commendable, remain inadequate. High-profile incidents such as the 2022 mass dismissal of 800 P&O Ferries staff via Zoom—with no prior consultation—demonstrate the limited effectiveness of current stakeholder protections.[9] Such cases underscore the need to reassess and reinforce the role of employees within the corporate constitutional framework. As asked at the previous chapters: how are stakeholders—especially workers, who are consistently the most directly and

[5] Ciarán O'Kelly, 'Corporate Governance and Resentment', *European Group of Public Administration: Annual Conference* (2019) 23.

[6] For a survey, see Jill Solomon, *Corporate Governance and Accountability* (John Wiley & Sons 2020) 195–232. John R Boatright, *Ethics in Finance* (John Wiley & Sons 2013). R Edward Freeman, *Strategic Management: A Stakeholder Approach* (Cambridge university press 2010). Peter A French, 'Collective and Corporate Responsibility', *Collective and Corporate Responsibility* (Columbia University Press 1984). Peter A French, 'The Corporation as a Moral Person' (1979) 16 *American Philosophical Quarterly* 207.

[7] John E Parkinson, 'The Contractual Theory of the Company and the Protection of Non-Shareholder Interests', *Corporate and Commercial law: Modern Developments* (Lloyds of London Press 1996) 121.

[8] Nina Boeger, Roseanne Russell, and Charlotte L Villiers, 'Companies, Shareholders and Sustainability' (2020) 7 *University of Bristol Law Research Paper Series* 10.

[9] 'Outrage and No Ferries after Mass P&O Sackings' *BBC News* (18 March 2022), https://www.bbc.com/news/business-60779001, accessed 26 May 2024. See also Gwyn Topham and Gwyn Topham Transport correspondent, 'P&O Ferries Boss Admits Firm Broke Law by Sacking Staff without Consultation' *The Guardian* (24 March 2022), https://www.theguardian.com/business/2022/mar/24/po-ferries-boss-says-800-staff-were-sacked-because-no-union-would-accepts-its-plans, accessed 26 May 2024.

adversely affected by corporate misconduct—to be situated in a shareholder-primacy system that purports to be constitutional in nature? This book argues that employees, including those affected in Carillion, must occupy a recognised and protected status within corporate constitutionalism. Workers are essential in establishing a legitimate and balanced power structure capable of holding corporate managers to account.

Chapters 6 and 7 explored the integrated roles of various corporate actors in maintaining this balance of power. Building on that analysis, this chapter asserts that the workforce itself represents a vital component of a healthy and legitimate corporate ecosystem. Parkinson rightly observed that any real improvement in employee conditions should not be based on existing market relations, but rather on a theory that challenges the current distribution of power and entitlements within the company.[10] Corporate constitutionalism, this book argues, offers just such a framework—a theory capable of challenging traditional contractual and hierarchical paradigms. This approach demands the democratisation of corporate governance, grounded in procedural justice. Though their roles differ from those of shareholders, employees should nonetheless enjoy equal standing in requiring corporate decision-makers to consider their interests. In Parkinson's words, "workers have a right that the company be operated in their interests that is at least equal to that of the shareholders."[11]

Various scholars have explored how to substantively elevate employees' roles in governance. Proposals include board-level employee representation,[12] the formation of workforce advisory panels, or appointing designated non-executive directors to represent employee interests in the boardroom—options already offered by the 2018 Corporate Governance Code.[13] Parkinson advocates for the establishment of "a system of works councils" as an initial reform step in the UK context.[14] In response to the scandals involving worker exploitation, Villiers has called for "a more genuine workplace democracy," encompassing both stronger boardroom representation and more robust union involvement in collective bargaining.[15] Meanwhile, Esser, MacNeil, and Chalaczkiewicz-Ladna have proposed a combined model involving

---

[10] Parkinson (n 7) 146.

[11] Parkinson (n 7) 145.

[12] Jeremy Waddington and Aline Conchon, *Board Level Employee Representation in Europe: Priorities, Power and Articulation* (Routledge 2015). Lionel Fulton, *The Forgotten Resource: Corporate Governance and Employee Board-Level Representation. The Situation in France, the Netherlands, Sweden and the UK* (Düsseldorf: Hans-Böckler-Stiftung 2007). Timothy J Lewis and others, 'Employee Roles in Governance: Contrasting the UK and German Experience' (2004) *Corporate Governance: The International Journal of Business in Society.*

[13] 'UK Corporate Governance Code 2018' provision 5, https://www.frc.org.uk/getattachment/88bd8c45-50ea-4841-95b0-d2f4f48069a2/2018-UK-Corporate-Governance-Code-FINAL.PDF, accessed 1 January 2024.

[14] Parkinson (n 7) 145.

[15] Charlotte Villiers, 'Corporate Governance, Employee Voice and the Interests of Employees: The Broken Promise of a "World Leading Package of Corporate Reforms"' (2021) 50 *Industrial Law Journal* 159, 195.

an advisory stakeholder panel—including employee representatives—and a designated non-executive director to represent all stakeholders collectively.[16] All of these proposals contribute to the broader project of enhancing employees' status and influence within corporate governance—an objective that aligns squarely with the values of corporate constitutionalism.

While these proposals are commendable in advancing employees' position within the corporation, this book argues that reforms must be grounded more clearly in the accountability, deliberation, and contestability mechanisms central to corporate constitutionalism. This requires not only formalised and transparent routes for stakeholders to express their views, engage in discussion, and challenge managerial decisions internally, but also the development of hard-law mechanisms to strengthen the enforceability of workers' and other stakeholders' rights. Space constraints prevent this book from examining employee protection in detail, but it recognises that this is a critical area warranting further and sustained scholarly attention.

9.3 Could Corporate Constitutionalism Have Prevented Carillion's Failure?

9.3.1 Key Observations of This Book

This book has undertaken a comprehensive study integrating empirical research, theoretical inquiry, and normative reflection, focusing on the collapse of Carillion as a case study through the lens of corporate constitutionalism. It begins with a detailed empirical examination of Carillion's failure, proceeds to a theoretical exploration of corporate contractualism and corporate constitutionalism, then evaluates the UK's corporate governance framework under the prevailing contractual paradigm, and finally offers a thought experiment applying the constitutional framework to the Carillion case.

The empirical investigation draws upon both primary and secondary sources, including Carillion's internal documents such as annual reports and accounts (2002–2017), board minutes, articles of association, and letters from institutional investors addressed to the House of Commons. Crucially, the Second Joint Report of the Parliamentary Committees on Business, Energy and Industrial Strategy and Work and Pensions provides a critical foundation for the book's arguments. That report observed that the enigma of Carillion was not merely its collapse, but how such a company could grow into a "corporate time bomb" within an ostensibly robust corporate governance system. It concluded that the participants in this system—directors, auditors, regulators, and shareholders—collectively failed in their duties and often acted in strict accordance with their own incentives, rather than the interests of the

[16] IM Esser, Iain MacNeil and Katarzyna Chalaczkiewicz-Ladna, 'Engaging Stakeholders in Corporate Decision-Making through Strategic Reporting: An Empirical Study of FTSE 100 Companies (Part 2)' (2020) 31 *European Business Law Review* 209, 234–235.

company or broader society.[17] In this light, Carillion's failure cannot be understood in isolation; it signals deeper systemic deficiencies in the architecture of UK corporate governance.

A key lesson from Carillion's collapse is that if those entrusted with corporate power lack an understanding of how that power should be legitimised, restricted, and subjected to checks, they are likely to exercise it in ways that erode long-term sustainability. Indeed, the overarching theoretical concern underpinning this book is what Mary Stokes has aptly described as "the problem of the legitimacy of managerial power."[18] The dominant UK legal form legitimises corporate control through a contractual paradigm, whereby managerial authority is presumed to flow from a web of private agreements. However, from this book's standpoint, that paradigm fails to convincingly justify or restrain managerial discretion, and it lacks the normative infrastructure necessary to prevent recurring corporate failures. The inadequacies of this contractual framework thus call for a more profound reconceptualisation of the theories on which corporate governance rests.

To this end, the book draws upon Bottomley's notion of corporate constitutionalism, seeking to transpose its normative commitments into the Carillion case. Corporate governance, as understood here, operates on both internal and external dimensions. Internally, power is exercised within the firm through formal roles and procedures; externally, corporate power radiates outwards and interacts with various stakeholders, including regulators, auditors, and the public at large.[19] Traditionally, the role of these actors has been framed within narrow accountability relationships—mechanisms through which corporate managers provide justifications to some external body, which may then pose questions or impose sanctions.[20] However, this model of accountability is too thin to support the kind of complex corporate governance needed in the contemporary landscape. Corporate constitutionalism, by contrast, envisions a more sophisticated system built on three interrelated principles: accountability, deliberation, and contestability. It aspires not only to justify power but also to design structures that prevent its abuse through meaningful stakeholder engagement and institutional checks and balances.

Applying these principles to Carillion, this book explores how corporate constitutionalism might reshape both the internal governance and the external oversight of the company. Internally, constitutionalism demands mechanisms that separate powers among directors, shareholders, auditors, whistle-blowers, and possibly workers. It

---

[17] House of Commons Business, Energy and Industrial Strategy and Work and Pensions Committees, *Carillion*, Second Joint Report from the Business, Energy and Industrial Strategy and Work and Pensions Committees of Session 2017–2019, HC 769, 16 May 2018, at 5, https://publications.parliament.uk/pa/cm201719/cmselect/cmworpen/769/769.pdf, accessed 31 October 2023.

[18] Mary Stokes, 'Company Law and Legal Theory' (1986) *Legal Theory and Common Law* 155.

[19] Bob Tricker, *Corporate Governance: Principles, Policies, and Practices* (Oxford University Press, 6 June 2019) 4.

[20] Mark Bovens, *The Quest for Responsibility: Accountability and Citizenship in Complex Organisations* (Cambridge university press 1998) 23–24. See also Andrew Keay and Joan Loughrey, 'The Framework for Board Accountability in Corporate Governance' (2015) 35 *Legal Studies* 252.

calls for meaningful deliberation spaces within corporate structures, allowing corporate actors to reflect on and influence key decisions. Moreover, it emphasises the right and ability of shareholders—and possibly other stakeholders—to challenge decisions through institutionalised contestation mechanisms. Externally, the book assesses Carillion's constitutional role in the broader public sphere. It emphasises the importance of written constitutions and formalised relationships with external actors, including regulators and public watchdogs. Chapter 8 further develops these ideas by speculating on how Carillion might have operated differently under a fully realised corporate constitutional framework. It offers a series of hypothetical reforms—both internal and external—grounded in the accountability-deliberation-contestability model, designed to enhance checks and balances and prevent corporate excesses.

In summary, the central observation of this book is as follows: the legitimacy of corporate governance lies not only in the outcomes it delivers but also in the processes by which decisions are made. Corporate constitutionalism places equal weight on procedural and substantive justice. Unlike the contractualist focus on efficiency and profit maximisation, constitutionalism insists that internal corporate processes must be structured to reflect normative commitments to transparency, inclusiveness, and restraint. It also acknowledges the complex reality of corporate life, recognising that power within corporations is relational, dynamic, and far from neutral.

Constituent corporate members—such as shareholders and directors—should no longer be regarded solely as private individuals acting in their own interest. Instead, they must also be viewed as collective actors with fiduciary and constitutional responsibilities toward the corporation as a whole. Through the framework of corporate constitutionalism, these various actors—including auditors, whistle-blowers, employees, and the public—can be woven into a broader web of power, mutual responsibility, and institutional coherence.

Above all, this book highlights that shareholder participation should no longer be a perfunctory or passive role. It must be reimagined as an active, meaningful, and constitutionally grounded part of corporate governance. Similarly, the role of the state must be reconceived—not as a distant overseer but as a decentralised regulatory partner embedded in corporate life. The insights drawn from Carillion's failure offer a powerful justification for this shift, and corporate constitutionalism provides the normative and structural tools to make it possible.

9.3.2 Answers to the Research Question

We may now return to the central research question that has guided this inquiry: Whether the corporate constitutionalism present a viable framework for addressing governance failures? The answer advanced in this book is an unequivocal yes.

This conclusion is not merely aspirational, but rather is underpinned by a detailed examination of the structural failures that precipitated Carillion's collapse and a comparative evaluation of how corporate constitutionalism, both in theory and in application, can address such deficiencies. The preceding chapters have laid the groundwork by establishing that corporate constitutionalism has the capacity both to rectify the weaknesses inherent in the prevailing corporate contractual paradigm and to align closely with the reform objectives set out in the Second Joint Report on Carillion. These two foundations lend strong support to the claim that corporate constitutionalism is not only a theoretically coherent model but also a normatively preferable and practically feasible alternative for modern corporate governance reform.

To elaborate further, we must first revisit the conceptual features of corporate constitutionalism and their relevance to Carillion's case. At the heart of this framework lies the constitutional principle of separating powers among various corporate organs and actors—shareholders, directors, auditors, employees, and regulators—thereby avoiding the concentration of decision-making authority in a single group or constituency. As John Pound argued in his seminal work, the rise of the political model of corporate governance necessitates the use of procedural mechanisms such as due process, substantive debate, and formal voting referenda to ensure legitimate and accountable decision-making processes within corporations.[21] Applied to the corporate context, this political—or constitutional—model prevents the entrenchment of managerial power and opens up avenues for genuine contestation, deliberation, and scrutiny across multiple decision-making sites.

In Carillion's case, one of the core failings was the unchecked dominance of executive management and the passive acquiescence of both non-executive directors and external auditors. There was insufficient scrutiny of strategic decisions and a lack of early warning signals, despite the increasingly unsustainable financial trajectory the company had embarked upon. A corporate constitutional approach would have introduced formalised mechanisms for multi-actor engagement, thereby allowing other stakeholders, including shareholders, workers, and even whistleblowers, to play a meaningful role in corporate deliberation. This multipolar governance structure, supported by institutionalised deliberation and contestation, could have enabled earlier detection and correction of problematic corporate strategies, potentially altering the company's fate.

Furthermore, corporate constitutionalism supports a governance culture that is long-term oriented, procedurally inclusive, and legitimacy-enhancing. It encourages shareholder activism and stakeholder accountability while also enhancing the capacity of external regulators to intervene meaningfully when corporate conduct veers off track. Through a more democratised and structured governance architecture, the likelihood of groupthink, regulatory capture, and excessive risk-taking is significantly reduced. In essence, this approach strengthens corporate resilience against failure by embedding checks and balances at multiple levels of decision-making.

The second part of the answer lies in how corporate constitutionalism aligns with the reform directions identified by the Second Joint Report following Carillion's collapse. That report outlined four principal reform areas, each of which resonates closely with the normative agenda of corporate constitutionalism.

---

[21] John Pound, 'The Rise of the Political Model of Corporate Governance and Corporate Control' (1993) 68 *NYUL Rev.* 1003, 1009.

First, the report criticised the UK's corporate governance framework for being overly reliant on investor engagement, despite the absence of sufficient mechanisms or incentives to facilitate such engagement.[22] This critique underscores the need for a structural transformation that goes beyond rhetoric. Corporate constitutionalism offers a pathway to recalibrate the balance of power and to embed shareholder participation more deeply and formally in corporate processes, rather than treating it as a voluntary or secondary concern.

Second, the report pointed to the chronic passivity and regulatory inertia exhibited by the Financial Reporting Council (FRC), the Pensions Regulator, and relevant government departments. It called for a cultural shift toward more assertive and timely intervention in the public interest, noting that effective enforcement and meaningful regulation are central to preserving market trust and stakeholder well-being.[23] Here again, corporate constitutionalism aligns with the reform call by envisioning a governance structure that empowers both internal and external watchdogs to fulfil their roles more effectively. It does so by establishing more robust channels for accountability and regulatory oversight, thereby ensuring that corporate misconduct does not go unnoticed or unpunished.

Third, the report urged radical reform of the audit market, including measures to increase competition and to separate audit from non-audit services provided by the "Big Four" firms.[24] Corporate constitutionalism does not directly prescribe audit market reform, but it does reinforce the need for institutional independence, transparency, and structural separation of functions. A corporate constitutional system would recognise the audit function as an independent pillar within the broader architecture of corporate governance, thereby avoiding conflicts of interest and restoring public confidence in the audit profession's integrity.

Fourth, and perhaps most importantly, the report highlighted the toxic corporate culture within Carillion. This included the systematic exploitation of workers, the ineffectiveness of Section 172 of the Companies Act 2006 in ensuring consideration of stakeholder interests, disproportionate executive compensation, and the poor treatment of suppliers. Corporate constitutionalism addresses this cultural malaise by mandating a more inclusive governance model—one in which stakeholder voices are institutionally recognised, and managerial discretion is subject to procedural constraints and normative standards. In this regard, corporate constitutionalism offers not just an institutional fix, but also a normative vision for what corporations ought to be in a democratic and socially responsible society.

However, even with a paradigm shift, we must recognise the limits of any governance framework. No model, including corporate constitutionalism, can completely eliminate bad faith, opportunism, or failure. There will always be individuals or groups who circumvent rules, act in self-interest, or fail to perform their duties with diligence. However, the central value of corporate constitutionalism lies in its preventive and corrective potential. It builds the institutional capacity to detect substandard

[22] Second Joint Report (n 17) 5.

[23] Ibid., 5–6.

[24] Ibid., 69.

behaviour earlier, to enable timely correction, and to avoid systemic collapse. It is precisely in its commitment to structural pluralism, deliberative governance, and distributed accountability that corporate constitutionalism demonstrates its long-term utility.

Ultimately, the contribution of this book lies not only in diagnosing the specific failures of Carillion or in challenging the prevailing contractual model. Rather, it lies in offering a coherent, principled, and practicable alternative that is attentive to the dynamics of power, the complexity of modern corporate structures, and the evolving expectations of corporate responsibility in the twenty-first century. Corporate constitutionalism is not merely a theoretical innovation; it is a viable policy proposal—capable of shaping the future of corporate governance in the UK and beyond.

9.4 Limitations and Further Steps

This book is, first and foremost, a thought experiment. It proposes and applies the framework of corporate constitutionalism to an already-collapsed company not to re-litigate the past, but to explore whether a different theoretical paradigm might have prevented its failure. In doing so, the book aims to challenge the prevailing orthodoxy of corporate contractualism, which has long dominated corporate governance theory and practice. Through this experimental lens, the book reimagines the corporation not merely as a nexus of contracts but as a constitutional polity—one that implicates political, social, and ethical dimensions alongside economic imperatives.

Yet, while ambitious in scope, the project is not without its limitations. It is, admittedly, a preliminary step—an initial and necessarily imperfect foray into an alternative conceptual terrain. Many of the ideas proposed in this book remain tethered, to varying degrees, to the assumptions and terminologies of contractualist thought. This is perhaps inevitable when attempting to shift paradigms from within the intellectual structure one seeks to challenge. The gravitational pull of existing doctrine and institutional forms cannot be easily escaped, and thus, some tensions and unresolved questions remain.

A key limitation, then, lies in the inherent abstraction of the theory itself. Corporate constitutionalism, as articulated in this book, is still largely a normative framework rather than an empirical one. It provides compelling philosophical and structural arguments but remains untested in large-scale practical application. Its viability, therefore, requires further scrutiny, not only through theoretical elaboration but also through comparative institutional analysis, empirical case studies, and engagement with legal reform debates.

Despite these limitations, the book opens several avenues for further research and development. In particular, one important direction involves interrogating whether corporate constitutionalism can be translated from theory into practice by examining existing alternative corporate forms. For instance, can Bottomley's vision of corporate constitutionalism be found, at least partially, in corporate models already available to us? Examples such as benefit corporations, worker cooperatives, John Lewis Partnership, and the social enterprises offer fertile ground for such inquiry. For example, in the John Lewis Partnership, all of the workers are paid as "owners". They receive a share of the profits. The worker-based cooperatives have very different representation and decision-making formats. The benefit corporations make very clear and emphasise their purposes. They are identified as purpose-led corporations.

Each of these forms departs from the traditional shareholder-primacy model and embeds within their structures various elements that resonate with corporate constitutionalism. While none of these forms perfectly realise the corporate constitutional ideal, they demonstrate its partial feasibility and provide useful experimental templates. Future research could therefore undertake comparative assessments of these alternative models, asking whether and how key constitutionalist features, such as checks and balances, pluralistic representation, formal deliberation, and transparency, are instantiated within them. Such comparative research could also begin to identify practical mechanisms for importing corporate constitutionalist features into more conventional firms. For instance, could reforms mandating stakeholder advisory councils, participatory budgeting processes, or independent whistleblowing tribunals serve as incremental steps towards a more constitutionalist model of governance? Could reforms to board composition, for example, mandatory employee representation or rotating stakeholder representative that introduce a constitutional logic into decision-making?

Another promising line of inquiry lies in the interaction between corporate constitutionalism and regulatory regimes. The rise of ESG disclosure mandates, sustainability due diligence requirements, and stakeholder engagement codes across various jurisdictions opens new opportunities to test whether constitutionalist principles could become embedded in hard or soft law instruments. For example, can the UK's Stewardship Code or Corporate Governance Code be amended to reflect procedural norms of deliberation and contestation? Could constitutionalist theory provide the normative foundation for new legislative or institutional reforms, particularly in areas like audit oversight, director accountability, and long-termism?

In conclusion, while this book is but an early attempt, it opens up a much-needed conversation about the structural foundations of corporate power and the normative assumptions of corporate governance. Its value lies not merely in its prescriptions for Carillion or other failed firms, but in its invitation to rethink the architecture of the modern company itself. In a world increasingly defined by climate crises, social inequality, and legitimacy deficits, the search for new governance paradigms is not only an academic exercise—it is a societal imperative. The constitutional approach to corporate governance may not yet be fully formed, but it is now firmly on the table.

Bibliography

Books

Aglietta M, Rebérioux A (2005) Corporate governance adrift: a critique of shareholder value. Edward Elgar Publishing
Aoki M (2001) Toward a comparative institutional analysis. MIT Press
Atiyah PS (1979) The rise and fall of freedom of contract. Clarendon Press
Bainbridge SM (2002) Corporation law and economics. Foundation Press
Bassey M (1999) Case study research in educational settings. McGraw-Hill Education, UK
Bellamy R, Castiglione D (1997) Constitutionalism and democracy-political theory and the American constitution. British Journal of Political Science 27:595
Berle A, Means G (1932) The modern corporation and private property. Macmillan, London
Berman H (1983) Law and revolution. Harvard University, Cambridge Mass. Sity Press, The formation of the western legal tradition
Bhaskar K, Flower J (2019) Financial failures and scandals: from Enron to Carillion. Routledge
Boatright JR (2013) Ethics in finance. John Wiley & Sons
Bottomley S (2007) The constitutional corporation: rethinking corporate governance. Ashgate Publishing, Ltd
Bottomley S (2021) The responsible shareholder. Edward Elgar Publishing Limited
Bovens M (1998) The quest for responsibility: accountability and citizenship in complex organisations. Cambridge University Press
Bowman S (2010) Modern corporation and American political thought: law, power, and ideology. Penn State Press
Charles EM (1944) Public and private government. Yale University Press, New Haven
Charkham J, Simpson A (1999) Fair shares: the future of shareholder power and responsibility. OUP Oxford
Cheffins BR (1997) Company law: theory, structure, and operation. Clarendon Press, Oxford
Coffee JC Jr (2006) Gatekeepers: the professions and corporate governance. Oxford University Press, Incorporated
Crouch C (2011) The strange non-death of neo-liberalism. Polity
Dignam A, Lowry J (2014) Company law. Oxford University Press
Dimock ME (1949) Business and government. The Business of Government
Dine J (2000) The governance of corporate groups. Cambridge University Press
Donaldson T (1982) Corporations and morality. Prentice-Hall, Englewood Cliffs, NJ
Davies PL et al (2016) Gower's principles of modern company law. Tenth edition /, Thomson Reuters (Professional) UK Ltd, trading as Sweet & Maxwell

Y. Yang, *Corporate Collapse and Corporate Governance*, CSR, Sustainability, Ethics & Governance, https://doi.org/10.1007/978-981-96-9666-6

Easterbrook FH, Fischel DR (1996) The economic structure of corporate law. Harvard University Press
Eells RSF (1960) The meaning of modern business: an introduction to the philosophy of large corporate enterprise. Columbia University Press
Eells RSF (1962) The Government of Corporations. Free Press
Emerson FD, Latcham FC (1954) Shareholder democracy: a broader outlook for corporations. Press of Western Reserve University
Fisse B, Braithwaite J (1993) Corporations, crime and accountability. Cambridge University Press
Freeman RE (2020) Strategic management: a stakeholder approach. Cambridge University Press
Frentrop P (2003) A history of corporate governance, 1602–2002. Deminor
Fulton L (2007) The forgotten resource: corporate governance and employee board-level representation. The Situation in France, the Netherlands, Sweden and the UK. Hans-Böckler-Stiftung, Düsseldorf
Gierke O (1913) Political theories of the middle age. Centro de estudios constitucionales
Gordon S, *Controlling the State: Constitutionalism from Ancient Athens to Today* (Harvard University Press 2009)
Gomm R, Hammersley M, Foster P (2000) Case study method: key issues, key texts. SAGE Publications
Gourevitch PA, Shinn J (2005) Political power and corporate control: the new global politics of corporate governance. Princeton University Press
Gomez PY, Korine H (2008) Entrepreneurs and democracy a political theory of corporate governance. Cambridge University Press
Grofman B, Wittman DA (1989) The federalist papers and the new institutionalism. Algora Publishing
Hannigan B (2015) Company law. Oxford University Press, USA
Habermas J (1996) Between facts and norms: contributions to a discourse theory of law and democracy. John Wiley & Sons
Hall PA, Soskice D (2001) Varieties of capitalism: the institutional foundations of comparative advantage. Oxford University Press
Hamilton WH (1957) The politics of industry. Knopf
Hobbes T, *Leviathan or The Matter, Forme and Power of a Commonwealth Ecclesiasticall and Civil* (Oxford : Clarendon Press 1651)
Honderich T (2005) The Oxford companion to philosophy. Oxford University Press USA - OSO
Jowell J, Oliver D, O'Cinneide C (2007) The changing constitution (8th edn). Oxford University Press
King A (2007) The British constitution. Oxford University Press
Knight A, Ruddock L (2009) Advanced research methods in the built environment. John Wiley & Sons
Kramer RM (1981) Voluntary agencies in the welfare state. University of California Press
Kukathas C, Pettit P (1990) Rawls—a theory of justice and its critics. Polity Press
Lukes S (2004) Power: a radical view. Macmillan International Higher Education
Lyons S (2016) Corporate defense and the value preservation imperative: bulletproof your Corporate Defense Program. CRC Press
McVea H (1993) Financial conglomerates and the Chinese wall: regulating conflicts of interest. Clarendon Press
Miceli MP, Near JP (1992) Blowing the whistle: the organizational and legal implications for companies and employees. Lexington Books
Mill JS (2009) Considerations on representative government. Floating Press
Moore M, Petrin M (2017) Corporate governance: law, regulation and theory Macmillan International Higher Education
Moore M (2013) Corporate governance in the shadow of the state. Bloomsbury Publishing
Ong A (2006) Neoliberalism as exception: mutations in citizenship and sovereignty. Duke University Press

Parkinson JE (2002) Corporate power and responsibility: issues in the theory of company law. Clarendon
Peters B (1993) Die Integration Moderner Gesellschaften. Suhrkamp
Pettit P (1997) Republicanism: a theory of freedom and government. Oxford University Press
Pfeffer J (1981) Power in organizations. Ballinger Pub Co
Posner RA (2014) Economic analysis of law. Wolters kluwer law & business
Rubin GR, Sugarman D (1984) Law, economy and society, 1750–1914: essays in the history of english law. Professional Books/Butterworths
Selznick P (1994) The moral commonwealth: social theory and the promise of community. University of California Press
Solomon J (2020) Corporate governance and accountability. John Wiley & Sons
Stout LA (2012) The shareholder value myth: how putting shareholders first harms investors, corporations, and the public. Berrett-Koehler Publishers
Talbot L (2015) Critical company law. Routledge
Tricker B (2019) Corporate governance: principles, policies, and practices. Oxford University Press, USA
Tyler T (1990) Why people obey the law. Yale University Press
Unger RM (1976) Law in modern society—toward a criticism of social theory. Simon and Schuster
Van Aaken A, List C, Luetge C (2004) Deliberation and decision: economics, constitutional theory and deliberative democracy. Taylor & Francis Group
Vile MJC (1967) Constitutionalism and the Separation of Powers. Liberty Fund, Incorporated
Villiers C (2006) Corporate reporting and company law. Cambridge University Press
Von Gierke O, Freyd B (2018) The development of political theory. Routledge
Walliman N (2006) Social research methods. SAGE Publications, Ltd
Williamson OE (1996) The mechanisms of governance. Oxford University Press
Wordsworth CFF (1837) The law relating to railway, bank, insurance, mining and other joint-stock companies: with an appendix, containing statutes, cases at law and in equity, resolutions of the houses of parliament as to railway and other bills, forms of deeds, &c. Henry Butterworth
Weber M (2009) The theory of social and economic organization. Simon and Schuster
Waddington J, Conchon A (2015) Board level employee representation in europe: priorities, power and articulation. Routledge

Articles

Ackerman B (1989) Constitutional politics/constitutional law. Yale Law J 99:453
Agrawal A, Knoeber CR (1996) Firm performance and mechanisms to control agency problems between managers and shareholders. J Financ Quant Anal 377:31
Alchian AA, Demsetz H (1972) Production, information costs, and economic organization. Am Econ Rev 62:777
Alcock A (2003) Higgs—the wrong answer? Co Lawyer 24:161
Bainbridge SM (2002) Why a board-group decisionmaking in corporate governance. Vand L Rev 55:1
Belinfanti TC (2013) Shareholder cultivation and new governance. Del J Corp L 38:789
Bellamy R, Castiglione D (1997) Constitutionalism and democracy–political theory and the American constitution. Br J Polit Sci 27:595
Blair MM, Stout LA (1999) Team production theory of corporate law. Va L. Rev 85:247
Blair MM, Stout LA (2001) Director accountability and the mediating role of the corporate board. Wash ULQ 79:403
Blumberg PI (1971) The politicalization of the corporation. BuL Rev 51:425

Boeger N, Russell R, Villiers CL (2020) Companies, shareholders and sustainability. University of Bristol Law Research Paper Series 7
Bonnafous-Boucher M (2005) Some philosophical issues in corporate governance: the role of property in stakeholder theory. Corp GovAnce: Int J Bus Soc 5:34
Bottomley S (1990) Taking corporations seriously: some considerations for corporate regulation. Fed Law Rev 19:203
Bottomley S (1999) The birds, the beasts, and the bat: developing a constitutionalist theory of corporate regulation. Fed Law Rev 27:243
Bottomley S (1997) From contractualism to constitutionalism: a framework for corporate goverance. Sydney L Rev 19:277
Braithwaite J (1997) On speaking softly and carrying big sticks: neglected dimensions of a republication separation of powers. Univ Tor Law J 47:305
Bratina B, Jovanovic D (2014) Shareholders positive voting duty. International OFEL Conference on Governance, Management and Entrepreneurship. Centar Za Istrazivanje I Razvoj Upravljanja Doo 150
Bratton WW (1991) Public values and corporate fiduciary law. Rutgers L Rev 44:675
Bratton WW (1989) The new economic theory of the firm: critical perspectives from history. Stanf Law Rev 1471
Brenner SN, Cochran P (1991) The stakeholder theory of the firm: implications for business and society theory and research. Proc Int Assoc Bus Soc 897
Brown JA, Forster WR (2013) CSR and stakeholder theory: a tale of Adam Smith. J Bus Ethics 112:301
Chapman R (2018) Ineffective risk management and the collapse of Carillion. PM World J VII
Chayes A (1959) The modern corporation and the rule of law. Corp Mod Soc 25
Cheffins BR (2015) The rise of corporate governance in the UK: when and why. Curr Leg Probl 68:387
Chiu IH-Y (2013) Reviving shareholder stewardship: critically examining the impact of corporate transparency reforms in the UK. Del J Corp Law 38:983
Chynoweth P (2008) Legal research. Adv Res Methods Built Environ 1:1
Clarke T (2005) Accounting for enron: shareholder value and stakeholder interests. Corp GovAnce: Int Rev 13:598
Clarke T (2014) High-frequency trading and dark pools: sharks never sleep. Law Financ Mark Rev 8:342
Clarke T (1998) Research on corporate governance. Corp. Governance 6:57
Coffee JC Jr (1991) Liquidity versus control: the institutional investor as corporate monitor. Colum L Rev 91:1277
Coffee JC Jr (2003) What caused enron-a capsule social and economic history of the 1990s. Cornell L. Rev. 89:269
Cohen J (1989) Deliberation and democratic legitimacy. In: Hamlin and Pettit (eds) The good polity: normative analysis of the state. Wiley-Blackwell
Conrad A (1982) Constitutional rights of the corporate person. Yale Law J 91:1641
Crouch C (2010) The global firm: the problem of the giant firm in democratic capitalism. In: The Oxford handbook of business and government. Oxford University Press
Daily CM, Dalton DR, Cannella AA (2003) Corporate governance: decades of dialogue and data. Acad Manag Rev 28:371
Dallas LL (1988) Two models of corporate governance: beyond Berle and means. U Mich JL Reform 22:19
Davies P (2020) The UK stewardship code 2010–2020 from saving the company to saving the planet? European Corporate Governance Institute-Law Working Paper
Davis K (1967) Understanding the Social Responsibility Puzzle. Bus Horiz 45:10
Daily CM, Dalton DR, Cannella AA (2003) Corporate governance: decades of dialogue and data. Acad Manag Rev 28:371

Dobson J, White J (1995) Toward the feminine firm: an extension to Thomas White. Bus Ethics Q 463
Dubnick M (2005) Accountability and the promise of performance: in search of the mechanisms. Public Perform & Manag Rev 28:376
Easterbrook FH, Fischel DR (1983) Voting in corporate law. J Law Econ 26:395
Eisenberg MA (1969) The legal roles of shareholders and management in modern corporate decisionmaking. Calif L Rev 57:1
Eisenberg MA (1983) Corporate legitimacy, conduct, and governance—two models of the corporation. Creighton Law Rev 17:20
Eisenberg MA (1998) The conception that the corporation is a nexus of contracts, and the dual nature of the firm. J Corp L 24:819
Esser I-M, MacNeil I, Chalaczkiewicz-Ladna K (2020) Engaging stakeholders in corporate decision-making through strategic reporting: an empirical study of FTSE 100 companies (Part 2). Eur Bus Law Rev 31:209
Fairfax LM (2013) Mandating board-shareholder engagement. U Ill L Rev 821
Fama EF (1980) Agency problems and the theory of the firm. J Polit Econ 88:288
Fama EF, Jensen MC (1983) Separation of ownership and control. J Law Econ 26:301
French PA (1979) The corporation as a moral person. Am Philos Q 16:207
French PA (1984) Collective and corporate responsibility. In: Collective and corporate responsibility. Columbia University Press
Fridman GHL (1967) Freedom of contract. Ottawa L Rev 2:1
Galbraith JK (1973) On the economic image of corporate enterprise. Corporate Power Am 3
Garriga E, Melé D (2004) Corporate social responsibility theories: mapping the territory. J Bus Ethics 53:51
Gevurtz FA (2004) The historical and political origins of the corporate board of directors. Hofstra L Rev 33:89
Gilson RJ, Mnookin RH (1984) Sharing among the human capitalists: an economic inquiry into the corporate law firm and how partners split profits symposium on the corporate law firm. Stanf Law Rev 37:313
Griffith J (1979) The political constitution. Mod. Law Rev 42:1
Hardin R (1989) Why a constitution. In: Grofman and Wittman (eds) The federalist papers and the new institutionalism. Algora Publishing
Hartman EM (1991) Donaldson on rights and corporate obligations. Ruffin Ser Bus Ethics 163
Hayek FA (1975) The corporation in a democratic society: in whose interest ought it and will it be run. In: Anshen and Bach (eds) Management and Corporations 1958. Greenwood
Heath J (2019) Is the "point" of the Market Pareto or Kaldor-Hicks efficiency? Bus Ethics J Rev 7:21
Hood C (1991) A public management for all seasons? Public Adm 69:3
Hopt KJ (2011) Comparative corporate governance: the state of the art and international regulation. Am J Comp Law 59:1
Horn L (2012) Corporate governance in crisis? The politics of EU corporate governance regulation. Eur Law J 18:83
Hughes JJ (1996) The Greenbury Report on directors' remuneration. Int J Manpow 17:1
Hutchinson T, Duncan N (2012) Defining and describing what we do: doctrinal legal research. Deakin L Rev 17:83
Hyde KF (2000) Recognising deductive processes in qualitative research. Qual Mark Res: Int J 3:82
Ireland P (2003) Property and contract in contemporary corporate theory. Leg Stud 23:453
Ireland P (1996) Capitalism without the capitalist: the joint stock company share and the emergence of the modern doctrine of separate corporate personality. J Leg Hist 17:41
Ireland P (2018) Corporate schizophrenia: the institutional origins of corporate social irresponsibility. In: Boeger and Villiers (eds) Shaping the Corporate Landscape Towards Corporate Reform and Enterprise Diversity. Hart Publishing

Jamali D (2008) A stakeholder approach to corporate social responsibility: a fresh perspective into theory and practice. J Bus Ethics 82:213
Jaques E (1991) In praise of hierarchy. Mark, Hierarchies Netw: Coord Soc Life 48
Jensen MC, Meckling WH (1976) Theory of the firm: managerial behavior, agency costs and ownership structure. J Financ Econ 3:305
Johnson L, Millon D (1989) Misreading the Williams Act. Mich Law Rev 87:1862
John K, Senbet LW (1998) Corporate governance and board effectiveness. J Bank & Financ 22:371
Kakabadse NK, Rozuel C, Lee-Davies L (2005) Corporate social responsibility and stakeholder approach: a conceptual review. Int J Bus Governance Ethics 1:277
Keay A, Loughrey J (2015) The framework for board accountability in corporate governance. Leg Stud 35:252
Kershaw D (2006) Waiting for enron: the unstable equilibrium of auditor independence regulation. J Law Soc 33:388
Klonoski RJ (1986) The moral responsibilities of stockholders. J Bus Ethics 35:85
Kosmin QCL, Roberts C (2013) Company meetings and resolutions: law, practice, and procedure. OUP Catalogue
Lahey KA, Salter SW (1985) Corporate law in legal theory and legal scholarship: from classicism to feminism. Osgoode Hall LJ 23:543
Lan LL, Heracleous L (2010) Rethinking agency theory: the view from law. Acad Manag Rev 35:294
Latham E (2013) The body politic of the corporation. In: Mason (ed) The corporation in modern society. Harvard University Press
Lee IB (2009) Citizenship and the corporation. Law & Soc Inq 34:129
Leff N (1976) Capital markets in the less developed countries: the group principle. Money Financ Econ Growth Dev 3:97
Lewis TJ et al (2004) Employee roles in governance: contrasting the UK and German experience. Corp Governance: Int J Bus Soc 4:16
Liebl J, Hartmann E, Feisel E (2016) Reverse factoring in the supply chain: objectives, antecedents and implementation barriers. Int J Phys Distrib & Logist Manag 46
Lin-Hi N, Blumberg I (2011) The relationship between corporate governance, global governance, and sustainable profits: lessons learned from BP. Corp Governance: Int J Bus Soc 11:571
Lloyd P (2010) Pareto efficiency. In: Blaug and Lloyd (ed) Famous figures and diagrams in economics. Edward Elgar Publishing
Millon D (1990) Theories of the corporation. Duke Law J 39:201
Moore M (2014) Private ordering and public policy: the paradoxical foundations of corporate contractarianism. Oxf J Leg Stud 34:693
Moore M (2015) Understanding the modern company through the lens of quasi-public power. University of Cambridge Faculty of Law Research Paper
Moore M (2015) The (Neglected) Value of board accountability in corporate governance. Law Financ Mark Rev 9:10
Moore M (2015) Corporate governance, pay equity, and the limitations of agency theory. Curr Leg Probl 68:431
Moore M (2016) The de-privatisation of Anglo–American corporate law? In: Routledge handbook of corporate law. Routledge
Morck R, Shleifer A, Vishny RW (1988) Management ownership and market valuation: an empirical analysis. J Financ Econ 20:293
O'Kelly C (2019) Corporate governance and resentment. In: European Group of Public Administration: Annual Conference
Parkinson JE (1996) The contractual theory of the company and the protection of non-shareholder interests. In: Corporate and commercial law: modern developments. Lloyds of London Press
Parkinson JE (2000) Evolution and polity in company law: the non-executive director. In: The polity economy of the company. Hart Publishing, Oxford

Pettit P (1999) Republican freedom and contestatory democratization. In: Shapiro and Hacker-Cordón (eds) Democracy's values (Contemporary political theory). Cambridge University Press
Pettit P (2000) Democracy, electoral and contestatory. In: Shapiro and Macedo (eds) Designing democratic institutions. NYU Press
Pound J (1993) The rise of the political model of corporate governance and corporate control. NYUL Rev 68:1003
Philip P (2000) Democracy: electoral and contestatory. NOMOS: Am Soc'y Pol Legal Phil 42:105
Rehg W, Bohman J (1996) Discourse and democracy: the formal and informal bases of legitimacy in Habermas' Faktizität Und Geltung. J Polit Philos 4:79
Riley CA (1992) Contracting out of company law: section 459 of the Companies Act 1985 and the role of the courts. Mod Law Rev 55:782
Ringe WG (2013) Independent directors: after the crisis. Eur Bus Organ Law Rev 14:401
Rule P, John VM (2015) A necessary dialogue: theory in case study research. Int J Qual Methods 14
Scherer AG, Baumann-Pauly D, Schneider A (2013) Democratizing corporate governance: compensating for the democratic deficit of corporate political activity and corporate citizenship. Bus & Soc 52:473
Scherer AG, Palazzo G (2011) The new political role of business in a globalized world: a review of a new perspective on csr and its implications for the firm, governance, and democracy. J Manag Stud 48:899
Schochet GJ (1979) Introduction: constitutionalism, liberalism, and the study of politics. Nomos: Am Soc Polit Leg Philos 20:1
Seidenfeld M (1992) A civic republican justification for the bureaucratic state. Harv Law Rev 1511
Stevenson RB Jr (1979) The corporation as a political institution. Hofstra L Rev 8:39
Stokes M (1986) Company law and legal theory. Leg Theory Common Law 155
Shearing C (1993) A constitutive conception of regulation. Bus Regul Australia's Futur 67
Sjåfjell B (2018) Dismantling the legal myth of shareholder primacy: the corporation as a sustainable market actor. In: Boeger and Villiers (eds) Shaping the corporate landscape towards corporate reform and enterprise diversity. Hart Publishing
Spender P, Bottomley S (2004) How to do things with contractarianism: Michael Whincop's contribution to corporate law scholarship. Griffith Law Rev 13:9
Talbot L (2013) Why shareholders shouldn't vote: AM Arxist-progressive critique of shareholder empowerment. Mod Law Rev 76:791
Turnbull S (1997) Corporate governance: its scope, concerns and theories. Corp GovAnce: Int Rev 5:180
Tsagas G (2018) Section 172 of the Companies Act 2006: desperate times call for soft law measures. In: Boeger and Villiers (eds) Shaping the corporate landscape towards corporate reform and enterprise diversity. Hart Publishing
Tse T et al (2014) Are we falling asleep at the switch, again? Some propositions for executive compensation. Int J Trade Glob Mark 7:53
Turnbull S (1997) Corporate governance: its scope, concerns and theories. Corp Governance: Int Rev 5:180
Vanberg VJ (2007) Corporate social responsibility and the "game of catallaxy": the perspective of constitutional economics. Const Polit Econ 18:199
Veldman J (2018) The separate legal entity and the architecture of the modern corporation. In: Boeger and Villiers (eds) Shaping the corporate landscape towards corporate reform and enterprise diversity. Hart Publishing
Villiers C (2008) Corporate law, corporate power and corporate social responsibility. Perspect Corp Soc Responsib 85
Villiers C (2010) Controlling executive pay: institutional investor or distributive justice? J Corp Law 10:309
Villiers C (2016) Executive pay: a socially-oriented distributive justice framework. Co Lawyer 37:139

Villiers C (2018) Corporate governance, responsibility and compassion: why we should care. In: Boeger and Villiers (eds) Shaping the corporate landscape towards corporate reform and enterprise diversity. Hart Publishing

Villiers C (2021) Corporate governance, employee voice and the interests of employees: the broken promise of a "World Leading Package of Corporate Reforms." Ind Law J 50:159

Wicks AC, Gilbert Jr DR, Freeman RE (1994) A feminist reinterpretation of the stakeholder concept. Bus Ethics Q 475

Williamson J (2018) Beyond shareholder primacy—the case for workers' voice in corporate governance. In: Boeger and Villiers (eds) Shaping the corporate landscape towards corporate reform and enterprise diversity. Hart Publishing

Williamson OE (1989) Transaction cost economics. Handb Ind. Organ 1:135

Wheeler D, Sillanpa M (1998) Including the stakeholders: the business case. Long Range Plan 31:201

Wong K (2019) The collapse of Carillion: regulatory failure in the contract state. LSE Law Rev 3

Wolin SS (1988) Collective Identity and Constitutional Power. In: Bryner and Thompson (eds) The constitution and the regulation of society. State University of New York Press

Yeoh P (2019) Corporate governance codes in the UK: the risk of over-reliance? Bus Law Rev 40:19

Reports

'After Carillion: Public Sector Outsourcing and Contracting - Public Administration and Constitutional Affairs Committee - House of Commons', https://publications.parliament.uk/pa/cm201719/cmselect/cmpubadm/748/74803.htm, accessed 10 April 2024

'Articles of Association of Carillion Plc 2010', https://find-and-update.company information.service.gov.uk/company/03782379/filing-history?page=6, accessed 29 January 2024

'Business, Energy and Industrial Strategy Committee, Third Report of Session 2016–2017, Corporate Governance, HC 702, April 2017', https://publications.parliament.uk/pa/cm201617/cmselect/cmbeis/702/702.pdf, accessed 3 March 2024

'Carillion Plc, Group Business Plan, January 2018', https://www.parliament.uk/globalassets/documents/commons-committees/work-and-pensions/Carillion-Group-Business-Plan-January-2018.pdf, accessed 18 March 2024

'Carillion Plc, Annual Report and Accounts 2006', https://www.annualreports.co.uk/HostedData/AnnualReportArchive/c/LSE_CLLN_2006.pdf, accessed 23 February 2024

'Carillion Plc, Annual Report and Accounts 2008', https://www.annualreports.co.uk/HostedData/AnnualReportArchive/c/LSE_CLLN_2008.pdf, accessed 23 February 2024

'Carillion Plc, Annual Report and Accounts 2011', https://www.annualreports.co.uk/HostedData/AnnualReportArchive/c/LSE_CLLN_2011.pdf, accessed 21 March 2024

'Carillion Plc, Annual Report and Accounts 2012', https://www.annualreports.co.uk/HostedData/AnnualReportArchive/c/LSE_CLLN_2012.pdf, accessed 21 March 2024

'Carillion Plc, Annual Report and Accounts 2014', https://www.annualreports.co.uk/HostedData/AnnualReportArchive/c/LSE_CLLN_2014.pdf, accessed 13 March 2024

'Carillion Plc, Annual Report and Accounts 2015', https://www.annualreports.com/HostedData/AnnualReportArchive/c/LSE_CLLN_2015.pdf, accessed 13 March 2024

'Carillion Plc, Annual Report and Accounts 2016', https://www.annualreports.com/HostedData/AnnualReports/PDF/LSE_CLLN_2016.pdf, accessed 12 March 2024

'Carillion Plc, Minutes of a Meeting of the Board of Directors, 2 April 2015', https://www.parliament.uk/globalassets/documents/commons-committees/work-and-pensions/Carillion-report/Carillion-Board-minutes-2.4.15.pdf, accessed 9 January 2024

'Carillion Plc, Minutes of a Meeting of the Board of Directors, 5 July 2017', https://www.parliament.uk/globalassets/documents/commons-committees/work-and-pensions/Correspondence/Carillion-Board-minutes-5-July-2017.pdf, accessed 26 March 2024

'Carillion-Two-Years-on.Pdf', https://www.instituteforgovernment.org.uk/sites/default/files/publications/carillion-two-years-on.pdf, accessed 14 November 2024

'Companies House, Carillion Plc Officers', https://beta.companieshouse.gov.uk/company/03782379/officers, accessed 13 November 2023

'Court and Tribunals Judiciary - Carillion Group', https://www.judiciary.uk/wp-content/uploads/2015/03/carillion-group-cmo1.pdf, accessed 17 March 2024

'Corporate Governance Reform: Green Paper', https://assets.publishing.service.gov.uk/government/uploads/system/uploads/attachment_data/file/584013/corporate-governance-reform-green-paper.pdf, accessed 10 October 2023

'Department for Business, Energy and Industrial Strategy, Insolvency and Corporate Governance, March 2018', https://assets.publishing.service.gov.uk/government/uploads/system/uploads/attachment_data/file/691857/Condoc_-_Insolvency_and_Corporate_Governance_FINAL_.pdf, accessed 3 March 2024

'Financial Reporting Council, The UK Stewardship Code (2020)', https://www.frc.org.uk/getattachment/5aae591d-d9d3-4cf4-814a-d14e156a1d87/Stewardship-Code_Dec-19-Final-Corrected.pdf, accessed 25 January 2024

Great Britain and Department for Business E& IS, *Restoring Trust in Audit and Corporate Governance: Consultation on the Government's Proposals* (2021)

House of Commons Business, Energy and Industrial Strategy and Work and Pensions Committees, Carillion, Second Joint Report from the Business, Energy and Industrial Strategy and Work and Pensions Committees of Session 2017–19, HC 769, 16 May 2018, at 3, https://publications.parliament.uk/pa/cm201719/cmselect/cmworpen/769/769.pdf, accessed 31 October 2023

House of Commons and Public Administration and Constitutional Affairs Committee, 'After Carillion: Public Sector Outsourcing and Contracting, Seventh Report of Session 2017–2019', https://publications.parliament.uk/pa/cm201719/cmselect/cmpubadm/748/748.pdf, accessed 27 May 2024

House of Commons Scottish Affairs Committee, Blacklisting in Employment: Final Report (Oral and Written Evidence, HC 272, 2015)', https://publications.parliament.uk/pa/cm201415/cmselect/cmscotaf/272/272.pdf, accessed 27 May 2024

House of Commons Work and Pensions and Business, Innovation and Skills Committees, *BHS*, First Report of the Work and Pensions Committee and Fourth Report of the Business, Innovation and Skills Committee of Session 2016–2017,
https://publications.parliament.uk/pa/cm201617/cmselect/cmworpen/54/54.pdf, accessed 27 May 2024

'Independent Review of the Financial Reporting Council – Kingman Review', https://assets.publishing.service.gov.uk/government/uploads/system/uploads/attachment_data/file/767387/frc-independent-review-final-report.pdf, accessed 27 May 2024

'Investegate |Carillion PLC Announcements | Carillion PLC: Half-Year Report', https://www.investegate.co.uk/carillion-plc/rns/half-year-report/201709290700092047S/, accessed 10 March 2024

'Investegate |Carillion PLC Announcements | Carillion PLC: Trading Statement', https://www.investegate.co.uk/carillion-plc/rns/trading-statement/201707100700105229K/, accessed 10 March 2024

'Investegate |Carillion PLC Announcements | Carillion PLC: Update', https://www.investegate.co.uk/carillion-plc/rns/update/201711170702318037W/, accessed 10 March 2024

'Letter from Andrew Dougal to the Chairs, 5 April 2018', https://www.parliament.uk/globalassets/documents/commons-committees/work-and-pensions/Carillion-report/Letter-from-Andrew-Dougal-to-Chairs-5-April-2018.pdf, accessed 25 March 2024

'Letter from Standard Life to the Chairs Regarding Carillion 2-February-2018', https://www.parliament.uk/globalassets/documents/commons-committees/work-and-pensions/Carillion/Letter-from-Standard-Life-to-the-Chairs-regarding-Carillion-2-February-2018.pdf, accessed 18 November 2024

'Letter from BlackRock to the Chairs, 8 February 2018', https://www.parliament.uk/globalassets/documents/commons-committees/work-and-pensions/Carillion/Letter-from-Blackrock-to-the-Chairs-regarding-Carillion-8-February-2018.pdf, accessed 2 April 2024

'Letter from Carillion to BlackRock, 7 March 2017', https://www.parliament.uk/globalassets/documents/commons-committees/work-and-pensions/Carillion/Carillion-letter-to-BlackRock-7-March-2017.pdf, accessed 2 April 2024

'Letter from Deloitte to the Chairs, 2 February 2018', https://www.parliament.uk/globalassets/documents/commons-committees/work-and-pensions/Correspondence/Letter-from-Deloitte-Chairman-to-the-Chairs-relating-to-Carillion-2-February-2018.pdf, accessed 29 March 2024

'Letter from Msheireb Properties to the Chairs Regarding Carillion', https://www.parliament.uk/globalassets/documents/commons-committees/work-and-pensions/Correspondence/Letter-from-Msheireb-Properties-to-the-Chairs-regarding-Carillion-27-Febraury-2018.pdf, accessed 26 February 2024

'Letter from Richard Howson to the Chairs Regarding Carillion', https://www.parliament.uk/globalassets/documents/commons-committees/work-and-pensions/Correspondence/Letter-from-Richard-Howson-to-the-Chairs-regarding-Carillion-21-February-2018.pdf, accessed 24 February 2024

'Letter from S&P Global to the Chairs', https://www.parliament.uk/globalassets/documents/commons-committees/work-and-pensions/Carillion-report/Letter-from-S-and-P-Global-to-the-Chairs-230318.pdf, accessed 7 April 2024

'Letter from Standard Life to the Chairs, 2 February 2018', https://www.parliament.uk/globalassets/documents/commons-committees/work-and-pensions/Carillion/Letter-from-Standard-Life-to-the-Chairs-regarding-Carillion-2-February-2018.pdf, accessed 2 April 2024

'Letter from Standard Life to the Chairs Regarding Carillion' https://www.parliament.uk/globalassets/documents/commons-committees/work-and-pensions/Carillion/Letter-from-Standard-Life-to-the-Chairs-regarding-Carillion-2-February-2018.pdf, accessed 27 February 2024

'Letter from Kiltearn Partners LLP to the Chairs Regarding Carillion 2 February 2018', https://www.parliament.uk/globalassets/documents/commons-committees/work-and-pensions/Carillion/Letter-from-Kiltearn-Partners-LLP-to-the-Chairs-regarding-Carillion-2-February-2018.pdf, accessed 25 January 2024

Mitchell I and others, 'Brexit and the UK's Public Finances' (Institute for Fiscal Studies 2016), https://www.ifs.org.uk/publications/8296, accessed 31 March 2021

'Memorandum of Association of Carillion Plc 2006', https://find-and-update.company-information.service.gov.uk/company/03782379/filing-history?page=8, accessed 30 January 2024

National Audit Office, 'Investigation into the Government's Handling of the Collapse of Carillion', https://www.nao.org.uk/wp-content/uploads/2018/06/Investigation-into-the-governments-handling-of-the-collapse-of-Carillion.pdf, accessed 30 January 2024

'Oral Evidence – Carillion – 6 Feb 2018', http://data.parliament.uk/writtenevidence/committeeevidence.svc/evidencedocument/work-and-pensions-committee/carillion/oral/78103.html, accessed 27 December 2023

'Oral Evidence - Carillion - 6 Feb 2018', http://data.parliament.uk/writtenevidence/committeeevidence.svc/evidencedocument/work-and-pensions-committee/carillion/oral/78103.html, accessed 26 March 2024

'Oral Evidence - Carillion - 7 Mar 2018', http://data.parliament.uk/writtenevidence/committeeevidence.svc/evidencedocument/work-and-pensions-committee/carillion/oral/79969.html, accessed 2 April 2024

'Oral Evidence: Carillion, HC 769', http://data.parliament.uk/writtenevidence/committeeevidence.svc/evidencedocument/work-and-pensions-committee/carillion/oral/78103.pdf, accessed 7 April 2024

'Oral Evidence - Sourcing Public Services: Lessons to Be Learned from the Collapse of Carillion - 24 Apr 2018', http://data.parliament.uk/writtenevidence/committeeevidence.svc/evidencedocument/public-administration-and-constitutional-affairs-committee/sourcing-public-services-lessons-to-be-learned-from-the-collapse-of-carillion/oral/82098.html, accessed 7 February 2024

'Private Sector Rail Investment - Thursday 18 January 2018 - Hansard - UK Parliament', https://hansard.parliament.uk/Commons/2018-01-18/debates/DFD3E110-A049-4D50-B467-22685AC5E06E/PrivateSectorRailInvestment, accessed 13 March 2024

'Prompt Payment Code', http://www.promptpaymentcode.org.uk/, accessed 6 April 2024

'Question for Department for Education - UK Parliament', https://questions-statements.parliament.uk/written-questions/detail/2018-01-16/123190, accessed 13 March 2024

'Question for Department for Transport - UK Parliament', https://questions-statements.parliament.uk/written-questions/detail/2018-02-20/HL5579, accessed 13 March 2024

Report of the Committee on the Financial Aspects of Corporate Governance - Cadbury Report (Gee and Co. Ltd., London, 1992)

Sacker and Partners LLP, Carillion Single Trustee - Meeting between Trustee Representatives and the Pensions Regulator Regarding Failure to Agree the 2011 Valuation', https://www.parliament.uk/globalassets/documents/commons-committees/work-and-pensions/Carillion/Carrillion.pdf, accessed 25 March 2024

'The Five Most Important Changes to the UK's New Stewardship Code | ACCA Global', https://www.accaglobal.com/ca/en/member/discover/cpd-articles/governance-risk-control/stewardship-codecpd.html, accessed 22 February 2024

'The Governance Lessons of Carillion's Collapse | ACCA Global', https://www.accaglobal.com/uk/en/member/member/accounting-business/2018/04/corporate/carillions-collapse.html, accessed 10 March 2024

'The Higgs Report: Review of the Role and Effectiveness of Non-Executive Directors' (*ECGI*, 27 January 2017), https://ecgi.global/code/higgs-report-review-role-and-effectiveness-non-executive-directors, accessed 17 May 2024

Thurley D and others, 'The Collapse of Carillion - House of Commons', https://commonslibrary.parliament.uk/research-briefings/cbp-8206/, accessed 13 March 2024

'UK Corporate Governance Code 2016', https://www.frc.org.uk/getattachment/ca7e94c4-b9a9-49e2-a824-ad76a322873c/UK-Corporate-Governance-Code-April-2016.pdf, accessed 27 December 2023

'UK Corporate Governance Code 2018', https://www.frc.org.uk/getattachment/88bd8c45-50ea-4841-95b0-d2f4f48069a2/2018-UK-Corporate-Governance-Code-FINAL.PDF, accessed 13 November 2023

'Wates Corporate Governance Principles for LPC 2018', https://www.frc.org.uk/getattachment/31dfb844-6d4b-4093-9bfe-19cee2c29cda/Wates-Corporate-Governance-Principles-for-LPC-Dec-2018.pdf, accessed 28 May 2024

'Written Questions and Answers - Written Questions, Answers and Statements - UK Parliament', https://questions-statements.parliament.uk/written-questions/detail/2018-01-15/122617, accessed 13 March 2024

'Written Statement Prison Competition and Efficiency, HC Deb 18 Nov 2014 C7WS', https://publications.parliament.uk/pa/cm201415/cmhansrd/cm141118/wmstext/141118m0001.htm, accessed 13 March 2024

News and Blogs

'Aberdeen Bypass Settlement Reached', https://www.theconstructionindex.co.uk/news/view/aberdeen-bypass-settlement-agreed, accessed 26 February 2023

'Accounting Tricks: How Carillion Duped the Market', https://www.globalconstructionreview.com/accounting-tricks-how-carillion-duped-market/, accessed 29 March 2023

Amir Qamar and Collinson S, 'Part A: The Causes of Carillion's Collapse – City REDI Blog', https://blog.bham.ac.uk/cityredi/the-causes-of-carillions-collapse-part-a/, accessed 27 February 2023

'Audit regime in the UK to be transformed with new regulator' (GOV.UK), https://www.gov.uk/government/news/audit-regime-in-the-uk-to-be-transformed-with-new-regulator, accessed 2 April 2023

'Balfour Beatty: Five Reasons Why the Carillion Merger Won't Work' (The Telegraph), https://www.telegraph.co.uk/finance/newsbysector/constructionandproperty/11035863/Balfour-Beatty-five-reasons-why-the-Carillion-merger-wont-work.html, accessed 23 February 2023

'Being Owed £200m on Qatar Job Helped Send Carillion under, Former Boss Admits' (Building), https://www.building.co.uk/news/being-owed-200m-on-qatar-job-helped-send-carillion-under-former-boss-admits-/5091953.article, accessed 26 February 2023

Bryant C, 'Hedge Funds Are the Good Guys In Carillion Debacle' (BloombergQuint), https://www.bloombergquint.com/opinion/hedge-funds-are-the-good-guys-in-carillion-debacle, accessed 31 March 2023

'Business Secretary Launches Major Overhaul of UK's Audit Regime in Wake of Big-Name Company Collapses' (*GOV.UK*), https://www.gov.uk/government/news/business-secretary-launches-major-overhaul-of-uks-audit-regime-in-wake-of-big-name-company-collapses, accessed 10 May 2023

'Carillion: 12 Months on from a PFI Perspective | Bevan Brittan LLP', https://www.bevanbrittan.com/insights/articles/2019/carillion-12-months-on-from-a-pfi-perspective/, accessed 6 February 2023

'Carillion Bosses Focused on Their Own Pay rather than the Company' (*Construction Enquirer News*), https://www.constructionenquirer.com/2018/03/07/carillion-investors-question-kpmg-auditing/, accessed 21 November 2023

'Carillion: A Case Study of a Corporate Defense Fiasco', https://www.linkedin.com/pulse/carillion-case-study-corporate-defense-fiasco-sean-lyons, accessed 16 March 2023

'Carillion Agreed Secret Bonus Account for Richard Howson' (Construction News, 26 March 2018), https://www.constructionnews.co.uk/news/contractors-news/carillion-agreed-secret-bonus-account-for-richard-howson-26-03-2018/, accessed 21 November 2023

'Carillion Collapse: Midland Metropolitan Hospital Work Resumes' BBC News (14 February 2020), https://www.bbc.com/news/uk-england-birmingham-51494374, accessed 26 February 2023

'Carillion Collapse Two Years on, Lessons Not Learned, Hospitals Unfinished and Guilty Unpunished', https://www.unitetheunion.org/news-events/news/2020/january/carillion-collapse-two-years-on-lessons-not-learned-hospitals-unfinished-and-guilty-unpunished/, accessed 13 April 2023

'Carillion Contracts Complete Transfer' (GOV.UK), https://www.gov.uk/government/news/carillion-contracts-complete-transfer, accessed 23 February 2023

'Carillion Declares Insolvency: Information for Employees, Creditors and Suppliers' (GOV.UK), https://www.gov.uk/government/news/carillion-declares-insolvency-information-for-employees-creditors-and-suppliers, accessed 24 February 2023

'Carillion Directors to Face FCA Action for Misleading Investors' Financial Times, https://www.ft.com/content/55a5136a-25a2-43a6-a085-3904ee72f60c, accessed 17 March 2024

'Carillion in Fresh Shares Plunge on Latest Profit Warning' (Sky News), https://news.sky.com/story/carillion-in-fresh-shares-plunge-on-latest-profit-warning-11129790, accessed 15 March 2024

'Carillion Issued 3 Profit Warnings. So Why Was It Still Getting Government Contracts?', https://www.newstatesman.com/politics/staggers/2018/01/carillion-issued-3-profit-warnings-so-why-was-it-still-getting-government, accessed 10 March 2024

'Carillion: Legal Bid Launched to Ban Former Directors' BBC News (14 January 2021), https://www.bbc.com/news/business-55659196, accessed 17 March 2024

'Carillion Shares Plunge after Third Profit Warning | Reuters', https://www.reuters.com/article/uk-carillion-outlook-idUKKBN1DH0QZ, accessed 31 March 2024

'Carillion Board Minutes Reveal Last CFO Blew Whistle on Accounting Irregularities - Committees - UK Parliament', https://committees.parliament.uk/committee/164/work-and-pensions-committee/news/97763/carillion-board-minutes-reveal-last-cfo-blew-whistle-on-accounting-irregularities/, accessed 19 March 2024

'Carillion Last Finance Chief Blew Whistle on Sloppy Accounting' (*Construction Enquirer*), https://www.constructionenquirer.com/2018/02/27/carillion-last-finance-chief-blew-whistle-on-sloppy-accounting/, accessed 18 March 2024

'Carillion: The Company Entrenched in Public Life' BBC News (15 January 2018), https://www.bbc.com/news/uk-england-42689717, accessed 27 February 2024

'Costs Double for Stalled Liverpool and Birmingham Hospitals, Report Finds' BBC News (17 January 2020), https://www.bbc.com/news/uk-england-51137640, accessed 26 February 2024

Davies R, 'Key Findings from the MPs' Report into Carillion's Collapse' The Guardian (15 May 2018), https://www.theguardian.com/business/2018/may/16/mps-dole-out-the-blame-over-carillions-collapse, accessed 29 December 2023

Emily Whiteley, 'Richard Adams (Finance Director of Carillion) - An Expert in Deceit.' (Richard Adams (Finance Director of Carillion) - An expert in deceit), http://emilywhiteleyfinance.blogspot.com/2019/11/richard-adams-finance-director-of.html, accessed 16 November 2023

Farrell S, 'Tesco Suspends Senior Staff and Starts Investigation into Overstated Profits' *The Guardian* (22 September 2014), https://www.theguardian.com/business/2014/sep/22/tesco-investigators-overstating-profit-250m, accessed 29 May 2024

Friedman M, 'A Friedman Doctrine– The Social Responsibility of Business Is to Increase Its Profits' The New York Times (13 September 1970), https://www.nytimes.com/1970/09/13/archives/a-friedman-doctrine-the-social-responsibility-of-business-is-to.html, accessed 24 February 2024

Financial Conduct Authority, 'Warning Notice Statement 20/2', https://www.fca.org.uk/publication/warning-notices/warning-notice-statement-20-2.pdf, accessed 17 March 2024

Goodley S, 'Carillion Chair Planned "Upbeat" Message before £845m Writedown' The Guardian (1 March 2018), https://www.theguardian.com/business/2018/mar/01/carillion-chair-planned-upbeat-message-before-845m-writedown, accessed 27 December 2023

Goodley S, 'The Four Contracts That Finished Carillion' *The Guardian* (15 January 2018), https://www.theguardian.com/business/2018/jan/15/the-four-contracts-that-finished-carillion-public-private-partnership, accessed 15 November 2023

Goodley S, 'Whistleblower Warned Carillion Bosses about Irregularities, MPs Told' *The Guardian* (27 February 2018), https://www.theguardian.com/business/2018/feb/27/carillion-whistleblower-emma-mercer-warned-bosses-about-irregularities-mps-told, accessed 18 March 2024

'Hedge Funds Are the Good Guys In Carillion Debacle' *Bloomberg.com* (16 May 2018), https://www.bloomberg.com/opinion/articles/2018-05-16/hedge-funds-are-the-good-guys-in-carillion-debacle, accessed 19 November 2023

HighPayCentre, 'CEO Pay Survey 2021: Median FTSE 100 CEO Now Paid £2.69 Million • High Pay Centre' (*High Pay Centre*, 18 August 2021), https://highpaycentre.org/ceo-pay-survey-2021-median-ftse-100-ceo-now-paid-2-69-million/, accessed 18 April 2024

'How the 2018 UK Corporate Governance Code and New Legislation Impacts Premium Companies | EY UK', https://www.ey.com/en_uk/assurance/how-the-2018-uk-corporate-governance-code-and-new-legislation-impacts-premium-companies, accessed 11 January 2024

Jolly J, 'Carillion Tribunal: Former KPMG Staff Turn on Each Other' *The Guardian* (11 January 2022), https://www.theguardian.com/business/2022/jan/11/carillion-hearing-former-kpmg-staff-turn-on-each-other, accessed 22 January 2024

Jolly J, 'KPMG Says Accounting Regulator "Was Misled" over Carillion Audits' *The Guardian* (10 January 2022), https://www.theguardian.com/business/2022/jan/10/kpmg-says-accounting-regulator-was-misled-over-carillion-audits, accessed 25 March 2024

'KPMG Sued For Billions Over Carillion', https://www.youtube.com/watch?v=rJI2dBqB3KE, accessed 25 March 2024

'Legal Bid Launched to Ban Ex-Carillion Directors from Top Boardroom Roles' (the Guardian, 13 January 2021), http://www.theguardian.com/business/2021/jan/13/legal-bid-launched-ban-ex-carillion-directors-top-boardroom-roles, accessed 20 March 2024

'Liverpool Hospital Completion Delayed by Two More Years', https://www.theconstructionindex.co.uk/news/view/liverpool-hospital-completion-delayed-by-two-more-years, accessed 9 January 2024

Makortoff K, 'KPMG to Be Fined £14m for Forging Documents over Carillion Audit' *The Guardian* (12 May 2022), https://www.theguardian.com/business/2022/may/12/kpmg-fined-frc-audit-carillion, accessed 18 May 2024

McCrum D and Plimmer G, 'Carillion Draws Short Sellers' Attention' *Financial Times* (12 October 2015), https://www.ft.com/content/d90be254-6e98-11e5-8608-a0853fb4e1fe, accessed 19 November 2023

'Moody's: Carillion's Collapse Exposes Flaws in the Accounting for Supply-Chain Finance Arrangements' (Moodys.com, 13 March 2018), http://www.moodys.com:18000/research/Moodys-Carillions-collapse-exposes-flaws-in-the-accounting-for-supply--PR_380769, accessed 31 March 2024

'Most Shorted Ahead of Earnings', https://cdn.ihs.com/www/blog/commentary/pdf/Most-shorted-ahead-of-earnings-21-August-2015.pdf, accessed 18 November 2023

Narwan G, 'Carillion's Problem Was Aggressive Accounting, Says Finance Chief', https://www.thetimes.co.uk/article/carillions-problem-was-aggressive-accounting-says-finance-chief-5rsskpjcw, accessed 28 March 2024

'News | Financial Reporting Council', https://www.frc.org.uk/news/june-2018/big-four-audit-quality-review-results-decline, accessed 17 March 2024

'Outrage and No Ferries after Mass P&O Sackings' *BBC News* (18 March 2022), https://www.bbc.com/news/business-60779001, accessed 26 May 2024

'Passive Investment and Ownerless Companies' *Financial Times* (11 March 2018), https://www.ft.com/content/0a23ddac-23b3-11e8-ae48-60d3531b7d11, accessed 18 April 2024

Plimmer G, 'Carillion Probe Pulls No Punches on Individuals or Institutions' Financial Times (15 May 2018), https://www.ft.com/content/aad5cb88-5820-11e8-b8b2-d6ceb45fa9d0, accessed 19 November 2023

Plimmer G, 'Carillion Probe Pulls No Punches on Individuals or Institutions' (15 May 2018), https://www.ft.com/content/aad5cb88-5820-11e8-b8b2-d6ceb45fa9d0, accessed 24 February 2024

PricewaterhouseCoopers, 'Carillion Group' (PwC), https://www.pwc.co.uk/services/business-restructuring/administrations/carillion.html, accessed 15 March 2024

Price D, 'Carillion Understated Hospital Costs by £70m' (*Construction News*, 26 March 2018), https://www.constructionnews.co.uk/news/contractors-news/carillion-understated-hospital-costs-by-70m-26-03-2018/, accessed 8 January 2024

Rol and others, 'What Carillion Plc Liquidation Means for Shareholders' (The Motley Fool UK, 15 January 2018), https://www.fool.co.uk/investing/2018/01/15/what-carillion-plc-liquidation-means-for-shareholders/, accessed 25 February 2024

Staff R, 'Carillion Collapse Exposed Flaws in UK Government Policy: Lawmakers' Reuters (9 July 2018), https://www.reuters.com/article/us-carillion-collapse-idUSKBN1JZ1H7, accessed 9 April 2024

Stewart H and Asthana A, 'Corbyn on Carillion: We'll End Outsourcing "racket" in Rule Change' *The Guardian* (18 January 2018), https://www.theguardian.com/politics/2018/jan/18/corbyn-on-carillion-well-end-outsourcing-racket-in-rule-change, accessed 27 March 2024

'The Ongoing Deconstruction of Carillion' (Restructuring GlobalView, 31 January 2018), https://www.restructuring-globalview.com/2018/01/the-ongoing-deconstruction-of-carillion/, accessed 14 March 2024

'The Collapse of Enron and the Dark Side of Business' *BBC News* (3 August 2021), https://www.bbc.com/news/business-58026162, accessed 28 May 2024

Tribe J, 'Carillion: Move to Disqualify Directors Signals UK Getting Tougher on "corporate Wrongdoing" - Articles - Liverpool Law School - University of Liverpool', https://www.liverpool.ac.uk/law/news/articles/carillion-move-to-disqualify-directors-signals-uk-authorities-getting-tougher-on-corporate-wrongdoing, accessed 7 January 2024

'The Tory 100: Captains of Industry, Party Donors (and a Few Tax Avoiders)' (*the Guardian*), http://www.theguardian.com/politics/ng-interactive/2015/apr/01/tory-100-industry-captains-party-donors-tax-avoiders, accessed 16 May 2024

Topham G and correspondent GTT, 'P&O Ferries Boss Admits Firm Broke Law by Sacking Staff without Consultation' *The Guardian* (24 March 2022), https://www.theguardian.com/business/2022/mar/24/po-ferries-boss-says-800-staff-were-sacked-because-no-union-would-accepts-its-plans, accessed 26 May 2024

'UK Intra-Firm Inequality: Stock-Based Pay for CEOs and Outsourcing of Lower Paid Jobs' (*LSE Business Review*, 7 December 2020), https://blogs.lse.ac.uk/businessreview/2020/12/07/uk-intra-firm-inequality-stock-based-pay-for-ceos-and-outsourcing-of-lower-paid-jobs/, accessed 18 April 2024

'UK Audit Giants Told to Build "Chinese Wall" after Collapses' (*independent*), https://www.independent.ie/business/world/uk-audit-giants-told-to-build-chinese-wall-after-collapses-39346427.html, accessed 30 May 2024

'Where Did It Go Wrong for Carillion?' BBC News (15 January 2018), https://www.bbc.com/news/business-42666275, accessed 24 February 2024

'Whistleblowing for Employees' (*GOV.UK*), https://www.gov.uk/whistleblowing, accessed 20 March 2024

Documentaries

Channel 4 (director), How to Lose Seven Billion Pounds: Dispatches, https://www.channel4.com/programmes/how-to-lose-seven-billion-pounds-dispatches, accessed 17 November 2023

The manufacturer's authorised representative in the EU is Springer Nature Customer Service Centre GmbH, Europaplatz 3, 69115 Heidelberg, Germany. If you have any concerns regarding our products, please contact ProductSafety@springernature.com

Printed and bound by CPI Group (UK) Ltd, Croydon, CR0 4YY
01/10/2026
02225921-0005